G-FORCE

FLYING THE WORLD'S GREATEST AIRCRAFT

G-FORCE

FLYING THE WORLD'S GREATEST AIRCRAFT

CHARTWELL
BOOKS

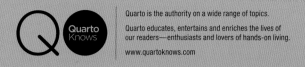

Quarto is the authority on a wide range of topics.

Quarto educates, entertains and enriches the lives of our readers—enthusiasts and lovers of hands-on living. www.quartoknows.com

This edition published in 2016 by

CHARTWELL BOOKS
an imprint of Book Sales
a division of Quarto Publishing Group USA Inc.
142 West 36th Street, 4th Floor
New York, New York 10018
USA

Editorial and design by
Amber Books Ltd
74–77 White Lion Street
London
N1 9PF
United Kingdom
www.amberbooks.co.uk
Appstore: itunes.com/apps/amberbooksltd
Facebook: www.facebook.com/amberbooks
Twitter: @amberbooks

Previously published in a different format in the partwork *Fighting Aircraft*

ISBN: 978-0-7858-3499-1

General Editor: James Bennett

Printed in China

10 9 8 7 6 5 4 3 2 1

Picture Credits

AIRtime: 182 (t & b, François Robineau; c, Frédérick Lert), 185 (t, François Robineau)

Amber Books: 117 (c)

Art-Tech/Aerospace: 14 (t), 16 (t), 20 (both), 21 (c & b), 23 (all), 27 (b), 34, 39 (t & c), 40 (t), 42/43, 44 (tl & tr), 45 & 46 (all), 47 (b), 48/49, 50 (both), 51 (tl), 54/55, 54 (l), 69 (b), 71 (t & c), 75 (t), 76 (c), 83 (t), 88 (t), 89 (t), 93 (b), 95 (t), 96/97, 98 (t), 99 (t & c), 100 & 101 (all), 104 (t), 105 (b), 116 (b), 117 (t), 120/121, 124 (b), 125 (t), 140 (c), 142, 148 (t), 150 (l), 152 (b), 153 (t), 154 (both), 155 (t), 157 (r), 158 (t), 159 (t), 160 (tl)

Art-Tech/MARS: 39 (b)

BAE Systems: 220 (t)

Austin Brown/Aviation Picture Library: 30/31, 31 (t), 35 (t & b), 53 (c), 128 (c)

Cody Images: 14 (b), 15 (c), 16 (b), 17 (all), 21 (t), 22 (all), 32 (cl), 33 (b), 35 (c), 52 (both), 81 (b), 130 (bl & br), 144/145, 146 (b), 148/149, 156/157, 158 (b), 160 (b), 161 (b), 164 (tl), 166 (b)

Corbis: 77 (b, Reuters), 150/151 (Sergei Chirikov/EPA), 152 (t, Kamal Kishore/Reuters), 153 (c, Sergei Chirikov/EPA)

Dassault Aviation: 162/163, 165 (both), 166 (tl & tr), 167 (b), 180/181, 183 & 184 (all), 185 (b)

Steve Davies: 66 (b), 68 (b), 70 (both), 106 (tr), 115 (r), 126/127 (both), 131 (b)

Eurofighter Typhoon: 198-203 (all)

Getty Images: 30 (b, Carl Sutton/Hulton Archive), 155 (b, AFP), 178 (b, Jeff Christensen)

Gripen International: 186/187 (Jonas Tillgren), 188 (t, Jan Gustavsson; b, Katsuhiko Tokunga), 189 (t, Katsuhiko Tokunga; b, Jan Gustavsson), 190/191 (Peter Liander), 190 (t, Peter Liander), 191 (r, Swedish Air Force)

Philip Jarrett: 92 (b)

NASA/Dryden Flight Research Centre: 37 (b), 44 (b)

Northrop Grumman: 80 (t), 216/217 (both), 218 (t), 219 (both), 221 (b)

O'Doyle: 133 (r)

Tyson V. Rininger: 211 (r)

TopFoto: 32 (b, PA)

U.S. Air Force: 18/19, 106 (b), 114/115, 116 (t), 117 (b), 118 & 119 (all), 122 & 123 (all), 124 (t), 125 (b), 159 (b), 160 (tr), 212 (both), 213 (t), 214 & 215 (all), 220 (b), 221 (t)

U.S. Department of Defense: 12/13, 15 (t & b), 24/25, 26 (all), 27 (t & c), 28 & 29 (all), 32 (t), 36/37, 38 (all), 40 (b), 41 (all), 47 (t & c), 51 (tr & b), 53 (t & b), 60/61, 63-65 (all), 66/67, 68 (t & c), 69 (t), 71 (b), 72/73, 74 (both), 75 (c & b), 76 (t & b), 77 (t), 78/79, 80 (c & b), 81 (t), 82 (both), 83 (bl & br), 84/85, 86 & 87 (all), 88 (b), 89 (c & b), 90/91, 92 (t & c), 93 (t), 94 (both), 95 (b), 98 (b), 99 (b), 108-113 (all), 129, 131 (t), 132/133, 134-139 (all), 140 (t & b), 141 (all), 143 (both), 145 (r), 146 (t), 147 (b), 148 (c), 149 (r), 164 (tr & b), 167 (t), 170-177 (all), 178 (t), 179 (all), 192-197 (all), 204-209 (all), 210/211 (Langley Air Force Base), 213 (b, Langley Air Force Base)

U.S. Navy: 62 (both), 102/103, 104 (b), 105 (t), 106 (tl), 107, 168/169, 218 (b)

Berry Vissers/Squadron Prints: 128 (t & b), 130 (t), 147 (t)

Jim Winchester: 32 (cr), 33 (t), 153 (b), 155 (c), 161 (t)

Contents

Introduction

RIGHT: Russia's MiG-15 was a capable fighter in the hands of a skilled pilot, and its small frontal cross-section made it notoriously difficult to visually acquire in a head-on engagement.

Since the advent of World War II in 1914, armed forces have utilised the aeroplane as a tool with which to strike the enemy. At that time, aeroplanes were gloriously simple machines, constructed of wood and canvas, and flown by pilots whose life expectancy was measured not in months, but in weeks. Aviation matured over the decades that followed, but while developments were made in construction techniques, materiel, weapons and electronic sophistication, the basics remained the same.

That all changed when Sir Frank Whittle conducted the first tests of his two-stage, single-sided centrifugal compressor in April 1937. The jet engine had been born. The jet engine would eventually take the aeroplane to new heights, quite literally. It offered superior thrust, and that meant faster airspeeds. Significantly, it allowed aircraft designers to re-think the aerodynamic shape of a fighter or bomber whose engines were mounted internally, and that resulted in new breed of combat aircraft unlike any seen before.

FIRST-GENERATION JET FIGHTERS

Perhaps the most iconic of this first generation of post-war jet fighters was the North American F-86 Sabre. By incorporating a swept wing on the F-86, North American had developed the first operational jet fighter that flew as comfortably above the sound barrier as it did below it.

'The [swept wing] *was the big difference: you had no Mach limitations. You could go into a dive against a target without going into a pitch-up...'* said Maj.

BELOW: The F-86 Sabre dominated the skies over North Korea, but had been superseded by newer US fighters by the end of the 1950s.

Gen. (ret.) Olav Aamoth, former Chief of Staff of the Royal Norwegian Air Force.

Over North Korea in the early 1950s, the most potent opposition to the Sabre came from the Russian-designed Mikoyan Gurevich MiG-15. The diminutive MiG's strength lay in its phenomenal manoeuvrability at very low airspeeds – a strength that could be exploited to give an advantage, according to Captain (ret.) Dmitri A. Samolyov: *'Although I had already begun to lose speed, my aircraft was still climbing… I turned and went after the last pair of F-86s. The Americans were taken completely by surprise. I caught up with them and shot one of them down.'*

Several classic designs followed the likes of the Sabre and MiG-15, most of which were beneficiaries not only of true supersonic performance brought about by rapid developments in the fields of propulsion and aerodynamics, but also by vast improvements in electronic wizardry. Among them was the Convair F-106 Delta Dart, a development of the somewhat flawed Convair F-102 Delta Dagger.

Lt Col (ret.) Earl Henderson, who flew both, recalled, *'The F-106 had variable ramps in the inlets to improve supersonic engine performance, and a fuel*

transfer system that activated above 1.4 Mach to automatically transfer fuel from one of the forward fuselage fuel tanks to the aft fuselage fuel tank. This shifted the centre of gravity, reducing supersonic trim drag and improving supersonic acceleration performance.' Such automation was a far cry from the likes of the Sabre.

ABOVE: US intelligence agencies estimated that the Soviet Union and its allies produced more than 19,000 examples of the MiG-21 during the Cold War.

LEFT: The last of the true 'Century Series' fighters, the F-106 Delta Dart combined electronics and interceptor performance that was unparalleled at the time.

ABOVE: Still in service today with the Royal Australian Air Force, the F-111 was the first strike fighter to offer automatic terrain-following down as low as 60 metres (200 feet) above the ground.

While the F-106 was packed full of sophisticated avionics, some of the designs of that came out of the late 1950s and early 1960s were built around a more humble design requirement: speed. The Lockheed F-104 Starfighter, the so-called 'missile with a man in it', personified this.

'*It was fast. Very fast. I have flown the jet out to 800 KIAS* [knots indicated air speed; 1,480km/h] *many times, and in the world of 1970s flying, that was really fast,*' Lt Col (ret.) Dud Larsen offered. Across the Iron Curtain, the MiG bureau had built its own interceptor, the MiG-21 Fishbed. '*In the*

hands of a good pilot, versus the F-4 [Phantom II], *the MiG-21 wins every time,*' USAF pilot Bob Sheffield explained.

MISSILES OR DOGFIGHTS?

The McDonnell F-4 Phantom II had been built at a time when advances in the miniaturization of electronics – making them small enough to fit inside a jet fighter – had come on leaps and bounds. It was heavily influenced by doctrinal shifts in the Air Force that decreed future air wars would be won with long-reaching air-to-air missiles. The Soviet Union, by contrast, lagged some ten years behind America's technical revolution and remained steadfast in its belief that winning air wars was all about simple, cheap designs that could be produced in great numbers. The Phantom was therefore not optimized for dogfighting, and had at least one savage handling quirk that cost lives when unsuspecting pilots flew it aggressively: '*The Phantom was not a forgiving jet if you didn't listen to it,*' confirmed Lt Col (ret.) Jerry Oney.

Ironically, America was still producing at least one jet fighter along the lines of Russia's MiGs, but it was initially only intended for export. The Northrop F-5 Freedom Fighter which, in its later incarnation as the F-5E Tiger II, can still hold its own today against a poorly flown McDonnell Douglas (now Boeing) F-15

RIGHT: The F-4 Phantom II represented a shift in strategic thinking by the United States. Built to tackle long range bombers at high altitude, it ended up in swirling dogfights with MiG fighters over Vietnam.

which is either a *'real pleasure, or quite terrifying, depending on the circumstances,'* according to one pilot.

Unsung workhorses also fill the catalogue of long-term Cold War warriors, the likes of which include the Grumman E-2 Hawkeye, the Lockheed P-3 Orion, and the Boeing E-3 Sentry. And one particular mainstay of the Cold War – and beyond – stands head and shoulders above them all: the Boeing B-52 Stratofortress, which has been in service for more than half a century, and yet still *'performs better now than it did when it was new,'* according to pilot Major Shane Vetter.

FIGHTERS PAST AND PRESENT

While the Orion, Sentry, Stratofortress and Hawkeye are all still stalwart platforms in the current global war on terror, it is the pointy-nose fighters and fighter bombers born in the early 1970s that continue to fascinate many observers the most. The Grumman F-14 Tomcat is the first of these to fall; retired by the US Navy in 2006, of which one pilot said, *'We used to say it took a good pilot to fly an average Phantom sortie. But you can put*

Eagle or General Dynamics (now Lockheed Martin) F-16 Fighting Falcon.

Swiss Air Force Colonel Oliver Spieth proclaimed the F-5, *'A typical pilot's airplane that does everything you ask of it and has no airs or graces: you just fly it!'*

While the glamour of these jet fighters is indisputable, the twenty years between 1950 and 1970 had produced other remarkable types, too. The General Dynamics F-111 Aardvark, crammed full of avionics to allow it to strike low, fast and with precision is one shining example. The Harrier jump jet, whose vertical take-off and landing characteristics allow it to be operated from small aircraft carriers –

an average pilot in an F-14 and he will fly a good Tomcat sortie.'

Then followed the enigmatic Lockheed F-117 Nighthawk, whose stealthy shape *'allowed the Air Force to go into places that they could never go before,'* but flew its final sorties in 2008.

The others continue to see frontline use. Foremost among these are the singularly impressive F-15 Eagle; the ubiquitous F-16 Fighting Falcon; France's Mirage 2000; and Russia's eclectic Sukhoi Su-27 Flanker, which can *'turn 360 degrees in ten seconds,'* and the MiG-29 Fulcrum. With the exception of the Su-27 'evolved Flanker', which is being developed into

ever-more sophisticated sub-variants, these are now known as 'legacy' jet fighters. Why? Because of the development and introduction to service of the 'four-and-a-half-generation' of jet fighters, and the 'fifth-generation' of stealthy types.

The four-and-a-half generation refers to the likes of the Dassualt Rafale, the Eurofighter Typhoon, the SAAB Gripen, and the Boeing F/A-18E/F Super Hornet. These aircraft make inroads into combining advanced handling, superior avionics and elements of stealth to give them an edge over legacy types. These fighters began to change the art of air warfare, automating and simplifying the pilot's duties.

Take the Rafale as an example; *'You can control it with two fingers on the*

sidestick. The thrust is enormous. As soon as one has understood the systems, one can concentrate fully on the mission and weapon deployment. Flying the plane then becomes a trivial matter,' according to one pilot.

FIFTH GENERATION

But it is the fifth generation of jet fighters that will complete this transformation. The Lockheed Martin F-22 Raptor is already in service, combining incredible stealth with previously unheard-of electronic capabilities. *'It's the fighter aircraft fighter pilots have been dreaming about,'* says one F-22 squadron commander, adding, *'There were so few compromises made for the aircraft's performance that it excels in virtually every arena...'*

Following the F-22 from the Lockheed Martin stable will be the F-35 Lightning II. Using some of the technology from the F-22, the Lightning II will provide Air Forces with a very stealthy strike platform that will also have a superb air-to-air capability. To its critics, one Lockheed Martin test pilot responded, *'You cannot shoot it down if you cannot see it!'*

Whatever the strengths and weaknesses of any given operational aircraft today, there is one thing that can be agreed upon. The role of the pilot has changed massively in the last 60 years of military aviation. Jet pilots in the 1950s would have spent a huge portion of their concentration just flying the aircraft, keeping it under control. That left little spare mental capacity to locate and prosecute the enemy. Today, the opposite is true. Computers have made flying so simple that it is now considered very easy to fly the F-22 or F-35. Computers have also taken away all the hard work associated with manipulating and operating the avionics systems, so today's combat pilots are more like battle managers than knights of the sky.

ABOVE: The F-22 Raptor is without question the world's most capable fighter. More than any other type, the Raptor turns those who fly it into battle managers, thanks to its sophisticated avionics and stealthy properties.

LEFT: The SAAB JAS 39 Gripen offers countries with modest budgets the opportunity to own an advanced fighter without breaking the bank.

Flying the F-86 Sabre

An all-time classic fighter, the North American F-86 Sabre is best remembered by many for its role in wresting air superiority from communist forces over Korea, but it also excelled in combat elsewhere and was developed to fulfil tasks ranging from all-weather interceptor to tactical nuclear bomber. Perhaps most importantly, the Sabre introduced the era of the swept-wing, supersonic warplane to air forces around the world.

Following such 'first-generation' US jet fighter designs as the P-80 Shooting Star and F-84 Thunderjet, the Sabre's critical advance was the employment of a wing with 35° of sweep. The original XP-86 design studies had incorporated a conventional straight wing and unswept tail surfaces, but evidence of Germany's advanced wartime research indicated the potential of swept flying surfaces, which would allow a new breed of jet fighters to slip into the supersonic realm.

Indeed, it has been suggested that the F-86 beat Chuck Yeager's rocket-powered X-1 through the sound barrier, and in early flight tests in

PILOT'S VERDICT

"[The F-86F was] designed to be a true fighter, and it was a very, very pleasant aeroplane to fly."

Major General Olav Aamoth
F-86F and F-86K pilot
Royal Norwegian Air Force

1947, test pilots certainly pushed close to the magic Mach 1.0 figure – if not beyond. Such was the Sabre's development potential, however, that later models, although heavier, were regularly going supersonic in a shallow dive.

ON THE FRONT LINE

Maj. Gen. Olav Aamoth has been described as the most experienced fighter pilot in Norway and was in the centre of Cold War activities with this NATO air arm, later being appointed Chief of Staff in the Royal Norwegian Air Force (RNoAF). He has flown the F-84, F-104 Starfighter and

F-16 Fighting Falcon, in addition to around 1,200 hours on the Sabre, and recalls the impression made by the first appearance of the F-86 in Norway: *'The* [swept wing] *was the big difference: you had no Mach limitations. You could go into a dive against a target without going into a pitch-up...'*

The F-86F model provided Aamoth's first experience of the Sabre, a variant first flown in March 1952 and which had been rushed to Korea before the end of that year, to bolster the F-86As and Es already deployed. Thanks to the 'all-flying' tail and 'irreversible' flight controls added from the F-86E onwards, the controls remained light and the handling precise throughout the transonic regime. *'The force required* [on the stick] *was the same at supersonic speed as it was*

MAIN PHOTOGRAPH: A Sabre performs a high-speed pass at NAS Oceana in 2004. A popular performer on the warbird scene, preserved Sabres can be seen at numerous airshows.

[MISSION REPORT]
+++++++++++++++++++++++++++++

ENTER THE MISSILE AGE
– TAIWAN VS CHINA

The F-86 Sabre holds the honour of introducing the era of the air-to-air missile (AAM) in combat. The first successful operational use of a guided AAM was made by F-86Fs of the Chinese Nationalist Air Force (CNAF) during confrontations with the Chinese People's Liberation Army Air Force (PLAAF) in the late 1950s. Numerically among the most significant export operators of the type, the CNAF received its first F-86s in late 1954 and would eventually accept 320 from USAF stocks, many of these being Korean War veterans. A first air-to-air kill was made against a PLAAF MiG-15 as early as 15 October 1955. When tensions between the Communists and Nationalists increased, a number of CNAF Sabres were quickly wired for the carriage of a pair of the first-generation AIM-9B Sidewinder AAMs, and they took this weapon into combat over the Taiwan Straits in 1958, during the Formosa Crisis. The crisis had begun when the Communists began a renewed artillery bombardment against the Nationalist-controlled islands of Quemoy and Matsu in the Straits in August. The first of numerous air-to-air confrontations soon began over the Straits, and these continued until October, and even extended to skirmishes fought over the Chinese mainland. Modern research supports Taiwanese claims that the Sabres destroyed no less than 31 PLAAF MiG-15 and MiG-17 fighters between August and September, for only two F-86 losses in air combat. In fact, confirmed 'kills' by the PLAAF amounted to just one F-86, achieved via collision with a MiG-17, although there are unconfirmed PLAAF claims detailing as many as 10 aerial victories against F-86s. Meanwhile, it is reported that only six examples of the Sidewinder were launched in anger during the crisis, these achieving four MiG 'kills', all recorded on 24 September; the other two AAMs caused damage to their intended targets. A further outbreak of fighting came in July 1959, when two more MiG-17s were confirmed as destroyed by the CNAF's Sabres – the CNAF made claims for five 'kills' in this period. The last of the CNAF F-86Fs were finally withdrawn in 1971.

at the lower speeds,' explains Aamoth. *'This was very different from what you had in the Thunderjet. So that made it a much more pleasant aeroplane to fly, and you could do things in the area of combat, which you couldn't achieve in the subsonic Thunderjet…It was a wonderful formation aeroplane because of the light controls – the hydraulic controls. You really had to fly it with some finesse – [it was] much more delicate than in the Thunderjet. It was very, very sensitive on the controls, but when you got used to it, it required less muscle power…'*

The Sabre's crisp handling made it an obvious mount for aerobatic teams in the 1950s: in addition to USAF teams, the air forces of Canada, Greece, Italy, Spain, Turkey, Yugoslavia and others all used the F-86 for formation aerobatics. In Norway, meanwhile, teams were formed on both the F-86F day-fighter and the F-86K all-weather interceptor: *'I had the aerobatic team on the "K"…'* explains Maj. Gen. Aamoth. *'It wasn't a very good display aircraft, because of the power, but still, if you did the right manoeuvres, and stayed at low altitude, you could do a fair amount of display with it, and we capitalised on that and had good fun with it…In southern Norway they had a very good aerobatic team on the "F", the 'Flying Jokers' they were called, and actually they were much better than we on the "K" up north, and they were a sort of a European high-standard… They were very good…'*

As well as continued aerodynamic refinements made throughout the F-86's development, the powerplant was progressively uprated to provide the pilot with more thrust. In the case of Aamoth's F-86F, a new engine was introduced in the form of the J47-GE-27. Although this provided a performance boost, Aamoth remembers that, *'We were, actually, a little underpowered…We had about 5,200 pounds [23kN] of thrust – actually a little less than in the Thunderjet, but the aircraft [was] lighter…When the Canadians put the Orenda engines in their Sabres, and the Australians the Avon, [the Sabre] became a fantastic aeroplane.'*

ALL-WEATHER FIGHTER

Aamoth's next mount was the F-86K, a radar-equipped all-weather fighter that was equivalent to the USAF's 'Sabre Dog' that featured a radar nose and rocket armament. The 'K' brought with it the J47-GE-33 engine, producing 7,650 pounds (34.02kN) of thrust with afterburning. However, the aircraft remained somewhat underpowered. *'It gave you about 2,000 pounds [8.89kN] more thrust, but that still – with a loaded aeroplane, with armament and so on – was not exhilarating, but it made possible for quick take-offs and acceleration to combat speed. The reheat itself had a very small area of control, so when you went into reheat you couldn't really modulate the power very much – very much different from today where you can modulate the afterburner over a great range of power settings. And it didn't always ignite.'*

Compared to the earlier day-fighters, the all-weather variants were a lot bigger and heavier, and this had a pronounced effect on their handling, as Maj. Gen. Aamoth recalls: *'Flying it, it was heavier – much heavier – than the "F"…Being much heavier, of course the manoeuvrability suffered; even with the afterburner on it was underpowered, and being an all-weather fighter, it wasn't really a dogfight aeroplane, it was an interceptor for all-weather conditions…It was a very good instrument aeroplane – flying in bad weather and up in northern Norway…It had ILS as well, which was a new thing for us, and a new navigation system – the TACAN system, tactical air navigation – so all this was new to us and very interesting [and] demanding. [It was] very satisfying to have such an advanced piece of machinery.'*

The pilots of the first F-86s thrown into combat over Korea's 'MiG Alley' could call upon the combined firepower of six 0.5in (12.7mm) Browning machine-guns – the same armament used by P-51 Mustang pilots in World War II. Although lacking the sheer firepower of the MiG-15, this remained the standard gun armament on US-built Sabres until the arrival of the 'Sabre Dog'. The F-86K for NATO, meanwhile, lacked the F-86D's rocket armament, but it added four hard-hitting 20mm cannon in place of the machine-guns. The advantage of the machine-guns was, as Maj. Gen. Aamoth reveals, the fact that *'the armament was concentrated; much more so than in the Thunderjet, which had two of its guns in the wings. And [the F-86F] was a delightful aeroplane to fire air-to-air gunnery with. It had a radar rangefinder coupled to the gyro gunsight – actually the same as in the Thunderjet, but combined with placing all the guns in the nose [this made it] a very good aeroplane for air-to-air gunnery. Now, for working as a fighter-bomber we used the standard weapons of the time, which was 500lb [227kg] bombs, or eight 5in [127mm] rockets. And we could carry napalm tanks as well…With the four 20mm cannon [of the F-86K], their rate of fire was less. It was a heavier gun than the Browning machine-guns, and having just four instead of six, the bullet pattern was of course not as dense as with the "F", but with the new gunsight which we had on the "K" – which was a great advance on the earlier "F" – we still had very good air-to-air results. We did a lot of air-to-air firing, obviously, since that was the only role. It was not a*

fighter-bomber and was never intended to be…'

In RNoAF service as elsewhere, the F-86K's cannon were soon supplemented by guided missile armament: *'We got the [AIM-9B] Sidewinder in about 1960, and that again was fantastic. We felt like masters of the sky with this thing on. We didn't realise, of course, all the limitations of the early Sidewinders. But we did fire it. We used rockets as the target; we had a rocket on one pylon on one wing, and we had a Sidewinder on the other wing, so we first fired off a 5in rocket and let it fly out for a couple of thousand feet and then you fired a Sidewinder to track it down and destroy it, which was quite good fun.'*

TACTICAL NUKES

Perhaps surprisingly for an aircraft that forged its reputation as a dogfighter in the air-to-air arena, the Sabre was also adapted for more offensive roles, even being equipped to carry tactical nuclear weapons. In the US, this requirement was met by the F-86H 'Sabre Hog' version, which was powered by the big J73 engine and which incorporated LABS (Low-Altitude Bombing System) toss-bombing equipment as standard. The primary nuclear store for the F-86H was the Mk 12 bomb, with a yield of 10-20 kilotons.

ABOVE: Leading US and UN ace of the Korean War was Capt. Joseph M. McConnell of the 39th FIS, 51st FIG. Seen here in his F-86F *Beauteous Butch II*, McConnell ran up a personal tally of 16 aerial victories over Korea, including three MiGs downed in one day, on 18 May 1953.

FAR LEFT: The cockpit layout of the F-86 – this is a Canadair-built CL-13 – was well laid out and advanced for its time. The pilot's 'office' was also spacious, and afforded excellent visibility.

BELOW: Former F-14 pilot Dale Snodgrass taxis his Sabre out for a display at the 2005 NAS Oceana airshow in Virginia Beach.

[MISSION REPORT]

+++++++++++++++++++++++++++

INDIA VS PAKISTAN
– AIR COMBAT

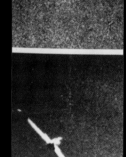

F-86 day-fighters of the Pakistan Air Force (PAF) went to war on two occasions against the Indian Air Force (IAF), in 1965 and 1971. At the time of the August–September 1965 conflict over the disputed Kashmir region, the Sabre was the most important warplane in the PAF inventory. In fact, the PAF F-86 had opened its account long before the 1965 war, with an IAF Canberra confirmed destroyed in April 1959. As well as being used for combat air patrols – with some aircraft being armed with Sidewinders – the PAF Sabres saw action during day and night air defence – including CAPs flown with Mach-2 F-104s as top cover, airfield strike, battlefield interdiction and close support missions.

Pakistan's assault began on 31 August, and PAF Sabres made a dawn raid on Indian army positions using rockets and machine-gun fire. Other roles included the escort of PAF B-57 bombers attacking Indian supply routes, and providing cover for trains delivering ammunition to friendly lines. A number of Indian aircraft fell to the Sabre's guns (and missiles), including examples of the Gnat, Hunter, Mystère and Vampire – at least three examples of the last-named type were claimed on 1 September alone, before the official outbreak of hostilities. On 2 September the Sabre force was committed to rocket attacks on Indian ground forces, and the following day saw the first, inconclusive, encounter with IAF Gnats, although an F-86 fell to this type on 4 September.

On 6 September – when the war 'officially' began – PAF Sabres claimed three Hunters in combat, while IAF Hunters destroyed three F-86s in turn. High-scorers among the PAF Sabre community included Sqn Ldr Mohammed Alam, who was eventually credited with nine 'kills', plus two damaged, as commander of No. 11 Squadron, one of at least eight units to have flown the type. On 7 September, in frantic actions during PAF raids on IAF airfields, Alam reportedly downed no less than five Hunters – four of these in a period of 30 seconds! Modern research suggests Alam destroyed two Hunters on this day, and made four 'kills' in total. Only one F-86 was confirmed lost on this day, with the two Hunters and a Mystère falling to Sabres. In the following days the F-86s were mainly involved in ground-attack missions, but a Gnat was destroyed by a Sabre/Sidewinder combination on 13 September. The next day saw the Gnat exact its revenge, with a manoeuvre 'kill' against an F-86.

On 16 September, Alam and his wingman, Lt Mohammed Shaukut-ul-Islam, were undertaking an offensive patrol at high altitude over Indian territory, with the aim of drawing IAF fighters up from their bases. The PAF pilots received a radio call indicating that two Hunters had taken off, and the four aircraft were soon locked in battle. While Alam destroyed the second Hunter with an AIM-9, the leader shot down Shaukut-ul-Islam, who ejected to be shot and then captured. A further two F-86s also fell to Gnats on this day. As the war drew to a

close, Sabres registered further confirmed 'kills' against the Hunter (two) and a single Gnat – all using gunfire – against one further loss credited to a Gnat.

After the 1965 war, the PAF boosted its F-86 stocks with the acquisition of 90 surplus West German Canadair Sabre Mk 6s, acquired by illicit means via Iran. These joined F-86Fs that comprised the survivors from the original deliveries of 120 aircraft from the US.

In both wars, the Sabre proved well matched with the IAF's Gnat fighters, and it was an engagement between these two types that precipitated the outbreak of the second major conflict, in December 1971. Again, the fighting broke out ahead of the official start of hostilities, as Gnats destroyed three F-86s as early as 22 November. On 3 December Sabres helped spearhead PAF strikes against IAF airfields, and in fighting the next day six examples fell to Hunters. In response, PAF Sabres destroyed five Hunters. On 5 December it was the turn of the IAF to wage war on PAF airfields, but Sabres avoided air-to-air combat. The following day saw an F-86 fall to a Hunter, and another was lost in combat on 7 December, to an HF-24 Marut. By now attrition was affecting the Sabre fleet badly, but the aircraft continued to be thrown into ground-attack missions, targeting airfields and Indian armour, with further action from 10 December, when two more Sabres were destroyed by a Hunter and a Marut.

Sabres would score four more confirmed victories: a Su-7 on the 11th, followed by a Gnat and a Krishak spotter aircraft on the 14th. Most impressively, a MiG-21 was destroyed on 17 December, the last day of the conflict, using machine-gun fire alone. The last two Sabres were lost in aerial combat on 13/14 December – in both cases to Hunters. Overall losses – to both IAF and anti-aircraft artillery – had been heavy, and the Sabre's days in PAF service were numbered. Nevertheless, the type soldiered on with the PAF until 1980.

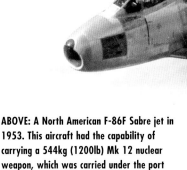

Over Korea, the earlier Sabre variants had been very well matched to their communist MiG-15 opposition in terms of performance and manoeuvrability, and it was inevitable that as the F-86 increased in weight through further development, its outstanding agility would be correspondingly eroded.

However, the day-fighter variants like the F-86F long remained a useful weapon in a turning dogfight, and this saw them remain in service into the 1980s with some air forces. On the other hand, the strengths of the F-86D/K 'one-man interceptor' lay in using a combination of its radar-based weapons system (albeit slightly downgraded in the F-86K export version) and afterburning engine to prosecute a hit-and-run attack on an unwitting enemy. Nevertheless, air combat manoeuvring remained on the all-weather Sabre pilot's syllabus, as Maj. Gen. Aamoth explains:

'We had to train on it, because we never knew exactly what we would have to expect…We just had to use the things we had to our advantage, and, for example, try to stay out of a turning fight with [fighters] like the MiG-15 or the F-86F, because as soon you start a turning fight, of course

ABOVE: A North American F-86F Sabre jet in 1953. This aircraft had the capability of carrying a 544kg (1200lb) Mk 12 nuclear weapon, which was carried under the port wing, while droptanks were attached under the starboard wing.

they have the advantage. So you really had to rather exploit altitude, you had to gain speed, diving and use your afterburner…Using the afterburner, and without the external fuel tanks, we got up to 50,000 feet [15,240m], as with the "F", but it took time and a lot of fuel. But we got there. With the "K", basically around between 20,000 and 30,000 feet [6,000–9,000m], that was the best altitude.'

The day and all-weather fighter models of the Sabre were also pitted against each other, as Aamoth explains: 'We were fighting each other every day, almost. Again, with the "F" being much lighter and much more

manoeuvrable, the "K" was no match for it in the daylight environment. But of course in darkness, then the roles were reversed completely.'

JET AGE MILESTONE

The Sabre has ensured its place in aviation history through a combination of its awesome achievements in combat, its pioneering operational use of missiles, various speed records and its long and distinguished service career. Perhaps its most important contribution, however, was in preparing a generation of Cold War pilots for the technological challenges of the sophisticated Mach 2 warplanes that awaited them.

Recalling the F-86, Maj. Gen. Aamoth remarked that the aircraft, like its US counterpart the 'Sabre Dog', represented 'a quantum leap, where a single pilot could operate a powerful search radar, with automatic pilot, electronic fuel control, afterburner for the engine, and later Sidewinder missile armament – it was a completely new ballgame for us day-fighter pilots…'

ABOVE: 52-3630, the prototype North American-built YF-86K, was converted from an F-86D and made its first flight in July 1954. Although the 'Sabre Dog' had been developed in some haste, the all-weather fighter versions of the Sabre gave good Cold War service.

LEFT: Assigned the vital role of protecting the continental US against the Soviet bomber threat, the F-86D 'Sabre Dog' entrusted its armament to unguided aerial rockets, carried in a retractable tray under the forward fuselage.

BELOW LEFT: This Japanese Air Self-Defense Force F-86F is one of 18 examples that were adapted for the reconnaissance role as the RF-86F. This added characteristic 'cheek' fairings on the sides of the cockpit, associated with the three under-fuselage K-14 and K-22 cameras.

Flying the MiG-15 and MiG-17

The MiG-15 was designed as a high-altitude interceptor, intended to destroy high-flying nuclear-capable American bombers like the Boeing B-29 and B-50 and the Convair B-36. It displayed its best aerodynamic qualities at heights of 6,100m (20,000ft) or more. Below that, it had dangerous tendencies. On several occasions in combat over Korea, UN pilots were mystified to see undamaged MiGs go into a spin during a combat manoeuvre and fail to come out of it, their pilots ejecting.

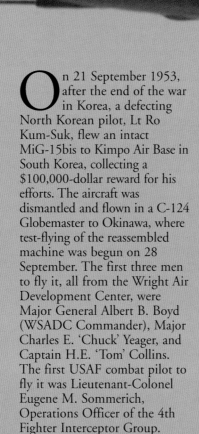

On 21 September 1953, after the end of the war in Korea, a defecting North Korean pilot, Lt Ro Kum-Suk, flew an intact MiG-15bis to Kimpo Air Base in South Korea, collecting a $100,000-dollar reward for his efforts. The aircraft was dismantled and flown in a C-124 Globemaster to Okinawa, where test-flying of the reassembled machine was begun on 28 September. The first three men to fly it, all from the Wright Air Development Center, were Major General Albert B. Boyd (WSADC Commander), Major Charles E. 'Chuck' Yeager, and Captain H.E. 'Tom' Collins. The first USAF combat pilot to fly it was Lieutenant-Colonel Eugene M. Sommerich, Operations Officer of the 4th Fighter Interceptor Group.

It was only now that western pilots could begin to understand the mysterious spinning troubles of the MiG. The cockpit of the MiG-15 featured a white line painted down the middle of the instrument panel, and if their aircraft got into a stall pilots were directed to shove the control column hard against it in an attempt to unstall the wings. If the MiG entered a spin and failed to recover after three rotations, the standard procedure was to eject. The problem was compounded by the fact that the cockpit was not fitted with a stall warning device. The aircraft also had a

MAIN PHOTOGRAPH: Pilot Bill Reesman puts his 'Red Bull' MiG-17 through its paces during an air show at March Reserve Air Base, California, on 3 May 2008. Reesman is an experienced combat veteran who flew 320 missions in Vietnam.

number of other unpleasant tendencies, including a tendency to oscillate – which made it a poor gun platform – and to pitch up without warning. The cockpit pressurization system worked intermittently, and the emergency fuel pump was prone to explode when turned on, tearing off the rear fuselage.

Summarizing his experience of flying the MiG-15, Colonel Sommerich rated the Russian type as '*not a bad airplane for acceleration, climb and maximum altitude, but I could still whip it with an F-86 any day of the week. Seeing them above us so often gave us only one problem – how to get them down where we were so we could fight. When he stayed over 50,000 feet [15,240m], he was safe. The MiG is nowhere near a match for the F-86, if the F-86 maintains a high Mach.*'

PILOT'S VERDICT

"*The Americans were taken completely by surprise. I caught up with them and shot one of them down.*"

Captain Dmitri A. Samolyov
523rd Fighter Air Regiment
VVS

LEFT: Although the MiG-17 was thought to be a simple improvement on the MiG-15, it was in fact virtually a new design, incorporating aerodynamic and other refinements that were developed as a result of the earlier jet's combat experiences over Korea.

BELOW: The Pakistan Air Force was a major user of the MiG-17 in its Chinese license-built version, the Shenyang F-5. Seen here is the FT-5 two-seat trainer version, the equivalent of the MiG-17UTI.

Lieutenant Ro, the North Korean pilot, stated that MiG pilots were told to limit their speed to 0.92 Mach and to avoid spins. American pilots found that buffeting began at 0.91 Mach, with the aircraft showing a tendency to nose up at 0.93. The speed brakes, normally manually controlled, opened automatically at 0.92. The MiG's turning radius was small, but this was compromised by its poor stalling characteristics. American pilots found no difficulty in pulling out of a spin, but disliked the instability and lack of stall warning.

The MiG's superiority over the Sabre at high altitude was revealed in a report by one of the Soviet fighter pilots who saw combat over Korea, Captain Dmitri A. Samolyov of the 523rd Fighter Air Regiment.

'On 9 September 1951 I flew as leader of a pair for the first time, and immediately shot down an F-86. It happened like this. Six of us were flying in the Andzu area where the fighting was particularly fierce, and where the Americans often used their fighter-bombers. From the GCC we suddenly received the urgent warning that we were being attacked by 24 Sabres. We started looking around, and found that the enemy was already very close to us. What were we to do? [Grigorii] Okhay suddenly led all six aircraft in a hard break, four to the left and two to the right. I was on the left, so I flew in this direction, and the other pair made the right turn. Suddenly we were alone. Eight Sabres followed us. They were attacking us from

[MISSION REPORT]
++++++++++++++++++++++++++++
ONE THAT GOT AWAY

In 1953 a Polish Air Force MiG-15bis pilot, Lt Zygmunt Gosciniak, defected to the neighbouring Danish island of Bornholm, only 25 miles (40 km) from his base. He had been briefed to take part in an air combat exercise with another pilot, a Russian.

'I was flying lower than he was, so that I could see him but he could not see me. Then the Russian peeled off to the left, and while he was engaged in this manoeuvre, I peeled off to the right – away from him instead of following him. From my height of 20,000 feet [6,100m] I dived right down to 400 feet [120m] at a speed of about 600 miles an hour [965km/h]. I knew that my only chance of avoiding the Russian artillery on the ground was to fly as near the deck as possible. I hopped over trees and hedges and made straight for the coast, and as the sea came up beneath me I set a course for Bornholm.'

Despite a compass malfunction, Gosciniak sighted Bornholm after searching for the island for several minutes, and to his relief spotted an airfield.

'I let down my undercarriage ready to land and then saw about twenty workmen busily engaged on the runway. They took no notice of me and would not go away to give me a clear space to land. So I climbed again and let off four rockets – yellow, green, blue and red. In Poland this had been a recognized signal of intention to land, but I did not realize that it had no significance to the workmen below.

'I had very little fuel left now, so I chose to land on the grass by the side of the runway. I raised the undercarriage and prepared for a belly landing. I came in low over the airfield, but my view of the immediate landing ground was obscured by a house. Quickly I pulled up over the house and came down again towards the grass. But, to my horror, I saw there was a bulldozer right in my path. I swerved crazily to the left to avoid it, and the wing of my plane grazed the ground. The impact jarred ever nerve in my body and smashed my head against the gunsight. My speed was about 150 miles an hour [240km/h] as I hit the ground, for 600 yards [550m] before coming to a halt. The dust was incredible – it rose 60 feet [18m] into the air. Soon officialdom surrounded me.'

above, were faster and really very close to us. At a range of 1000 metres [3,280ft] they began to shoot at us. I shouted "Hold on!" to my wingman, Misha Zykov, and started turning.

'I was turning round, to the left, up and down again. The Sabres attacked us at a height of about 6,000 or 6,500 metres [19 or 21,000ft] and followed us as high as 11,000 metres [36,000ft].

'Somewhere in the region of 10,500 metres [35,000ft] I saw that four of them had given up and were on their way down. Although I had already begun to lose speed, my aircraft was still climbing. Then I saw that two of the other four pursuers had also given up and were on their way down too. I looked around; the sky was clear with nobody in sight, so I turned and went after the last pair of F-86s. The Americans were taken completely by surprise. I caught up with them and shot one of them down.'

INTENTIONAL STALLING

Experienced Russian pilots also had no trouble in coping with the MiG's stalling and spinning characteristics, and sometimes used them as evasive combat manoeuvres, as revealed by Lieutenant Nikolai Ivanov of the 726th Fighter Air Regiment.

'I practised stalling frequently and made my pilots do the same, so that they learned to recognize it and deal with it. On one occasion, with a Sabre on my tail, I stalled deliberately and he overshot. We were at medium altitude, and as I recovered from

the stall I saw the Sabre directly in front of me. I fired twice and hit him. A second Sabre appeared ahead of me. I fired, seeing strikes on his left wing, and he began to smoke. I fired again and the Sabre exploded in flames. It fell away to the left, trailing smoke.'

RIGHT: The MiG-15 was powered by an imported version of the Rolls-Royce Nene turbojet, supplied to the Soviet Union by the post-war British government in a misplaced gesture of goodwill.

MiG-15 pilots in Korea often preferred to circle at altitude and then carry out diving attacks on United Nations aircraft. One advantage of this type of attack was that gravity assisted, rather than hindered, the trajectory of the MiG's heavy 37mm (1.46in) shells. In a level attack, the trajectory of the 37mm(1.46in) rounds dropped much more sharply than that of the 23mm

(0.91in), to the extent that UN pilots under attack from astern often saw the 37mm (1.46in) tracer rounds pass underneath them while the 23mm (0.91in) rounds passed overhead.

THE MIG-17

When the MiG-17 first appeared in the early 1950s, western observers at first believed that it was an improved MiG-15, with

ABOVE: A MiG-15UTI jet trainer coming in to land. Thousands of Eastern Bloc pilots received their advanced jet training on this type, as did pilots of many more nations who purchased MiG-15s.

LEFT: Seen here in USAF markings, this is the MiG-15 flown to the Republic of Korea in 1953 by Lt Ro, a defecting North Korean pilot. It is flown here by Capt Tracey B. Mathewson, who became a qualified instructor on the type.

American pilots were astounded by the MiG-17's manoeuvrability when they first encountered it in combat over North Vietnam. It came as a severe shock to the USAF and US Navy to discover that the MiG-17 was a serious match for their modern, radar-equipped, automated supersonic fighters. The MIG-17 had a far lower wing loading than its opponents; its span was almost as great as that of the F-4 Phantom, but its loaded weight was about the same as that of the F-4's internal fuel load. The result was that the MiG-17 could enter a relatively slow but very tight turn that no US aircraft could match.

COCKPIT REFINEMENTS

One of the most important refinements incorporated in the MiG-17 was a new ejection seat. Introduced in 1953, it was similar to the well-tried British Martin-Baker design, and was fitted with a face blind, leg restraints, and stabilizers to prevent the seat from tumbling. A rear-view

mirror was also fitted on top of the canopy.

The aircraft was also fitted with an RP-1 Izumrud (Emerald) AI radar, the search radar antenna being mounted in a 'lip' installation on top of the intake and the tracking radar antenna in a radome on the intake splitter. The cockpit was modified to accommodate the radar scope. The radar, known as 'Scan Odd' under the NATO codename system, was used in the terminal stage of an attack, the pilot being guided to the vicinity of the target by ground controlled interception (GCI).

The MiG-17F featured modified airbrakes, as did the last variant, the MiG-17PF. The latter was also fitted with the improved Izumrud 2 radar, which had a greater range and a larger radome on the centreline intake bulkhead. A Sirena-2 radar warning receiver (RWR) was also fitted.

One problem common to both the MiG-15 and MiG-17, from the pilot's point of view, was the small clearance between the

ABOVE: This close-up of the nose of a MiG-15bis clearly shows the installation of the 37mm cannon. This weapon was not much use in fighter-versus-fighter combat, as gravity had an adverse effect on the ballistic trajectory of its shells.

RIGHT: A stricken MiG-15 goes down over Korea, the victim of a Sabre's guns. American claims that they destroyed ten MiGs for every Sabre lost were later drastically revised.

BELOW: This MiG-15bis, pictured at the Monino Air Museum near Moscow, has been configured in the ground attack role.

new features that reflected the technical lessons learned during the Korean War. In fact, design of the MiG-17 had begun long before the war in 1949. The new type incorporated a number of aerodynamic refinements that included a new tail on a longer fuselage and a thinner wing with different section and planform.

The MiG-17's highly swept wing was virtually untapered and incorporated some anhedral to reduce stability in the rolling plane. The wing was relatively lightly loaded, giving good manoeuvrability, especially in terms of turning performance. Three full-chord fences were fitted to each wing; these stop the span-wise migration of boundary-layer air, significantly reducing induced drag.

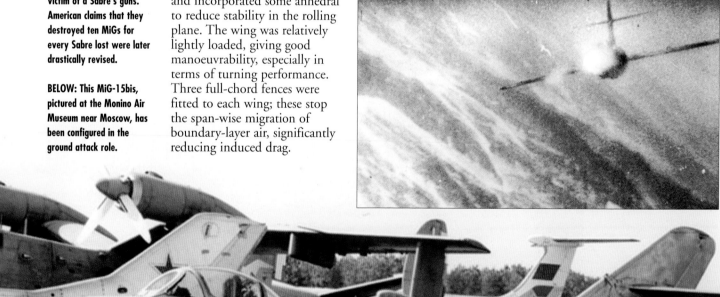

[MISSION REPORT]
++++++++++++++++++++++++++
EQUIPMENT BRIEFING

The west had little technical information on the MiG-15, other than that which could be gleaned from combat encounters with the type over Korea, until July 1951, when a wrecked example was salvaged from shallow waters off the North Korean coast. A thorough examination of the wreckage by US and British Intelligence experts, and data obtained from intact MiG-15s whose pilots defected in later years, resulted in the following abridged report on the aircraft's cockpit and associated equipment.

RADIO EQUIPMENT
The early model MiG-15 had no radar, not even IFF (Identification Friend/Foe), and the electronic equipment appears to have consisted solely of a high-frequency radio and navaid (RSI-6M-1), and a low-frequency homing receiver (RPKO-10M). The only antennae are the wire aerial stretching between the fin and the mast behind the cockpit, and a flat loop which is buried in the underside of the rear fuselage. The MiG-15bis is better equipped, although there is no record of radar ranging ever being fitted. In this case the radio transceiver is a VHF set (RSIU-3M), feeding a blade antenna behind the cockpit. Navigation is assisted by a beacon receiver (MRP-48P) and a radio compass (ASRK-5), the latter using the wire aerial (which now goes directly to the front fuselage) and a directional antenna mounted under a plastic panel in the rear fuselage. In addition, a radio altimeter (RV-2 or -10) was introduced in this model, and an IFF set (type SRO) feeding the antenna mounted on top of the centre fuselage. None of the series appears top have a standby radio, or provision for tele-briefing.

COCKPIT LAYOUT AND EJECTION SEAT
The MiG-15's cockpit is somewhat cramped by Western standards, and during evaluation pilots complained of trouble with canopy defrosting. The cockpit heating and

ABOVE: The MiG-15's cockpit was simple, and Western pilots who flew the Russian aircraft were often critical of the layout.

environmental systems are poor, and if a pilot is forced to dive rapidly from high altitude the canopy tends to fog up, limiting visibility. The cabin is designed for the surprisingly high pressure differential of 4.2 psi (0.3 kg/cm2), but the mass flow of the air-conditioning system is rather low for operation in hot climates. The ejection seat is simplicity in the extreme, there being no drogue to stabilise the seat, no leg restraining straps, and no protection for the pilot's face other than that provided by his goggles. In ejecting he simply places his feet on the rests provided, grasps the firing handles built into the armrests, jettisons the canopy with his left hand, and fires the seat by pulling the trigger on the right side. The seat is then ejected, and after three seconds the straps are automatically released, enabling the pilot to fall clear and open his parachute. (It was recognised that the ejection lever only being fitted on the right side might cause problems if the pilot should be injured, so later MiG-15s were reconfigured with levers on both sides, activating the canopy release as well as the seat firing mechanism).

The air brakes are deployed by depressing a button on the control column, and automatically retract when the pressure is released. The airbrakes are deployed automatically if there is a danger of the aircraft exceeding its limiting Mach number of 0.92. The 37mm (1.46in) cannon button is on top of the control column, and the twin 23mm (0.91in) triggers on the front. (On later models the latter were reconfigured in a single gun button).

INSTRUMENT LAYOUT
The instrument layout is conventional, although space is saved to some extent by combining two or more instruments in a single case. For example, one unit shows both IAS (Indicated Air Speed) and TAS (True Air Speed). Another acts as both voltmeter and ammeter, and a third combines fuel pressure, oil pressure and oil temperature. The gunsight is believed to be based on a British design, with a maximum range setting of 2650ft (800m) The aircraft has no parking brake, and no anti-G equipment for its pilot.

cockpit canopy and the pilot's head. Pilots often opted to wear leather flying helmets, rather than the bulkier 'bone dome'.

Pilots also suffered from lack of space as the cockpit equipment underwent progressive refinements. For example, the gun sight occupied most of the space in the front of the canopy, restricting the pilot's view. In addition, a rocket control panel was added to the

RIGHT: A MiG-17F of the East German Air Force. The latter was unique among Warsaw Pact air forces in that it was often equipped with the most advanced Soviet fighters, instead of downgraded export models.

cockpit when the plane was equipped with rocket pods. The large tail fin and mid-set tailplane also restricted the pilot's view to the rear, creating a dangerous blind spot.

Flying the B-52

With its eight engines in four underwing pods, bicycle landing gear and wingtip outrigger wheels, the Boeing B-52 Stratofortress is remarkably ungainly and far from pretty. Yet for many, the venerable Stratofortress occupies a soft spot in their hearts.

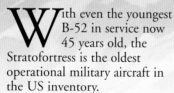

With even the youngest B-52 in service now 45 years old, the Stratofortress is the oldest operational military aircraft in the US inventory.

Major Shane 'Magnum' Vetter, a United States Air Force pilot with 1,300 hours' flying time in the B-52, explains the B-52's modern mission.

'It is tasked with pretty much every air-to-ground mission around. That includes nuclear, strategic attack, interdiction, close air support, offensive counter-air (bombing airfields), non-combat peacetime support (dropping leaflets), and naval mine-laying.'

The aircraft's sheer size and unconventional looks have led crews to call it the Big Ugly Fat Fellow, or BUFF, although the last word is sometimes replaced with an expletive.

Carrying as many as ten people, but with a usual combat crew of five, the Stratofortress is a complicated weapons system to operate, and each member of the crew brings a unique set of skills to the flight deck.

Vetter explains: *'The navigator is responsible for basic navigation; being at the right place on time. We can fly for thousands of miles and arrive at a precise location within seconds of our planned time. The radar navigator is primarily responsible for weapons employment. They are the experts on all of the weapons we carry, and they enter data into the targeting computer to target the weapons. In addition, the radar navigator supervises the navigator and backs them up. The electronic warfare officer [EWO] defends the aircraft by using a variety of sensors to know when enemies are looking at our aircraft, and then he can jam enemy radars, and dispense chaff and flares. The copilot shares flying*

duties with the aircraft commander, and he is also essentially a flight engineer: he is responsible for the radios and communication, engine performance, fuel distribution, and maintaining our centre of gravity within limits, and he coordinates with outside agencies such as ground controllers. Finally, the aircraft commander is ultimately responsible for the safe and effective employment of the aircraft. He takes in inputs from the various aircrew members, and then makes a decision on what to do with the jet.'

By way of example, Vetter says, 'If the EWO says we have to turn left to avoid getting shot, and the nav says we have to turn right in order to hit the target, the aircraft commander must make the decision on what to do based on experience, Rules Of Engagement, etc. Of course, I say "he" for convenience, but we also have female aircrew members in all crew positions.'

FLYING THE BUFF
With the B-52 design now almost 60 years old, it might be thought that the aircraft would show its age from a pilot's perspective.

'Not really,' replies Vetter, explaining, 'The B--52 actually

The B-52 is equipped with eight TF33 turbofans contained within four engine pods. Outboard of these are two external fuel tanks, and inboard are two weapons pylons originally designed to carry nuclear weapons to supplement those housed in the big jet's cavernous bomb bay. This B-52 was photographed over Afghanistan during a close air support mission.

ABOVE: Nose art on B-52s is common: 'Guardian of the Upper Realm' is a B-52H stationed at Minot Air Force Base (AFB), North Dakota. It is assigned to the 5th Bomber Wing, 23rd Bomber Squadron.

performs better now than it did when it was new due to a variety of upgrades that have been made over the years.' Even so, *'It can be sluggish, and yes its controls are a little heavy. The control surfaces themselves are not mechanically linked to the yoke or rudder pedals; instead they are all hydraulically actuated with an artificial feel system for the pilots. However, there are some heavy springs in the system, resulting in*

some very significant control forces. For example, holding in full rudder requires approximately 200 pounds [900N] of force.

'The B-52 is a very large, heavy aircraft with a large wingspan, which gives it a considerable moment of inertia. In addition, it uses spoilers instead of ailerons for lateral controls, which act by destroying lift, which is very sluggish. This, in turn, means that the aircraft does not react instantly to a control input like a small fighter aircraft will. Instead, the control input must be made, and then removed before it fully takes effect. If the control input is held in place long enough for the turn, climb, or bank to develop, you have just over-controlled and the aircraft will shoot past your desired attitude. All the same, with practice and good pilot technique, we are capable of air-to-air refuelling and maintaining a precise heading for weapons release within 0.1 degree of

desired heading while hand-flying the aircraft,' Vetter concludes.

And what of the flight envelope? Vetter says that, *'Within its flight envelope, it is fairly forgiving. It is an aerodynamically stable aircraft, meaning that it will return to its trimmed airspeed after a control input is made. It is capable of some fairly aggressive manoeuvring, but of course we do not try to go upside down in it.'*

Although the B-52 is impressively sized externally, its cockpit, split into two levels, is far from spacious, and creature comforts are basic indeed.

'There is a crew bunk, but the cockpit is so small that we are forced to use it for storage. There is a small electric oven that gets used quite a bit on long flights. There is not a real toilet on the jet, but we have a urinal in the corner. The ceiling is very low in the aircraft, so you can't actually stand up inside it. Therefore, you are forced to crouch

[MISSION REPORT] B-52 FUTURE
+++++++++++++++++++++++++++++

The USAF intends to keep the B-52 in service until at least 2040, but the Department of Defense has recommended that the number of aircraft in the B-52 fleet be halved in order to save money. Vetter put forward his view on the proposals:

'Congress repeatedly turns down suggestions to reduce the bomber fleet, so I don't know if it will ever happen. However, with fewer bombers, it will actually make it easier to maintain the aircraft. There is a possibility that it will affect individual crewmembers, who would be deployed more often, since reducing the fleet would probably be followed by a reduction in personnel. However, our mission is always growing, and we are deployed more now than ever.'

As for enhancing the jet itself, there is talk of a re-engining programme, but a stand-off radar jammer upgrade for the jet has already been axed, and Vetter is concerned about the B-52's *'lack of modern avionics and crew comfort.'* He closes by saying, *'A weather radar, TCAS [traffic collision avoidance system], and RVSM-compliant [Reduced Vertical Separation Minima] equipment would make the aircraft safer and more efficient to fly.'*

TCAS and RVSM would make it much safer for the BUFF to operate in the ever more crowded skies, particularly where there is an abundance of aircraft but no air traffic control, such as in a war zone.

MAIN PHOTOGRAPH: The BUFF is able to carry a vast array of conventional munitions, including these Mk.82 Air Inflatable Retard, or 'Balute', 227kg (500lb) general purpose bombs. With parachutes opening immediately after release, the bombs decelerate to allow the low-level BUFF to escape their blast radius. Flares are used to distract heat-seeking missiles.

PILOT'S VERDICT

"Within its flight envelope, it is fairly forgiving. It is an aerodynamically stable aircraft, meaning that it will return to its trimmed airspeed after a control input is made. It is capable of some fairly aggressive manoeuvring, but of course we do not try to go upside down in it."

Maj. Shane 'Magnum' Vetter
USAF B-52 pilot

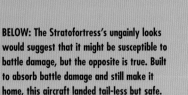

BELOW: The Stratofortress's ungainly looks would suggest that it might be susceptible to battle damage, but the opposite is true. Built to absorb battle damage and still make it home, this aircraft landed tail-less but safe.

down whenever moving, including while using the urinal. Upgrading our poor cockpit layout and uncomfortable seats, lack of latrine, etc. would reduce fatigue and make it more comfortable to fly. But the

aircraft was built during the Cold War to fly a nuclear mission, and nobody was too concerned about comfort. We fly it much more now than they did then – it primarily sat on ground alert back then – and the lack of crew comforts is much more noticeable.'

STRATOFORTRESS PECULIARITIES

At the time the B-52 entered service, its undercarriage was classified secret and closely protected from prying eyes. The reason for this is simple: it was the first aircraft to be designed to land in crosswinds by swivelling the undercarriage to line up with the runway.

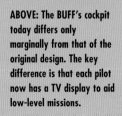

ABOVE: The BUFF's cockpit today differs only marginally from that of the original design. The key difference is that each pilot now has a TV display to aid low-level missions.

ABOVE: With the flight line at Minot AFB covered in snow, a line-up of B-52s awaits the day's flying schedule in the bitter Dakotan cold. The B-52 once stood nuclear alert 24 hours a day, 7 days a week, 365 days a year. With the Cold War over, the BUFF has turned its hand to conventional missions.

RIGHT: The Radar Navigator's station on the lower deck of the B-52's rather cramped cockpit.

'It can swivel left and right up to 20 degrees, so the aircraft can land in a crabbed attitude,' Vetter clarifies. 'Part of the reason for this design is the huge 185-foot [56m] wingspan. If we tried to land pointing straight down the runway in a "wing-low" attitude, we would scrape a wing tip. We use the crosswind crab landing gear system on virtually every landing, even if there are only a few knots of crosswind. On a typical day with about five to ten knots of crosswind [10–20mph], we will set between two and five degrees of crab. Using the full 20 degrees of travel, we can handle much more crosswind than most aircraft.'

Another of the BUFF's idiosyncrasies is the pronounced nose-down take-off attitude. This, says Vetter, is because 'the wing itself is not horizontal with respect to the fuselage. It is actually angled upwards towards the nose. This gives the wing a positive angle of attack when the fuselage is horizontal. Therefore, when we climb out, the nose of the fuselage is pointed down slightly, but the angle of attack of the wing is substantially positive.'

Unusually, some of the B-52's crew sit on downward-firing seats, resulting in a minimum altitude limit of 75m (250ft) in level flight. In emergency

situations, Vetter reveals, 'Our specific guidelines are the same as those for the rest of the Air Force: if you are at low altitude, don't stay in a bad jet below 2,000 feet [600m] trying to troubleshoot malfunctions, such as re-starting a flamed out engine. Since we have eight engines and many other multiple redundant systems – hydraulics, electrics – this is less of a problem for us. In fact, one of the best things about the Buff is its redundant systems. It was designed about five years after World War II, using lessons learned from B-17 and B-29 missions. It is designed to get shot at and keep going, with eight engines, six hydraulic systems, with back-up standby pumps, 12 independently controlled fuel tanks, and four 120 kilowatt [160hp] generators. We can fly and safely land the aircraft with less than half of our systems working. Also, B-52s have landed before with extensive battle damage, including large holes in wings and even missing the entire vertical stabilizer!'

WEAPONS PLATFORM

While the B-52's flying qualities and unique aerodynamic features are of great interest, the aircraft was of course built to be a heavy bomber. It is a role that it performs extremely well.

LEFT: Despite the aircraft's age – the youngest is 45 years old – the BUFF retains an impressive maintainability record and mission-capable rate. The aircraft's huge flaps, used to help it take flight, are clearly visible in this image of a B-52H taking off from Minot AFB during an exercise.

'We're capable of carrying virtually every type of munition in the inventory,' Vetter states. 'Nuclear bombs and cruise missiles, conventional gravity bombs, guided and unguided cluster bombs, GPS- [global positioning system] *guided bombs, GPS-guided cruise missiles, the AGM-158 Joint Air-to-Surface Standoff Missile – a new, highly precise stealthy cruise missile – sea mines, and laser guided bombs. Our range is about 8,000 miles* [12,800km] *one-way empty, or about 5,000 miles* [8,000km] *with a full combat payload, and we can fly indefinitely with air-to-air refuelling.'*

The B-52 finds its targets through a combination of GPS, inertial navigation system, radar, and Litening II laser targeting pods, the latter of which is gradually being introduced to the B-52 fleet. Litening II will, for the first time, give the B-52 the ability to optically target both static and moving targets on the ground. In doing so, the B-52 will become a much more flexible weapons platform that is

also far less reliant on other sources to generate target coordinates for it. With the introduction of these new targeting and avionics systems, carpet-bombing in the B-52 is firmly a thing of the past.

Vetter expands on that: *'We are still capable of dropping gravity bombs, and we have done so in Afghanistan. However, with our precise navigation system, we can drop unguided weapons from high altitude and have them land within about 200 feet* [60m] *of a target. Given the blast radius of*

the weapons, that is virtually a direct hit. Therefore, while we can lay down a "stick" of weapons of a given length that we can select in the cockpit, it is definitely not the WWII carpet bombing tactic.

'This precision capability is 'absolutely critical,' says Vetter. 'The vast majority of aerial combat today is in close support of friendly ground forces. A B-52 is able to employ close air support from high altitude using the JDAM, dropping very precisely while mitigating risk to friendly forces and collateral damage.'

BELOW: The B-52 has been used by the US Air Force to test alternative fuels that will help the USA reduce its dependence on imported petroleum. This BUFF participated in one such test in 2006: once safely airborne, two of the aircraft's eight engines were operated on the natural gas-based Fischer-Tropsch fuel blend.

BELOW: The brake parachute is used routinely on landing to help decelerate the massive jet and to reduce wear and tear on the main landing gear brake pads.

Flying the Avro Vulcan

Designed from the outset to carry British nuclear weapons, the Avro Type 698 Vulcan was the most important of the RAF's first generation of jet medium bombers, and a key component of Britain's nuclear deterrent force for over a decade.

From the moment of the first flight, Avro's Chief Test pilot, Wing Commander Roly Falk, was left in no doubt that the company had produced a winning design.

'From the start, the Vulcan was laid out with a view to simple operation, both on the ground and in the air. The cockpit was arranged in such a way that the complexity necessary in a modern aircraft was reduced as much as possible. For this reason, there did not appear to be any necessity for a crew of more than one on the early flights. In fact, only one seat was fitted. In some quarters surprise was expressed at this unusual decision, but as all the controls required in flight – even in an emergency – were within reach of the pilot, the Vulcan could in this respect be considered in the same light as a single-seater.'

PILOT'S VERDICT

❝ The Vulcan set an entirely new standard of manoeuvrability for an aircraft of this size.❞

Wing Commander Roly Falk
Chief Test Pilot

'Further flights were made as soon as possible and the required flying hours were completed just in time to fly to Boscombe Down and appear in the air over the SBAC Show [the annual Society of British Aircraft Constructors' display, at Farnborough]. Unfortunately, for security reasons, clearance could not be given for a landing to be made at Farnborough for the 1952 display. In the few hours' flying which I did before the display I was able to satisfy myself that the handling of the Vulcan came fully up to the high standard that we had been led to expect from our trials on the [BAC] 707. And I think that anybody who witnessed the aircraft flying at the display that year would confirm that it set an

ABOVE: After many years of painstaking and costly restoration work, Vulcan B.2 XH558 took to the air again on 18 October 2007.

MAIN PHOTOGRAPH: By no means a small aircraft, the vast wing area of the Vulcan gave it a considerable advantage at altitude, and its handling characteristics were highly praised by its pilots.

MAIN PHOTOGRAPH: With fighter-like manoeuvrability, the Vulcan could evade most interceptors of its era. Its rate of climb and descent were equally impressive.

ABOVE: A Vulcan casts its shadow on the desert during a 'Red Flag' exercise in Nevada, USA.

RIGHT: The Vulcan's entry/exit hatch was somewhat complicated. The three rear crew members, not having ejection seats, had to get out this way in the event of an emergency.

BELOW: A Vulcan releases its full salvo of twenty-one 454kg (1,000lb) bombs on a test range. The bomber's conventional weapons were used in anger during the 1982 Falklands War.

entirely new standard of manoeuvrability for an aircraft of this size.'

By the summer of 1953, a Royal Air Force liaison team was working closely with Avro in the test programme; it was headed by Squadron Leader Charles C. Calder, who in March 1945, while flying with No 617 Squadron, had captained the first Lancaster to drop a 10-tonne (22,000lb) 'Grand Slam' bomb on an enemy target, the Bielefeld Viaduct. Calder had gone to Avro in December 1952 and had made his first flight in the Vulcan on 18 February 1953, with Roly Falk as first pilot. The trip lasted about an hour and Calder handled the aircraft for 20 minutes.

DOCILE MANNER

'I had heard various rumours regarding the Vulcan's stalling characteristics,' recounted Calder, 'and I was determined to find out for myself. So I asked Roly if he would stall the machine. This he promptly did. To my surprise, the aircraft behaved in such a docile manner that I felt there must be some catch in it. Roly must have read my thoughts, for he immediately released the controls and said, "Now you do it!" I stalled the aircraft twice before I was finally convinced.'

COCKPIT LAYOUT

Squadron Leader Calder's team went on to evaluate the Vulcan at the Aeroplane and Armament Experimental Establishment, Boscombe Down, Wiltshire. One of the RAF test pilots involved described the aircraft's cockpit layout:

'The crew entered the Vulcan's pressure cabin by the under-fuselage hatch position just in front of the nosewheel, an arrangement which caused some misgivings among the three rear crew members, who had no ejection seats and who, being required to make their exit through the hatch in an emergency, felt there might be problems if the undercarriage was lowered at the time. The hatch itself opened to an angle of about 45 degrees and inside had a ladder, a section of which slid down to hang vertically from the lower edge to make the climb-in easier. Inside the pressure cabin, the two navigators and the air electronics officer sat facing rearwards in bucket seats on a raised platform a little above and behind the door, their instruments positioned in a semi-circle and filling the space above a table running from one side of the fuselage to the other. Their only view of the outside world was through two small portholes, situated high up on either side of the cabin.

'Another short ladder led up to the flight deck, with its twin ejection seats. This arrangement appeared somewhat cramped, as though the second seat had been pushed into what looked like a single-seat cockpit as an afterthought, and worming one's way through the narrow gap between the seats was a definite art which required practise to perfect without undue contortions, especially as the throttle console was positioned between the two pilots.

FIGHTER-TYPE CONTROLS

'The cockpit was equipped with dual control columns on the ends of tubes which slid into the lower part of the blind flying panels. Pilots coming to the Vulcan from other bombers expressed surprise that the control columns were not of the traditional "spectacle" type, but the fighter-type sticks had one big advantage: they made snatch units [devices which quickly move the control column out of the way of the pilot's legs] unnecessary as part of the ejection system, and if the pilots were forced to eject it was with the comforting knowledge that their legs were unlikely to be parted

ABOVE: The three rear crew members sat facing rearwards in front of their instrument panels, separated from the two pilots by a curtain. Escape for the two navigators and the air electronics officer at low level was practically impossible.

[MISSION REPORT]
+++++++++++++++++++++++++++++

QUICK REACTION ALERT

By 1963 the 'V-Force' – the Vulcan, Valiant and Victor bombers – had become an extremely efficient organization. This expertise was embodied in and reflected by the QRA (Quick Reaction Alert) concept and in the ability of the V-bombers to 'scramble' in ninety seconds. Crews were assigned to QRA on a one-a-week basis, plus one weekend in every three. For the most part, there was little to do except read and play cards, the crews living in their QRA caravans beside the 'Bomber Box', the teletalk system connecting the crew to the Bomber Controller in the Bomber Command Operations Room.

When a crew was called to readiness or summoned for an alert exercise, crew members reported to the Operations Wing (with sufficient kit for an indefinite stay away from base) and were briefed on the nature of the alert. Each crew would undergo the usual pre-flight briefing routine, and then all the crews would be subjected to further specialist briefings; the Air Electronics Officers (AEOs) would be briefed by the Wing AEO, for example. The crews would then go into a waiting posture while the aircraft was made combat ready, each having to meet a stringent preparation level. When this was achieved, crews would go out to their aircraft to carry out the appropriate checks; the cockpit door would then be locked and no one allowed inside except crew members. In the worst possible case, early warning radar would have given the V-Force only four minutes' warning of an enemy missile attack. A more likely margin, even in the event of a surprise attack, would have been eight or even fifteen minutes, and intelligence indications would probably have increased this margin still further to hours or even days.

With the Vulcan ready to go, the crews would then await the alert call, explains a former Vulcan AEO, which was sounded either by klaxon or station broadcast over the tannoy. The initial call brought them to 'Readiness One-Five' (15 minutes) and they would remain inside the cockpit with the door locked and ground crew standing by, the bomber crew connected to the

Bomber Command Operations Room via the 'Bomber Box'. Over the teletalk, the crew would be able to hear dispersal instructions being issued to other units; these usually followed a set pattern, with units being brought to five-minute readiness, followed by two-minute readiness, then scrambled. Engines were started at Readiness Zero Two; later, a simultaneous start technique (Mass Rapid Start) was evolved, enabling all four engines to be started at the same time.

Once a scramble had been ordered, all the pilot had to do was to press the Mass Rapid Start Button and everything else happened automatically, the engines lighting up and the aircraft starting to move off the Operational Readiness Platform, set at an angle to the runway, as thrust developed. The cockpits of both Vulcan and Victor were fitted with shields for protection against nuclear flash; only the forward vision panels were exposed during take-off and initial climb. During the remainder of the sortie the whole of the cockpit was blacked out, the route being flown by radar. The crew's task in this respect became more exacting when the V-Force went over to the low-level role, for the continual use of terrain-following radar required a high level of concentration on the part of the two pilots.

ABOVE: Scramble! The five crew members race for their Vulcan during a practice alert. Thanks to a technique whereby all four engines could be started simultaneously, four Vulcans could be airborne in less than two minutes.

from them in the process.

'The cockpit layout was good; most of it, in fact, had been designed by Roly Falk. Unlike that of most bombers, the cockpit roof was devoid of any controls or switches, fostering its fighter-type appearance; on the main instrument panel the blind flying instruments were duplicated in front of each pilot, with the engine control panel between. The throttle quadrant was positioned just below the engine control panel, and apart from the throttles it served as a mounting for airbrake switches, parking brake lever and the four fuel contents gauges. The first pilot's console on the port side of the cockpit housed the engine starting, radio, bomb door and power flying control stop panels, while the second pilot's console on the starboard side contained the pressurization, air-conditioning and de-icing controls. Production Vulcans also had a spring-loaded retractable console housing the fuel system

[MISSION REPORT]
+++++++++++++++++++++++++++++++

VULCAN SWAN SONG: BLACK BUCK

In May 1982, Vulcans operating from Ascension Island in the Atlantic carried out attacks on the Falkland Islands in support of British operations to recapture them from Argentina. These operations, code-named 'Black Buck', were the longest ever flown at the time and involved both conventional bombing sorties and anti-radar missions by individual aircraft, each mission being supported by no fewer than 11 sorties by Victor K.2 tankers.

ABOVE: A Vulcan B.2A of the Waddington Wing pictured at Ascension Island during the Falklands war of 1982, when Vulcans flew the longest-range bombing missions ever attempted at the time.

On the night of 30 April–1 May 1982, Vulcan B.2 XM607 (Black Buck One) dropped a stick of 21 x 453kg (1,000lb) bombs across the main runway at Port Stanley airfield. One bomb hit the runway; the rest caused damage to the surrounding installations. The Vulcan recovered safely to Ascension Island after a flight of 15 hours and 45 minutes. Vulcan XM607 carried out a second bombing attack (Black Buck Two) against Port Stanley airfield on the night of 3–4 May, with a similar bomb load; no significant damage was caused.

Black Buck Three was aborted because of strong headwinds encountered en route, and on 28–29 May Vulcan XM597, armed with four AGM-45A Shrike anti-radar missiles, also had to abort its mission when one of the Victor tankers became unserviceable before the penultimate fuel transfer. The mission was re-scheduled on the following night as Black Buck Five, and three Shrikes were launched against radar targets. A similar mission (Black Buck Six) was flown on 2–3 June, again by XM597, two Shrikes being launched at radar targets. On this occasion, the Vulcan crew encountered trouble on the homeward flight, when the aircraft's flight refuelling probe fractured. The Vulcan diverted to Rio de Janeiro, Brazil, where it was detained for a week before being allowed to depart.

There was one more Vulcan operation, Black Buck Seven, before hostilities ended on the Falklands. It was flown on 12 June by XM607. This time, the Vulcan was armed with a mixture of 453kg (1,000lb) high explosive and anti-personnel bombs, fuzed to burst in the air, and the target was enemy troop concentrations holding on around Port Stanley. The mission was held to be a partial success, and all the aircraft involved in Black Buck Seven recovered safely to Ascension Island.

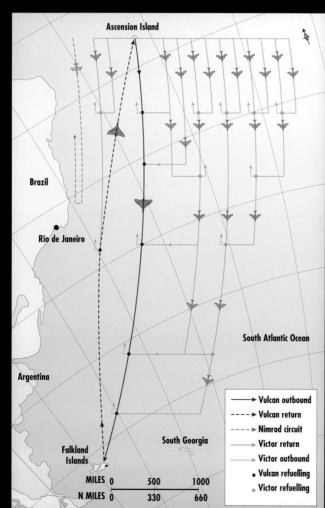

Ascension Island

Brazil

Rio de Janeiro

South Atlantic Ocean

Argentina

South Georgia

Falkland Islands

→	Vulcan outbound
---→	Vulcan return
---→	Nimrod circuit
→	Victor return
→	Victor outbound
●	Vulcan refuelling
●	Victor refuelling

MILES 0   500   1000

N.MILES 0   330   660

controls and the power control start buttons; when not in use, it was tucked away in a recess under the instrument panel.'

VIEW FROM THE COCKPIT

The only real problem with the Vulcan's cockpit – and it was a major one – was the view. The canopy covering was completely opaque, broken only by two circular side panels, which meant that the pilots had no vision above or to the rear; they could only just see the wingtips though the panels by leaning as far forward as possible and twisting their heads round.

The forward view on the ground was restricted, too, because the cockpit coaming was some way in front of the pilots and the cabin itself was at a considerable height from the ground; this created a 27m (30yd) blind spot immediately in front of the nose. Other blind spots occurred between the front windscreen panels and the circular side panels. All this created marshalling problems, as the pilot was quite unable to see a marshaller who positioned himself in front of or on the starboard side of the aircraft. There were also problems in checking the full and free operation of the power controls. This had to be

confirmed by the crew chief, standing outside the aircraft and plugged into the intercom system, and as an additional check the pilot could refer to a visual indicator, rather like an artificial horizon but with moveable indicators to represent the flying control surfaces, which was fitted to the engine control panel.

The reason for the lack of cockpit transparency was twofold. The first was a question of strength, given the altitudes at which the Vulcan was designed to operate and the possible operating conditions; the second was to give the crew maximum protection from nuclear flash. Once the bomber

was on its way to the target there would no longer be any need for the crew to see outside; the windscreen was fitted with anti-flash screens, and the side windows could be completely blacked out with sliding panels.

ABOVE: A Vulcan shows off its capacious bomb bay at an air show. As well as British and US nuclear weapons, it could carry more than nine tonnes of conventional bombs.

ABOVE: Vulcan B.2 XJ781, seen here landing, was written off in a crash landing during a visit to Iran in 1973, when its port undercarriage failed to lower.

MAIN PHOTOGRAPH: Vulcan XH558 was the first B.2 delivered to the RAF, joining No 230 OCU in July 1960 and later serving with No 50 Squadron.

Flying the F-102/F-106

Convair's two delta designs, the F-102 Delta Dagger and F-106 Delta Dart, together protected the continental United States from the threat of Soviet nuclear bombers for more than two decades. While the F-102 was problematic from the start, those who flew the F-106 fell in love with it instantly, and today many view the 'Six' as the last of the truly beautiful jet fighters.

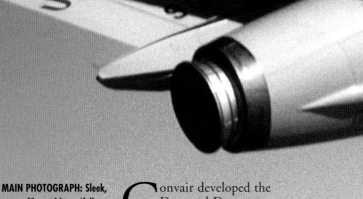

MAIN PHOTOGRAPH: Sleek, arrow-like and beautifully proportioned, the F-106 Delta Dart was a truly beautiful spectacle.

Convair developed the Dart and Dagger as interceptors for the United States Air Force's (USAF) Air Defense Command (ADC). The big delta wing was well suited to the high-altitude interceptor role, and according to Col. (ret.) Daniel 'Doc' Zoerb, *'The F-106 was a true pleasure to fly. It did, however, require that the pilot pay attention to subtle and not-so-subtle signs that the airplane was unhappy. Failure to pay attention during heavy manoeuvring resulted in violent departures from controlled flight,*

BELOW: The F-106 Delta Dart was later fitted with new 'vertical tape'-style instruments, replacing the older round gauges that were common in fighter cockpits at that time.

and a strong proficiency was required to employ the airplane to its optimum. It was a very stable, steady, fuel-efficient jet at high altitudes and mach numbers, with optimum cruise mach of 0.92, and ability to perform intercepts against targets at altitudes over 65,000 feet [20,000m].'

SUPERSONIC DASH

Intercepting Soviet nuclear bombers meant that a solid supersonic dash performance was essential. Lt.Col. (ret.) Earl 'Obi Wan' Henderson explained that the F-106 had a

number of clever improvements over the F-102, also known as 'the Deuce', to facilitate this.

'It had variable ramps in the inlets to improve supersonic engine performance, and a fuel-transfer system that activated above 1.4 Mach to automatically transfer fuel from one of the forward fuselage fuel tanks to the aft fuselage fuel tank. This shifted the centre of gravity, reducing supersonic trim drag and improving supersonic acceleration performance. The top speed of the F-106 was said to be 2.3 Mach, but the reality was that getting to Mach 2.0 was

difficult unless the outside air temp was unusually cold – lower than minus 56 degrees [-68°F].'

BELOW: The F-102 may have had a short lived life with the Active Duty Air Force, but in the service of the Air National Guard it continued to sit on intercept alert for many years.

POWER-TO-WEIGHT RATIO

Henderson, who flew the Deuce for 80 hours before converting to the much-improved F-106 (in which he

accrued more than 1,600 hours), added: 'The F-106 had a lot more power than the F-102, so the thrust to weight ratio was much better. The F-106 had the J-75 engine whereas the F-102 had the J-57.'

Making a supersonic intercept in the F-106 was not without its quirks, as Zoerb, who flew the Six for five years, recalled. 'One distraction was termed the "g-tuck", which was experienced during deceleration from super- to sub-sonic speeds, resulting in the g-loading suddenly increasing to 3g or 4g as the aerodynamic trim shifted and elevons became more effective. There were several instances in which pieces of wingtip were shed as the airplane experienced a sudden over-g while decelerating.'

RIGHT: Two F-106s cut through the air en route to intercept a radar contact. Some intercept missions took the pilots hundreds of miles from the shore, and well out of radio contact range.

STATE OF THE ART GEAR

'For its time, the F-106 had state-of-the-art avionics,' Henderson recalled, adding, 'The airborne radars before the F-106 had designators like MG-10, MG-13. The F-106 radar was so new it was called the MA-1 fire control system – a total new beginning. However, it was still a pulse radar and had difficulty with ground clutter [spurious radar returns from the ground] at low altitude. The two primary improvements over previous radars were ECCM [electronic counter counter

MAIN PHOTOGRAPH: The Dagger's intercept range, speed and endurance capabilities made it an ideal choice as chase plane for the Rockwell B-1 Lancer programme.

measures] *and an automated data link.'*

'*The enemy electronic counter measures threat of the 1960s and 1970s were primarily brute-force "noise jammers" that could be tuned to a range of frequencies. The MA-1A had an ultra-fast tuneable magnetron that gave it excellent frequency agility at up to 80,000MHz per second, which no tuneable jammer could match.'* This rendered the Soviet bombers' noise jammers ineffective.

FORMIDABLE INTERCEPTOR

Zoerb continued, '*Speed, endurance and range, coupled with advanced avionics and weapons, made the F-106 a formidable air defence interceptor. Although primitive by today's standards, the Hughes MA-1A radar was very capable against the threat it was designed to go up against. And in its day, the radar's connectivity to the semi-automatic ground environment* [SAGE] *data link provided enormous improvements*

LEFT: The F-102 deployed to Southeast Asia to guard Thailand from airborne attack by the North Vietnamese Air Force. As the threat of that diminished, the Deuce was repainted in a camouflage pattern and started flying light strike missions in South Vietnam.

ABOVE: The F-106's delta wing design was based on work by Dr. Alexander Lippisch, a German aerodynamicist who had worked for the Luftwaffe during World War II.

[MISSION REPORT]

+++++++++++++++++++++++++++++

GENIE AND FALCON

The most potent weapons the F-106 could employ were the AIM-2A Genie, and later, the AIM-26 Falcon. '*The Genie was a "never-never-land" weapon,'* Henderson recounted. '*It was designed to destroy Soviet bomber formations with overpressure from the nuclear blast above, and fighters would probably suffer the same fate. Its actual use in combat would have only been allowed if there were an all-out nuclear war. It was a very large, unguided, ballistic rocket with a 1.5 kiloton nuclear warhead – one-tenth the size of the Hiroshima A-bomb. The rocket weighed around 820lb [372kg] and was carried at the top of the missile bay on a special weapons rack. The rocket motor had 32,000lb [14,500kg] of thrust and the missile accelerated to Mach 3.3 almost instantly. It went for 5.5 seconds and then detonated. Right after launch you performed a 6g break turn for 120 degrees to escape the nuke blast, which would wipe out one cubic mile of airspace.'*

TIGHT TOLERANCES

Zoerb added that the real trick to firing the unguided Genie lay in acquiring and locking the radar to the target. '*From that point until the weapons launch cycle began was just a few seconds, during which time it was required to steer the steering*

ABOVE: The Falcon, a guided derivative of the nuclear-tipped Genie, was the most potent weapon in the F-106's arsenal. Four Falcons are proudly displayed here.

dot into the exact centre of a steering circle which collapsed from a full screen circle. And no yaw was allowed. The tight launch tolerances reflected the ballistic nature of the rocket and the need to precisely place the nuclear warhead within a lethal radius of the target or group of targets. The effects on friendly fighters, unaware of the Genie launch, would have also been unpleasant, with at least temporary blindness being the biggest fear. In fact, we carried an eye patch in the survival vest in the hope of preserving sight in at least one eye.'

The AIM-26 Falcon was a later development that could be slaved to the radar to allow it to guide after launch.

RIGHT: This photograph of the F-102 prototype clearly shows the location of the intakes almost parallel with the forward canopy. This gave the Dagger a somewhat 'stubby' appearance.

to air defence effectiveness through precise voice and non-voice intercept communications. Automation enabled large numbers of threats to be intercepted while maintaining a reasonable controller workload. The data link greatly reduced the amount of radio communications required and increased effectiveness in a communications jamming environment.

INFRARED DETECTOR

'The F-106 also had an IRSTS [infrared search and track system] *which was retractable when not in use,*' Henderson added. '*The IR detector head scanned in azimuth and was controlled in elevation with the thumb wheel on the control stick. The range of the system was very dependent on atmospheric conditions. On a clear night at altitude you could detect a target in the stern at about 20 miles [32km] if the target was in cruise power. You could detect a night target in afterburner at about 15 to 20 miles [24 to 32km] in the front, but at low altitude the detection range was very degraded if there was haze or visible moisture. The radar could be slaved to the IR antenna after IR lock on to allow for accurate range.*'

TACTICAL SITUATION DISPLAY

The SAGE data link was used to allow ground based Ground Control Intercept (GCI) radars to pass target data to the F-106 pilot without the need for verbal instructions over the radio, and to provide the MA-1A with the general location of the target. Henderson noted, '*We received command heading, speed and altitude from GCI and they were displayed on the flight instruments, the radar scope and on the Tactical Situation Display [TSD].*'

While the radar scope was located at the top of the instrument panel in line with the pilot's sight, the TSD was located at the bottom of the panel. '*As you got within about*

40 miles [72km] of your target, a data link target designation circle about the size of a quarter would appear on your radar scope and the target was supposed to be within that circle. A target "bug" would also appear on the TSD,' he concluded.

While the F-106's onboard radar and IRST were cutting-edge for their day, the radar rarely picked up fighter-size targets beyond 36km (20 miles), and

[MISSION REPORT]
+++++++++++++++++++++++++++++
INTERCEPT PROFILE

Henderson described a typical intercept. 'GCI would vector you to a point where you could achieve a heading crossing angle of 150 degrees or higher. For training, the initial range was 40 to 50 miles [64–80km] and your intercept speed was generally just subsonic, 0.9 Mach, and your power setting was around 85% rpm to maintain that speed. Against a fighter-size target, lock-on was normally achieved at 15 to 20 miles [24 to 32km], following which you would receive steering information on the radar scope. You would then manoeuvre so as to place the steering circle, about the size of a pencil

diameter, inside the three-inch [75mm] diameter target designation circle. As you approached launch range the large circle began to shrink. When it shrank to zero you were at optimum launch range and you pulled the trigger. At launch an "X" appeared on the scope, and shortly thereafter an "8-ball" symbol appeared, indicating the pilot should initiate a breakaway from the collision course. If a stern re-attack was to be accomplished, you would pull off to the side and let the target pass head-on, then turn in behind him at about 3 to 4 miles [5–6.5km].'

'After lock-on,' Zoerb picked up, 'the radar would track and provide steering guidance to the selected weapon's launch parameters. As the firing point was approached, assuming the trigger was depressed, the launch sequence would begin. The missile bay doors would open, the missile rails would extend into the air stream, and missiles would fire. Following the missile firing pulse, the rails would retract and the doors would close... and you became an ace... simple!'

LEFT: Streaming a thick cloud of burnt rocket propellant during missile launch was bound to give away the F-106's position, but against a bomber target this mattered little.

bomber-size targets at greater than 48km (30 miles), according to Zoerb. Key to a successful interception therefore lay with the SAGE data link.

'After takeoff, or an active air defence scramble in which we were off the ground less than five minutes from the time the klaxon sounded, we would check in with the Air Defense Region controller, perform weapons system and data link checks and if all was normal we'd begin receiving data link commands to the intercept or holding point. The data link commands included type of intercept – forward quarter/stern intercept – and intercept objective – identify, kill, shadow, etc, and the small data link target designation circle on the

LEFT: Unlike the two-seat TF-102 with side-by-side seating for instructor and student, the F-106B trainer employed a tandem arrangement that allowed it to keep its good looks.

radar scope indicating where, in azimuth and range, the target should appear. If desired, the autopilot could be coupled to the data link, in which case, the only

pilot action required was maintaining desired airspeed, initiating radar or IR track on the target, and arming and firing weapons.'

LEFT: The Air Force originally intended to purchase 1,000 F-106s to equip 40 Air Defence Command interceptor squadrons, but delays with the Dart meant that those figures were culled dramatically.

BELOW: Two of the most obvious physical differences between the F-102 and the F-106 shown here were the Dart's relocated engine intakes (moved aft) and squared-off vertical tail.

Flying the F-104

The Lockheed F-104 Starfighter, which saw service from 1958 until 2004, was the brainchild of legendary aircraft designer Clarence 'Kelly' Johnson. Also known as the 'Zipper', or 'Zip', the F-104 was reminiscent of a rocket ship, with short wings and a pencil-thin fuselage.

MAIN PHOTOGRAPH:
A Royal Netherlands Air Force F-104 climbs skywards, bearing wingtip fuel tanks and twin AIM-9 Sidewinder missiles.

Perhaps the most talked-about aspect of the Starfighter is its incredible acceleration and thrust. Lieutenant Colonel (retired) Andy Bush, who began flying the F-104 in 1976 as an instructor at Luke Air Force Base, Arizona, and later became an instructor at the F-104 Fighter Weapons School, recalled, *'It was fast. Very fast. I have flown the jet out to 800KIAS* [knots indicated air speed; 1,480km/h] *many times, and in the world of 1970s flying, that was really fast. I never went anywhere near that speed when I flew the F-4 Phantom. In that*

jet, we thought of 500-plus KIAS [925km/h] *as fast!'*

SHARP AS A KNIFE

Lt. Col. (ret.) Dud Larsen, another US Air Force pilot who flew the Starfighter on exchange with the Royal Canadian Air Force, and who has also flown the

from 0.9 Mach to 2.0 Mach at 35,000 feet [10,000m] while flying straight and level. This equalled about 1,200 knots [2,200km/h] ground speed. Trying to turn the airplane at 2.0 Mach was one gigantic sweeping turn that took up a bunch of airspace,' Larsen reflected.

'I remember our Maintenance test pilot taking off one day,' he mused, 'and having reached 498KIAS [922km/h] by the end of the runway. A Phantom on a good day would have about 420 [777km/h] and an F-105 Thunderchief would be lucky to have 375 [695km/h]!'

FAST THINKING REQUIRED

Bush observed that there was more to the Starfighter than just its speed. 'Getting the most out of the F-104 in air-to-air required the pilot to fly the jet to the edge of its manoeuvring envelope, both in speed and turn capability. This required most pilots to go into areas of the flight envelope that they had never been

F 4 and MiG 21, commented on one oft-recounted fact about the F-104:

'The common "gee-whiz" fact was that the wing was as sharp as a butcher's knife, and in essence that was true. Not a sharp butcher's knife, but sharp enough to break the skin if you hit it just right.

'The Zip was an incredibly fast airplane for its design era. I remember that it took about three minutes 15 seconds to accelerate

before. It was exhilarating to operate the airplane like we did, but it was something that was not for every pilot. It was a risky business, the jet was a demanding airplane, and it was not for pilots who were complacent or slow thinkers. This aspect was a major limitation in that the jet had to be flown to its limits to be competitive. Not every pilot was willing to do that.'

The F-104 was designed from the outset as an interceptor that

ABOVE: The F-104's razor-thin wings cut the air like a knife through butter, but the total wingspan of these 'lifting surfaces' was also impressively small: not quite 6.7m (22ft) across, for a total surface area of just under 18.6m² (200 sq ft).

ABOVE: The US Air Force's Air Defense Command (ADC) was the launch customer for the F-104A, using it as an interceptor that could reach out and destroy Soviet high-flying nuclear bombers before they came within range of the continental United States.

could engage high- and fast-flying Soviet fighters and bombers, but it was never intended to dominate in the dogfight arena where manoeuvrability was key. Even so, the little Zipper's ability to turn has been much maligned over the years, and most of what has been said is factually incorrect when put into historical context, according to Bush.

'When flown properly, the F-104 could sustain a turn that was about the same as a F-4. It had as good an energy capability as the F-4, and better than a MiG-21. When flown below 15,000 feet [4,500m], we could sustain a 6–7 g turn at about 420KIAS [777km/h], and this gave us a turn radius of about 4,000 feet [1,200m] or so. Against 1960s-era aircraft, this was competitive – against an F-15 Eagle or F-16 Viper, obviously not so. With manoeuvre flaps down, the jet would turn

a lot better than most other folks realized.'

Larsen was an experienced F-4 pilot who'd specialized in air-to-ground tactics at low altitude, but was also an accomplished air-to-air pilot who had graduated from the USAF's F-4 Fighter Weapons School. Of the CF-104, he said, 'In the low altitude environment it was as capable as the F-5 and

BELOW: Photographed in May 1960, F-104A Starfighter serial number 734 sits on a dry lakebed at NASA's Dryden Flight Research Center.

F-4, save the lack of viable weaponry. At low altitude the energy diagrams were very good, and in the high altitude environment the turn rates and radii were comparable to the MiG-23 Flogger. In the multi-bogey environment the Zip was formidable. The airplane would accelerate like the trip-hammers of hell and was very tiny head on. In fact it was difficult to see from almost any aspect. The radar cross-section was also very small, and until the modern radars in the F-15, F-16 and F/A-18, other fighter radars found it very difficult to pick us up.'

When the F-104 pilot combined the jet's dash speed with its best turn capability, he

RIGHT: The Starfighter carried an M61A1 20mm Gatling gun in the port fuselage, for which 725 linkless rounds were stored in an adjacent ammunition drum. Seen here installed in a Luftwaffe F-104G, the gun gave the jet a good capability for close-in dogfighting, and also offered an effective option for strafing attacks on ground targets.

'ended up with air-to-air tactics that were "straight lines and hooks",' said Bush. 'We would enter the fight supersonic, usually at 600KIAS [1,110km/h] or above, make a pass, and then extend away at max afterburner. Once separation had been gained, we'd go idle and boards [extend the air brakes], slow down to 0.85 Mach or 450KIAS [833km/h], then extend the manoeuvre flaps and

[MISSION REPORT]
+++

FLYING THE ZIPPER WITH THE CANUCKS

Dud Larsen spent almost four years flying the CF-104 with the RCAF in the early 1980s, and is probably the only man to have flown both the Zip and the MiG-21 Fishbed – Russia's answer to Kelly Johnson's design – operationally. Larsen flew the MiG-21 as a member of a secret USAF squadron in the 1980s following his CF-104 tour.

'I was posted to the Canadian 417 Squadron. We were a training squadron for all the NATO pilots that were posted to Europe. We were also a teaching squadron for all pilots transitioning to the CF-104 or being requal'ed in the airplane. At the time, low-altitude ingress was the tactic de jour and we spent considerable time in the low altitude environment. We had the luxury of the free world's greatest training area: the Cold Lake Air Weapons range, which at the time was the only large range that could even come close to the European environment and was therefore ideal for training pilots that were to be posted to Europe. The biggest difference was that most of the year round the weather at Cold Lake was too good!

ABOVE: The original role of the Royal Canadian Air Force's CF-104 was as a photo-reconnaissance and nuclear delivery platform. When the Canadian government decided to delete nuclear weapons from its arsenal, the Zipper was 're-roled' as a conventional ground-attack fighter bomber.

'We flew some very big multi-bogey packages and the Zip did well. You would enter the fight at at least 600KIAS [1,110km/h], never slow down, never turn more than 30 degrees (even to get a shot), and just keep on going. Follow that with a huge sweeping turn at the edge of the area and re-enter the fight even faster for another slash through the fur ball: it is hard to convert on a target doing 600+ KIAS and get a valid shot. Of course, nowadays, with all-aspect heaters [heat-seeking missiles] and radar missiles, this tactic is moot. But at that time we were King Kong at 650 [knots – 1,200km/h] on the deck. Bottom line, streak through the area at great speed and try to be invisible, if you get a valid shot leave the fight, go to the bar and brag because by that time you were out of fuel.'

ABOVE: The most obvious difference between the F-104G multi-role version and the F-104A and C that preceded it (furthest from camera) was the enlarged vertical stabilizer. Other less obvious differences included a strengthened fuselage and wings, increased internal fuel capacity, revised flaps and beefed-up landing gear.

make a 6–7 g turn back into the fight. With our nose on the fight, we'd raise the flaps and shove it back up to "warp 5".'

DOWN LOW

Despite being designed as an interceptor, the F-104 was also employed as a low-level nuclear and conventional bomber. At the heart of both the interceptor and low-level conventional and nuclear bomber missions was a simple AN/ASG-14T pulse radar. Bush summarized the F-104 as having an air-to-ground capability *'that was better than the F-4 but not as good as the F-111. We could carry "the bomb" as far as the F-4 and get better radar accuracy results.'*

Larsen elucidated: *'The Zip was a joy to fly low-level due to* the extremely high wing loading. The Canadian airplane had a rudimentary INS [inertial navigation system] *called the LN-3 but it was hideous to use and not very accurate, therefore good old dead reckoning was the way to go. The LN-3 did, however, have a system called the GSRO – Ground Speed Read Out – that allowed you to set a ground speed [GS] you wanted to*

[MISSION REPORT]

++++++++++++++++++++++++++++++++

THE WIDOW MAKER? FACT OR FICTION

Bush explains the origin of the F-104's Widow Maker nickname. *'That name comes from the German experience. The Luftwaffe were the primary users of the jet and were the first to operate it in NATO. Sadly, the German Air Force was not quite ready for a jet with that kind of performance: the pilots were used to subsonic, non-afterburning F-86s and F-84s with limited avionics, and the maintenance folks were used to working on those kinds of aircraft. Plus, NATO airfields are 8,000 feet [2,500m] long, which presents a challenge in low visibility approaches and at the speeds the 104 flew at.*

'The airplane itself had a long history of mechanical issues. NATO tended to fly the jet at low altitudes, and when something went wrong there, bad things often happened. The F-104 also had a unique flying characteristic known as the "pitch-up." This resulted from the T-tail design and was a uncontrolled pitch-up that happened when the angle of attack (AoA) went past a certain value. This characteristic was the cause of a number of accidents and became something that many pilots feared. I've flown out of a number of pitch ups and it was no big deal; it was just the result of the pilot just pushing the jet too far.'

Larsen made clear, *'Kelly Johnson was no dope... [he] designed an AoA limiter into the flight controls that initially would give the pilot a stick shaker, warning the pilot he was approaching the AOA limit, and if he continued to pull past the shaker ... a stick kicker that forced the stick forward with an*

ABOVE: As the first air force to get to grips with the Zipper in the fickle and unobliging climate of western Europe, the F-104 presented the Luftwaffe with a learning curve that was steeper than anything they had experienced since the introduction of jet fighters in World War II.

approximate force of 50 pounds [23kg]. This in and of itself was not disheartening unless you were in the strafe pattern and you were a little steep!

'Primarily the aircraft was on the far end of the design world when Kelly Johnson put it on paper. The airplane had very few back-up systems and if the engine quit it had the glide characteristics of a bowling ball. Engine failure or malfunction often led to a delayed decision to eject, as pilots tried unsuccessfully to get a restart or guide the aircraft to a safe crash site.'

It was delays such as this that would get a pilot killed.

Bush concluded, *'I do not agree that the jet deserves its name. Other fighters of that era had similar accident numbers. Additionally, the other air forces that flew the jet did not have the same record as the Luftwaffe. Part of that was because the Luftwaffe worked out many of the problems before the other users bought the airplane.'*

fly on a dial on the left console. When you reached the desired GS the equivalent of the glide slope indicator for an ILS [instrument landing system] would come into view on the ADI [attitude directional indicator], and you would modulate the power to maintain an "on glide slope" indication. When you were "on glide slope" it meant that you were on your GS, and therefore dead reckoning became easier. Then, to maintain course, you flew a solid heading and turned on a accurate time that you kept with a stopwatch that was mounted on the glare shield. The stopwatch on the glare shield allowed you to glance at the watch with the horizon still in view. No looking at your lap to look at a chart or clock to navigate. It was easy to map-read with a little practice by holding your map up to eye level and looking through the map and keeping your eyes on the horizon. No unwanted pitch changes that lead to "close encounters of the worst kind". With the stability of the airplane at low level, plus a lot of practice, it became very easy to find your target. After all, how close do you need to get with a 65-kiloton blast?'

SIMPLE GUN SIGHT

'In conventional air-to-ground,' Bush admitted, *'we were limited by our Korean War-era gun sight. It was not a heads-up display in any respect, nor did we have any automated delivery systems, so when compared to the F-16 or A-7 Corsair, our results were not as good. When compared to the F-4, we were about equal.'*

'In air-to-air mode, we could search out to at least 40nm

[nautical miles; 74km] *for fighter-sized targets, and had a lock-on limitation of 20nm [37km],'* Bush recalled, before adding, *'We did not have an autopilot, and so all radar operation was done while hand-flying the jet. We operated the search and acquisition controls with our left hand using a control unit on the left console. We also has a short-range "auto-lock" capability, using the boresighted gun sight as a reference.'*

Dud Larsen characterized the air-to-air radar mode as being *'very difficult to use, requiring the dexterity of a six-fingered juggler with four eyes to make it lock on.'*

ABOVE: The Japanese Air Self-Defence Force (JASDF) operated the F-104J (pictured) based on the F-104G, and the two-seat F-104DJ, based on the TF-104G trainer.

LEFT: The F-104's primary air-to-air armament for the majority of its operation service was two or four heat-seeking AIM-9 Sidewinder missiles mounted on the wingtips and fuselage. This aircraft, of the 69th Tactical Fighter Training Squadron, 58th Tactical Training Wing, 12th Air Force, carries two inert Aim-9J training rounds.

BELOW: Italy's F-104S could carry the AIM-7 Sparrow radar-guided missile, which improved the range at which it could engage other aircraft. As the last force to operate the Starfighter, the Italian Air Force extensively modernized the venerable jet over the course of two major programmes, to include modern avionics, radar and weapons systems.

Flying the A-4 Skyhawk

The Douglas A-4 Skyhawk's production run spanned almost 30 years and totalled almost 3,000 examples. Flown by navies and air forces around the globe, the small, agile A-4 is still operated by a few nations today.

The A-4 is perhaps unique among aircraft designed strictly for their ability to drop bombs and fire rockets in that, whenever its pilots speak of the airplane's abilities, it is not about how good it is in combat, but rather what a nimble and manoeuvrable machine it is. Indeed, the United States Navy's vaunted display team, the Blue Angels, were so impressed by the Skyhawk's aerobatic abilities that the unit flew the A-4F for six seasons before changing to the F/A-18 Hornet.

SMALL AND LIGHTWEIGHT

From the outset, the A-4's designers were obsessed with saving weight and reducing its dimensions. This would allow more aircraft to fit on US Navy aircraft carriers in the days before the introduction of the huge Nimitz-class aircraft carriers. Anywhere a few grams could be saved, even in such places as the ejection seat, it was done. And where centimetres could be shaved off, they were, giving the Skyhawk its famously cramped cockpit, which is insulated with nothing more than a thermal blanket tacked to the cockpit walls. Radar was deemed a luxury on the first Skyhawks, and even advanced models had little radar coverage.

In the paranoid days of the early Cold War, when the Skyhawk was still in the prototype stage, it was viewed as, among other things, a tactical nuclear bomber, Crews trained for that role by toss-bombing nuclear 'shapes,' knowing they would be flying one-way missions if the call ever came. This nuclear role was

euphemistically called 'special weapons capability'.

SIMPLE AND SAFE

Skyhawk pilot Major Arthur Padios (Ret.), who flew it in combat during the Vietnam War, boiled down the A-4's shortcomings to two: *'I considered the aircraft to have two emergencies: an airborne flameout which couldn't be restarted, and an uncontrolled fire. Period. End of emergencies.'*
As Padios tells it, the Skyhawk had a handle in the cockpit that could be pulled for every problem that cropped up.

MAIN PHOTOGRAPH: A Royal New Zealand Air Force (RNZAF) A-4K looses two unguided rockets from underwing pods. New Zealand has now retired all its Skyhawks without replacement.

PILOT'S VERDICT

❝*I never observed a flight of A-4s that didn't get the job done first time, every time.*❞

Maj. Arthur Padios (Ret.)
US Marine Corps
Skyhawk pilot

'If half the tandem hydraulic system gets shot away, the other half flies the airplane. If the whole system gets blown away, pull the handle to disconnect it and fly it by wire. If the generator fails, pull the handle and deploy the RAT [Ram Air Turbine]. If the landing gear won't come down hydraulically, pull the handle and it falls out. If it will not come down at all, land on the [external] tanks. If you need to get rid of external ordnance in a hurry, pull the jettison handle and "chain" it off safe.'

All other problems could be overcome, he said, and a safe landing effected. That may be an exaggeration, but the A-4 was designed to be an extremely simple airplane compared with other tactical jets – simple to fly, simple to maintain, with relatively few moving parts. Of course, this became a liability when the Skyhawk went to war in the unfriendly skies over Vietnam, where pilots had to cope not only with vicious air defences, but also unpredictable

monsoon weather, as well as terrain that rose and fell abruptly and was often hidden by cloud cover.

CARRIER OPERATIONS

Pilots generally found the Skyhawk easy to land on aircraft carriers, though catapult launches, because of the A-4's light weight, could be violent affairs. Lt. Phil Thompson flew the A-4G in the Royal Australian Navy in the early 1970s. He

[MISSION REPORT]
+++++-++-+++++++++++++++++++
ARGENTINA'S FALKLANDS LOSSES

When the six-week Falklands conflict broke out in 1982, Argentina's primary strike aircraft was the Skyhawk. The aircraft was almost 30 years old by then and Argentina's estimated 60 Skyhawks were among the earliest models.

The A-4s were further hobbled by a US arms embargo that had deprived them of spare parts, the Skyhawks' ejection seats being especially unreliable. Nevertheless, flying at the limit of their range, the Skyhawks did considerable damage to the British assault fleet.

But it came at a terrible cost. The Skyhawks carried few, if any, defences. British anti-aircraft fire was accurate and lethal. And then there were the deadly Harriers.

No fewer than 22 Skyhawks fell during the war: three losses were blamed on operational accidents. According to the most reliable statistics available, six of the A-4s were downed by ship-based anti-aircraft missiles; one was shot

ABOVE: Eight Argentine Skyhawks fly in echelon formation. Argentine A-4s suffered terrible losses in the Falklands conflict – these are replacement aircraft purchased after the war.

down by friendly anti-aircraft artillery while another fell to British AAA on the islands themselves; five were shot down by Harriers armed with the AIM-9L Sidewinder heat-seeking missile, and one more was lost to a land-based AIM-9 battery; one loss was credited to a combination of artillery and missiles and, finally, one was shot down by a ship-mounted 40mm Bofors gun.

ABOVE: A TA-4F from Marine Training Squadron VMAT-102 fires a Zuni unguided rocket.

LEFT: A Royal New Zealand Air Force (RNZAF) Skyhawk takes to the sky with flaps lowered for takeoff.

described what it was like to be shot off the deck of HMAS *Melbourne*, and how such shots could get dicey:

'In heavy seas the catapult firing had to be timed so that the aircraft was launched as the bow started to rise on the swell. Being launched while the bow was going down into the swell was not something to contemplate for the two seconds between saluting the catapult officer and being actually launched.

'The Skyhawk rotated naturally to the correct angle of attack off the catapult and the stick automatically flicked back into your stomach – we held our hand there to catch the stick while at the same time holding on to the launch bar and throttle to ensure that the throttle did not reduce during launch. There is at least one story of an A-4G [the Australian model of the Skyhawk] *being launched into the swell such that the wheels skimmed the sea surface for a few seconds before the plane got airborne.*'

Padios' reference to the Skyhawk's ability to land safely with wheels up on its two underwing tanks was not exaggerated. It could be and was done quite frequently (and happened as recently as 2006 in an incident involving a civilian-registered Skyhawk in Canada), and those who achieved this dubious distinction became members of the 'Skyhawk Ski Club'. Former Skyhawk pilot Scott Rogers related:

'I had heard stories of the Skyhawk Ski Club, but we got a chance to watch it gain a new member. The engine was shut down just before touchdown and the Skyhawk slid along on the drop tanks showering the runway with sparks.

'After enough of the aluminium had disappeared from the bottom of the tanks, gravity took over and the tanks collapsed slightly within a second of each other and a small explosion as the last few ounces of fuel ignited. The flames disappeared quickly and the Skyhawk slid to a stop with only

BELOW: Seven A-4J Skyhawks of VF-43 are connected to NC-8A starter carts at Naval Air Station Oceana prior to taking off on their last flight before the A-4 was retired from the US Navy after 39 years of service.

[MISSION REPORT]
+++++++++++++++++++++++++++++++++

VARIATIONS ON A MASTERPIECE

ABOVE: This trainer version of the A-4S was produced for the Royal Singapore Air Force with a distinctive raised cockpit for the instructor.

If production numbers, longevity of service and the number of countries which flew it are any indication, the A-4 Skyhawk was the most popular strike fighter of the post-war era. The Skyhawk was produced over 25 years in a dazzling array of variations on the original theme, and flew with the air forces or navies of Argentina, Australia, Brazil, Indonesia, Israel, Kuwait, Malaysia, New Zealand, Singapore and the Navy and Marine Corps of the United States.

Designed in the early 1950s as a small, lightweight, daylight bomber, that role would change radically as more uses were found for the Skyhawk. Engines became more powerful, weapons loads grew, and as electronic kit became more sophisticated, the A-4E and F grew a 'hump-back' to accommodate all the black boxes it carried for, among other

things, self-defence. Each country using the Skyhawk had its own requirements. The Israelis lengthened the exhaust pipe to protect against heat-seeking missiles. Singapore's A-4S had a mightier engine and some machines featured a separate, elevated cockpit to give all-round vision and control to the instructor. The US operated the dual A-4F and J as its advanced naval trainer for more than 30 years. A total of 2,960 Skyhawks were built.

BELOW: A RNZAF TA-4K fires a guided Maverick missile over the target range. The Maverick could be either infrared- or television-guided.

a skinned nose, a couple of wrecked 300 gallon [1,135 litre] drop tanks, and a starboard main landing gear to repair.'

FLYING THE SKYHAWK

While the Skyhawk was capable of spectacular takeoffs and landings, its true legend, of course, was born in the air. Pilot Budd Davisson described his first Skyhawk flight in a Blue Angels two-seat TA-4J in the mid-1970s:

'I can't begin to tell anybody how incredibly stupid I felt when I placed my – so I thought – well-trained hand upon the stick and couldn't even hold level flight! Just the pressure of my hand holding the stick sent the airplane into a three-dimensional gyration that probably had [Front-seater] Lt. Patton in gales of laughter. Control pressures? There aren't any. None. Zero. Zip. Zilch.

'After I overcame my initial shock, I settled down to make this thing fly. The controls are hydraulically boosted and there's a very slight dead spot in the

middle; so the stick kind of floats between four hydraulic contacts until you move it a bit to touch one. Then the airplane leaps to your command. Noting that, I relaxed my grip on the stick and just kept a couple of fingers close to it. After five minutes of gentle turns – it's darned hard to fly them gently in this airplane – and Dutch rolls, I began to get a little feel for where centre was.'

Any airplane that has a roll rate of 400 degrees per second is bound to be a bit touchy on the controls.

'In flitting around the sky,' Davisson recalled, 'altitude losses and gains happened so quickly that I found I had to study the altimeter to be sure I read it correctly. One second, we'd be bombing along at 18,000 feet [5,500m]; moments later the second altimeter, the radar job, would light up as we screamed down the beach 70 feet [20m] above the waves.'

Paradoxically, the Skyhawk, for all its lightness on the controls, was deemed tame enough to be the US Navy's advanced jet trainer for more than 30 years before being replaced by the US version of the BAe Hawk, the T-45 Goshawk.

Because of its sprightly performance, the Skyhawk's last duty with the US Navy, and one it performed for more than 30 years, was as a stand-in for Warsaw Pact fighters at the famed Top Gun school and other bases where US and NATO pilots trained.

'Every single person I've ever fought in one of these airplanes has "died" the first time I fought him. Every...single...one.'

BELOW: The US Navy display team, the Blue Angels, seen here taking off in diamond formation, flew the A-4F for more than a decade.

That was the observation of Randy Clark, a former aggressor pilot, referring to mock dogfights with much more sophisticated aircraft like the F/A-18 Hornet and the F-14 Tomcat.

BAD GUYS' MOUNT
The Navy and Marine Corps' aggressor Skyhawks, alongside the F-5 Freedom Fighter, flew against newer pure fighter aircraft at Top Gun, and only the best pilots were selected to play the bad guys. That combination, with the Skyhawk as their mount, meant that the

baddies won considerably more often than they lost. Now, Clark works for one of the private firms that own up to a squadron's worth of civil-registered A-4s, and contract with the US, Canada, and the militaries of other nations to help train their pilots in air combat tactics.

More than a half-century after its first flight and more than two dozen variations on the original design, the A-4 continues to fly with a few of the world's air forces, as well as training squadrons such as this. It seems the 'Scooter' will be around for many more years to come.

LEFT: An A-4F of VF-126 in 'aggressor' colours. These aircraft were used by the US Navy and Marines to simulate Warsaw Pact aircraft in mock dogfights.

BELOW: A two-seat US Navy TA-4J trainer takes off from a land base. Skyhawks trained US Navy and Marine Corps aviators for more than 30 years.

Flying the MiG-21

One of the most widely exported and iconic Cold War fighters, the Mikoyan-Gurevich MiG-21 has been operated by no fewer than 50 countries around the world in its five-decade career. More than 10,000 MiG-21s are thought to have been built.

The MiG-21 entered service in 1959, and was assigned the NATO call sign 'Fishbed', but was known to Soviet operators as the 'Balalaika' because its planform resembled the triangular stringed musical instrument of Russian origin.

As a result of the lessons learned by Russian advisors during the Korean War, Mikoyan's designers aimed to build a Mach 2-capable lightweight fighter. What resulted was an aircraft constructed mostly of aluminium alloy, boasting a slender fuselage with a circular intake in the nose. Inside the intake, a cone governed the airflow to the compressor blades of the Tumansky R-11 motor – a turbojet that produced upwards of 37.7kN (8,500lb) of thrust at military power, and 56.2kN (12,655lb) in afterburner.

There were five main versions of the R-11, each producing slightly different amounts of thrust. With a normal operating weight of around 6,800kg (15,000lb), the R-11 gave the Fishbed a decent thrust-to-weight ratio for its time.

The MiG-21 was an attractive design, with triangular delta wings, cropped at the tips, that were swept at 57° and spanned 7.15m (23ft 5in). A swept tailplane raked sharply

backwards at 60°. The MiG-21 had tailerons for roll and pitch control, a brake parachute fairing, and airbrakes under the fuselage.

Over the years, the MiG-21 would be upgraded to create more than 30 sub-types, each with slightly different capabilities and performance.

EXPORT MODELS

The MiG-21F-13 export model was one of the most numerous of the early Fishbeds, flying with many 'satellite' customers of the Soviet Union. It featured twin Nudelmann-Richter NR-30 30mm automatic cannons installed internally and below the cockpit, and each wing could carry a single weapons pylon for bombs or unguided

rocket pods, or could accommodate a single AA-2 Atoll air-to-air missile. It was this marque of MiG-21 that inflicted heavy losses on US aircraft operating over North Vietnam. The US would eventually operate a squadron of these jets in total secrecy in order to exploit their weaknesses and neutralize their strengths.

Colonel Jose Oberle, one of the US pilots who flew the type, recalled, 'The MiG-21 is a super

MAIN PHOTOGRAPH: The Indian Air Force has been one of the largest export operators of the MiG-21 since it first used the Fishbed in combat against Pakistan in 1971.

PILOT'S VERDICT

' *The MiG-21 is a super airplane that flies as good as it looks. You can pull 7gs in it, look over your shoulder and still be very comfortable.* '

Colonel Jose Oberle
MiG-21 evaluation pilot
US Air Force

ABOVE: India operates in the region of 450 license-built MiG-21s, many of which are of the MiG-21M shown above, the MiG-21S, and the MiG-21Bis varieties. However, India has upgraded some of these to the 'Bison' standard, which mixes Russian and Western avionics improvements in a bid to modernize the type.

BELOW: A classic propaganda photograph showing a group of Soviet pilots receiving a last-minute briefing prior to launching on an interception sortie in their MiG-21MF 'Fishbed J' aircraft.

airplane that flies as good as it looks. You can pull 7gs in it, look over your shoulder and still be very comfortable. The MiG-21 had a drag chute we could deploy with a little button, so it had a pretty good stopping distance, and it landed a lot like the Northrop F-5E. Compared to the MiG-17, it was faster, but still had a very similar cockpit picture – they both sit close to the runway and about the same distance to look out over the nose.'

Colonel Gail Peck, who commanded the secret squadron in 1979, added, 'It had a tall control stick and its rudder became effective from about 30 knots [55km/h]. On take-off the nose would lighten at 140 knots [260 km/h], you rotated the nose wheel off the ground at 170 knots [315km/h], and then you climbed at 0.88 Mach.'

The manoeuvre characteristics and slow-speed flight handling of the Fishbed were both compelling, and absolutely out of the ordinary. The MiG-21 could fly manoeuvres that contemporary US aircraft could not, at least not without their jet

engines stalling and flaming out. Bob Sheffield, one of the first US Air Force MiG-21 pilots, remembered, 'You could actually do a hammerhead turn in it – go straight up to around 100 knots [185 km/h], at which point you start to lose control authority. You push the stick forward and add right aileron and full left rudder, and around she would come. You would never really want to get that slow in a dogfight, but it could be done.'

When turning, the Fishbed could scribe tight circles around the sky. Col Mike Scott had found that the MiG-21 could be coaxed into a quick departure from controlled flight to further tighten the turn.

'Since the MiG-21 turned so well, our American airplanes would inevitably overshoot, and all you had to do was put a little uncoordinated control into the Fishbed and it would depart. But it would depart in roll, usually through 180 degrees. That could be done either positively, so the canopy rolled towards the sky, or negatively, where the canopy rolled towards the ground. It was a great manoeuvre because you turned faster than you could move the airplane with the controls. All you did was release the controls and the airplane would enter controlled flight again. It was that forgiving to fly.'

DOGFIGHTS AND AIR COMBAT MANOEUVRING

The Fishbed was a formidable opponent in air combat when flown properly, although there were very few nations that flew it anywhere near as aggressively as the American test pilots.

Against the venerable McDonnell Douglas F-4

Phantom, 'Below 20,000 feet [6,100m] and above 400 knots [740km/h], the MiG-21 was at a disadvantage. But the MiG-21 still had better "instantaneous g" available than the Phantom and could snatch a bat turn on you,' Peck had discovered. The F-4 would out-accelerate the Fishbed at low level, but 'the MiG's wing generated enough lift to produce a climb at any airspeed above 250 knots [465 km/h], which the Phantom could not follow.'

Sheffield had been pleasantly surprised by just how good the Fishbed was. 'In the hands of a good pilot, versus the F-4, the MiG-21 wins every time,' Sheffield stated. While he never used the hammerhead manoeuvre during dogfights with American pilots, he did use a similar technique. 'I would go into the vertical and then at fairly low speed, around 150 knots [275km/h], I would put in a boot-load of right rudder and right aileron to really make that thing turn around. It was a fairly good manoeuvre not only to get someone off your six, but also to get behind someone who had fairly low energy.'

'The biggest problem everyone had was seeing it, finding it, and tracking it,' Peck said. 'I remember being behind it in gun-tracking situations and thinking, "There's nothing to this thing. All I can see is the wing."'

Trying to acquire the MiG-21 visually was a learning experience in itself, Sheffield concurred, adding, 'Believe it or not, finding the MiG-21 visually the first time actually makes it easier to do it again the second time.' Sheffield also warned, 'Perhaps the most important lesson on fighting the MiG-21 was that it was very manoeuvrable and that it was

POTENT VARIANTS

In addition to the MiG-21F-13, Peter Misch flew the MiG-21U Mongol trainer, MiG-21SPS, SPS-Ka, M, MF, MF 75, US, and USM. He also gained extensive experience on the most potent of the Fishbed family, the MiG-21Bis (Bis-SAU and Bis-Lazur).

'The MiG-21SPS [a variant made especially for East Germany], was an improvement over the F-13 because it had a new RP-21 radar that provided much more information to the pilot – previously, the MiG-21 had only been equipped with a basic radar to provide range to a target directly in front. The SPS also had flaps that could be lowered to 45° [a greater angle than those on the F-13], and had boundary layer air control – hot air taken from the engine and blown over the wing – that reduced the landing speed by about 20 km/h [12mph] and therefore made it a little easier to land. The MiG-21M had four hardpoints for air-to-air missiles, and the 23mm GSh-23L two-barrel cannon, which was a better weapon than the 30mm Nudelman-Rikhter NR-30 cannon it replaced, but made the aircraft heavier and reduced its manoeuvrability. The MiG-21MF saw the introduction of a new, more powerful engine, and therefore had the manoeuvrability of the MiG-21SPS with the armament of the MiG-21M.

'The Bis had a better autopilot and a new motor, and the Bis-SAU could auto land down to a height of 40 metres [130 feet] before the pilot had to take over. It was really an impressive capability: you controlled the engine and speed, flaps etc, but the aircraft did the rest. I often sat in bad weather, with my right hand resting on my lap, watching in wonder as the stick moved around on its own and brought me to within visual distance from the runway.'

ABOVE: The MiG-21Bis, seen here in Slovakian Air Force markings, was the most potent of the original Fishbed series, and India continued to produce the Bis until as late as 1987.

better to take care of it before you got into a tussle with it. The only aircraft that was more or less unbeatable against the MiG-21 was the F-16. It could sustain the energy [airspeed] and it could pull 9gs. Our MiG-21s could only pull 7.33gs and bled energy. So, the F-16 can get inside the MiG's turn [and point his nose at me]. And if he's not running out of energy, he can still do something to me when he gets there.'

IMPROVED FISHBEDS

Peter Misch, a former East German Air Force pilot, flew a succession of Fishbed variants between 1973 and 1991, accruing 800 hours on the type.

'The main role of the MiG-21 in the East German Air Force was to attack enemy fighters and bombers, although we had secondary roles of reconnaissance and ground attack. We practised making use of Ground Control Intercept [GCI] radar stations to execute slashing attacks from the stern quarter on aerial targets, and we would fly formations of two and four aircraft in dogfights, by day and night, and even in the cloud. Our MiG-21s had an 8.5g limit in optimum conditions, but

we were usually limited to 7gs in order to reduce the stress we put on the aircraft. The most experienced pilots would fly only 60 hours per year, but new pilots were required to fly 100 hours, and moderately experienced pilots flew 75 hours. For all pilots, the requirement was to fly at least one dogfight per month, and one sortie in bad weather every two months in order to maintain their instrument rating.'

A typical intercept in the MiG-21Bis, Misch recalled, consisted of the following: 'Take off with minimum afterburner, which we would come out of to conserve fuel as we reached 600km/h [370mph]. We would continue to accelerate to 900 km/h [560mph] while we received commands from the GCI to steer us towards the target. They would give us directions in height and heading

BELOW: The North Vietnamese Air Force used the MiG-21 to good effect during the South East Asia air war against the United States. Its pilots conducted supersonic slashing attacks against vulnerable American fighter bombers, loosing AA-2 Atoll missiles at short range with devastating results.

OPERATORS

CURRENT OPERATORS:
Angola
Armenia
Azerbaijan
Bangladesh
Bulgaria
Cambodia
Croatia
Cuba
Egypt
Guinea
India
Iran
Laos
Libya
Madagascar

Mali
Mongolia
Mozambique
Nigeria
North Korea
Romania
Serbia
Sudan
Syria
Turkmenistan
Vietnam
Yemen

FORMER OPERATORS:
Afghanistan
Bangladesh

Algeria
Belarus
Burkina Faso
Republic of the Congo
Czechoslovakia/Czech
  Republic
Democratic Republic of East
  Germany
Ethiopia
Finland
Guinea-Bissau
Hungary
Indonesia
Iraq
Kazakhstan
Kyrgyzstan
Yemen

Poland
Russia
Slovakia
Tajikistan
Soviet Union
Uganda
Ukraine
Socialist Federal Republic of
  Yugoslavia/Federal Republic
  of Yugoslavia
Zambia

BELOW: A Polish MiG-21M lands following an interception sortie. The Fishbed was straightforward to land, provided that the pilot kept power on the jet until he was over the runway.

ABOVE: While seen here in Russian markings, the MiG-21MF was actually an export model based on the MiG-21M. Russian removed some of the avionics (and downgraded the motors, in some cases) for the export versions of the Fishbed.

for a stern conversion, and as they did so, we would switch on radar to locate [the] target. Once acquired, we then checked if target was hostile or friendly by interrogating them with the IFF [identification friend or foe]. Depending on the height of the target, we could locate the target from 18km [11 miles] away, identify it by 10km [6 miles], and then launch our missiles within about 7km [4 miles].'

Key to this capability was the improved radar installed in newer variants of the Fishbed. *'The SPS onwards had the RP-21 radar,'* Misch clarified, *'which was effective out to 20km [12 miles] for searching for targets, and had a lock-on capability from about 10km [6 miles]. It was very effective when combined with our R-3S infrared air-to-air*

missiles. This radar also gave you launch ranges to make sure we were within the correct engagement envelope for the missiles. The MiG-21Bis had the R3R radar guided missile and the RP-22 radar, which had a 30km [19 mile] search range, but the same 10km [6 mile] lock-on distance as the RP-21. However, this radar could see targets that were as low as 500m [1,600ft] above the ground, whereas the RP-21 had trouble seeing anything lower than 1,200m [4,000ft] above the ground.'

Continuing his discussion of the intercept, Misch explained that the MiG-21Bis and MiG-21SPS had a data link that allowed the GCI controller to send instructions from the ground without transmitting voice commands over the radio.

'We would look at our cockpit instruments to see the speed, altitude and direction that we were required to fly. A separate instrument featured the commands to turn on the radar, arm the missiles and so on. And there was one more instrument that showed us our position in relation to the target via two needles: vertical needle that told us if we were aligned directly behind the target, or to its left or right; and a horizontal one that indicated if we were at the same altitude as it, or above or below it.'

WARTIME REALITIES

Completing the intercept in wartime conditions relied on the Fishbed pilot being able to position himself for a missile shot. With the older generation air-to-air missiles, this was not always easy because of their austere firing constraints. The East German Air Force eventually received the newer R-60 (AA-8 'Aphid'), which was far more flexible, as Misch revealed: *'From the SPS to the Bis, we could employ the R-60, which was an improved missile that we could launch at 7g. It could even automatically launch itself once it was locked onto the target – we just held down the release button,*

LEFT: The Czech Air Force upgraded its MiG-21MFs to MiG-21MFN standard in order to comply with NATO compatibility regulations, but the type is no longer in Czech service having been replaced by the JAS 39 Saab Gripen.

and as soon as it was locked-on, away it would go. Of course, we had to be careful with that mode of operation, as you could end up shooting down a friendly! The R-60 was highly manoeuvrable, and could turn at 45g. We could carry four of these missiles on the SPS.'

In the very heavy communications and radar jamming environment that was anticipated in a war in central Europe, the East German Air Force knew that its MiG-21 pilots could find themselves without GCI assistance.

'The visibility out the front of the MiG-21 was good enough to see most targets, and from the MiG-21M model onwards we got a periscope and mirrors to look behind us. It became a matter of training for us to teach our new pilots to make visual checks of the airspace not just ahead of them, but all around them, too. In reality, we knew that if there was a war in central Europe, that a lot of our electronic equipment was not going to work, and that there was going to be a lot of electronic warfare. So, we were going to rely on a visual check to see if the target was a friendly or enemy

aircraft, and to keep an eye out around us for unseen enemy aircraft.'

Misch has fond memories of the MiG-21, enthusiastically recalling: 'The MiG-21Bis-SAU was the complete package, and a big improvement over the previous MiG-21 modifications. You felt better in the Bis from the moment that you taxied it. You could take-off and land on grass, and we practised this frequently; it required a longer take off run, and longer landing run, but it was just like driving down a bad road! We would do formation take-offs on grass, too. We did this because our MiG-21 Wings had secondary runways that were grass strips, and we used to even practise this by night! We had a low accident rate, with only 5 or 6 incidents per year, of which not many resulted in us losing a pilot. Every pilot I knew who flew the MiG-21 loved this aircraft. Lots of us wanted to move to more advanced fighters like the MiG-29, but we made the most of what we had and we enjoyed every moment.'

BELOW: The MiG-21F-13 'Fishbed C/E' was the first export version of the Fishbed, and this is a Finnish Air Force example. One recognition feature of the F-13 is the forward-hinging canopy, which latches to the ejection seat when closed and serves as a wind-breaker for the pilot during bailout.

Flying the F-4

The F-4 Phantom II is one of the most prolific and best-loved jet fighters of all time. In all, 5,195 Phantoms were built, and as recently as 2001 there were still more than 1,000 examples remaining in operational service with air forces around the world.

MAIN PHOTOGRAPH: Flying the Phantom at low speeds required the pilot to apply aileron control inputs carefully lest he induce the infamous adverse yaw that would cause the aircraft to go out of control.

The first thing that strikes most people about the Phantom is its sheer size, the awkward protuberance of its collection of antennas, air scoops and aerials, and its overall lack of aesthetic finesse – all of which led to its unofficial nickname, 'Rhino'. Col. William 'Shadow' Schaal, who flew the F-4 before moving to the F-15E Strike Eagle, attests to this:

'It was bigger than anything I had ever flown up to that point.

It had a heritage that made every aircrew proud to join its history. As you walked around the aircraft, it was generally leaking fuels or other hydraulics which you learned over time was normal. You also had to watch out for antennas and other objects on the jet that you could strike your head on. Many an aircrew had "Rhino bites" to remind them of this lesson. As you strapped into the aircraft, it was amazing how much you really couldn't see and

how big the aircraft was. The Martin-Baker seat sat low compared to the canopy rails. You had to look in a rear view mirror to see behind you, and the WSO [weapons systems officer] was situated behind a large bulkhead.'

SIZE AND COMPLEXITY

One such Phantom WSO, now-retired Lt. Col. Jerry 'One-Y' Oney, recalled that his

introduction to the F-4 was an up-close and personal visit to a mini control tower RSU (runway support unit) at the edge of the runway, *'to see an active-air scramble by the guys who sat alert ready to intercept Soviet bombers. Their full-afterburner takeoffs were spectacularly loud; the RSU windows just about popped out of their mountings, we had to cover both ears, and both jets almost dragged their wingtips on the runway while turning towards where the bombers were. I was absolutely awestruck.'*

With the shock of the size and sheer complexity of the Phantom overcome, the next jolt came from the Phantom's crowded cockpits. Sitting in it, said Mike 'House' Hauser, *'it seemed like you were down in a tub; only your head stuck up out of the maze of switches and dials.'* Hauser, a retired Lt. Col. who eventually flew the F-16, added, *'compared*

to the fighters that came after it, the cockpit was not well engineered for human factors.'

Oney, who went on to fly the roomy F-15E, concurred:

'After being in the Eagle for a couple of years I had the chance to hop back into the Phantom's back seat – boy, was it small! Up in Iceland we had to wear tons of cold-weather gear when we flew: "Chinese" underwear, long-johns, a flight-suit, a poopy [immersion] suit, a g-suit, and the parachute harness. The first couple of times all that gear seemed horribly restrictive and tight in the cockpit.'

[MISSION REPORT]
++++++++++++++++++++++
HIGH-LIFT DEVICES

Up until the F-4E in 1972, F-4s had utilized bleed air from the two GE-79 turbojets and fed this via internal piping into the wing leading edges, and then through vents over the wing itself. This 'boundary layer air' control system increased lift at low speeds and was ideal for carrier landings since it gave Navy pilots extra room for error during the approach.

The USAF's F-4Es were the first to feature high-lift slats to improve low-speed manoeuvrability and to reduce adverse yaw. Lt. Col. Mike 'House' Hauser commented: 'The F-4 was heavy and really didn't turn all that well, even with the slats. Dogfighting in the F-4 required using a lot of vertical to keep the jet on the offensive. With the slats adverse yaw was not as bad until you got to high angles of attack. Our jets also had slotted horizontal stabilizers that increased lift at the back of the jet; you could actually pump the stick at slow speed and "jack the nose up". Doing this, you could control nose position at slow speed pretty well.'

ABOVE: Although the carrier would attempt to get 55km/h (30 knots) of wind over its deck, landing a 25-tonne (27.5 ton) jet on it was best done with as low an airspeed as was safe. Bleed air was routed over the Phantom's wings to allow it to maintain control at slow speeds.

Lack of physical space aside, Schaal's comments reflected Hauser's:

'The cockpit was not mechanized for hands on throttle and stick switch [HOTAS] activations; there were switches on the every side of the cockpit for employing the aircraft and working systems during emergencies. The left side of the front cockpit panel was mechanized for weapons employment and radar illumination for the AIM-7 Sparrow radar-guided missile, and also for switching between missile stations. Some pilots even placed a straw or other type item on the missile station select switch to make sure they toggled

the right switch the heat of combat. The pilot had to manually select stations to drop weapons, as well as rotating a switch to indicate release quantity and interval.'

'HEADS-DOWN' CONTROLS
Unlike today's jet fighters with Head-Up Displays (HUD) to aim ordnance and view flight information, *'the Phantom did not have a HUD with a pipper that indicated where the ordnance would hit. The aircraft had a combining glass that displayed a fixed sight that you would input miliradian settings into for each delivery,'* Schaal concluded. Hauser said of the front office's combining glass that, *'next to it there was a*

column of lights that said ARM, RADAR, HEAT, and GUN, to tell us which weapon was selected. It was up near the glare shield, so you could refer to it without lowering your head, but there was nothing "heads-up" otherwise. The bombing system controls were all "heads-down" and not very intuitive to a new guy.'

THE BUCKING RHINO

The US Navy, for whom the F-4 had originally been built, showed in the course of the Vietnam conflict that if the right tactics were used and the pilot knew how to aggressively manoeuvre the Phantom without exceeding its limits, then the Rhino could dominate any MiG in service in the 1960s and '70s in a dogfight.

Although the USAF killed more MiGs than the Navy, it lost more to MiGs and had a lower kill ratio. Part of the reason for this was the tactics they employed, but another

factor was that Air Force pilots at the time were not as familiar with handling the big jet at the limits of its performance capabilities. Early Phantoms had

some very dangerous flight characteristics at certain points of their flight envelopes, and these killed more Air Force pilots than Navy pilots.

'The Phantom was not a forgiving jet if you didn't listen to it – once you learned to listen to it, the jet was awesome. The first thing a new pilot learned was not to use aileron inputs at high angles of attack [AoA] unless you wanted to depart – instead, you used the rudder to roll the jet left or right. We joked that Instructor WSOs had a stick that they would use to hit the side of your helmet if you did use ailerons. Most of the WSOs I knew would

PILOT'S VERDICT

❝ The Phantom was not a forgiving jet if you didn't listen to it – once you learned to listen to it, the jet was awesome. ❞

Col. William 'Shadow' Schaal
F-4 Phantom II Pilot, USAF

MAIN PHOTOGRAPH: Poor pilot visibility was one of the Phantom's real weaknesses. The pilot had to look through a forward windscreen encased in an obtrusive metal framing, and visibility to the rear was almost non-existent.

[MISSION REPORT]
++++++++++++++++++++++++
THE 'FLARETTE'!

While Navy pilots recovered to 'the boat' in what amounted to an undignified, controlled crash, land-based pilots employed a small flare – gently raising the nose just as the wheels touched-down in order to slow the jet's sink rate – on landing. British Royal Air Force pilots who flew the F-4K/M (a modified version of the USN F-4J) humorously referred to this as a 'flarette'. *'I flew a 17° AoA approach, and doing that, the jet would flare real nice. You could make a very smooth touchdown in an F-4E, especially if there was*

a nice wind blowing. If you flew "on speed", which gave a steady aural tone in the aural angle of attack system, instead of "on-AoA", you'd land a little hard by Air Force standards,' confirmed Mike 'House' Hauser, a retired USAF pilot.

For increased stopping power and to counter the Rhino's comparatively weak brakes, the jet's drag parachute could be deployed as the nose was lowered onto the runway, or at about 10m (30ft) above the runway. Deploying the parachute before the main wheels had touched down generated such sudden deceleration forces that one RAF pilot said it usually resulted in 'my teeth embedded in front console'. *'Still',* he grinned, *'that was the technique I always favoured!'*

BELOW: It was down to the pilot to decide whether to flare, and how early to deploy the brake parachute. The more aggressive the stop, the more likely that the WSO would utter a string of expletives from the back!

BELOW: U.S. Air Force F-4s received a range of camouflage patterns that varied from the familiar two-tone grey, to the three-tone green/brown, and this three-tone green/grey wrap-around pattern.

place their legs closer to the sides of the stick during this phase of flight to prevent young pilots from inputting lateral stick movements,' Schaal said of the infamous 'adverse yaw' – where the nose rapidly sliced through the air and caused the Rhino to go out of control. When the departure from controlled flight did occur, Hauser counsels, *'it was fairly easy to handle as long as you got the controls neutral. The nose was heavy, so it would tend to nose over and get you right out of the departure. If you were very nose high and departed, you could tail slide the jet a little, but again, the* nose would come over, and as long as you got the controls neutral, it would fly right out.'

Schaal adds that there were other things to keep an eye out for, too:

'You also had to know what flight regime you were in; low airspeeds at medium altitude and high AoA required small throttle inputs – If you went from afterburner or military [maximum] thrust and then to idle and back, the motors generally stalled or stagnated briefly as you did so. During high-g manoeuvring, you also had to watch out for "MACH tuck" or "dig in" – this phenomenon would add about 1g to your aircraft and usually generated an over-g condition.'

YOU ROW, I'LL SHOOT THE DUCKS!

While the pilot controlled the Rhino through all of these combat manoeuvres, the WSO was busy riding it out and working the weapons systems. Despite the violence of the manoeuvres and the confines of the rear cockpit (RCP), *'I'd venture to say the vast majority of WSOs had cast iron stomachs* and nobody could get us sick,' Oney reckoned.

Schaal still uses today some of the basics of crew coordination he learned in the F-4:

'We always joke – "The FCP [front cockpit] rows the boat and the RCP shoots the ducks."'

In reality, the pilot also shot the missiles but in the Phantom the RCP was required to acquire all radar contacts, although AIM-9 Sidewinder IR missile shots would occur without the help of the rear cockpit. Each person backs up each other in navigation, with the RCP spending most of his time using the radar to find and identify our targets. As Schaal reveals, the RCP also serves as a safety valve during visual attacks and other scenarios:

'More than one friend of mine was saved when the WSO yelled,

"pull-up!" during a diving delivery to avoid hitting the ground; or, as the aircraft descended through weather and the pilot got special disoriented, the WSO recognized it first and helped direct the aircraft to a safe flight condition.'

DOMESTIC PHANTOM VARIANTS

F-4A: Prototype variants for the U.S. Navy and the U.S. Marine Corps

F-4B: First operational model used by the Navy and Marines

RF-4B: Tactical reconnaissance version of F-4B

F-4C: USAF derivative of F-4B optimized for land-based operations

RF-4C: Tactical reconnaissance version of F-4C with internal cannon and radar removed, and provision for cameras in redesigned nose

F-4D: Improved F-4C used by both USAF and USMC with improved weapons systems

F-4E: Much-improved F-4D with internal M61A1 gun and revised radome arrangement, cockpit and the addition of leading-edge slats (on most examples) and slotted vertical stabilizers

RF-4E: Tactical reconnaissance version of F-4E with internal cannon and radar removed, and provision for cameras in redesigned nose

F-4G: 'Wild Weasel' suppression of enemy air defence (SEAD) version of the F-4E with extensive avionics refit and SEAD weapons such as the AGM-88 HARM.

F-4J: Improved F-4B with new radar, new J-79 engines and the deletion of the IR detector found on F-4B

F-4N: Upgraded F-4B that included the slotted stabilizer of the F-4J and the locking of the inboard leading edge slats

F-4S: Upgraded F-4J with an advanced radar and smokeless J-79 engines. Leading edge slats were also installed

QF-4B/E/G/N: Retired aircraft converted into pilotless target drones

MAIN PHOTOGRAPH: The U.S. Marine Corps, arguably the most versatile of all three U.S. armed forces, operated the Phantom primarily in support of its ground troops. Although eclipsed by the USAF and USN Rhinos in Vietnam, USMC F-4s nevertheless provided grunts on the ground with protection in the form of a robust close air support capability.

Flying the F-5

Sleek lines, a classically curved 'coke bottle' fuselage and small wings lend Northrop's F-5 an air of both grace and menace. Having seen service with no fewer than 36 nations around the world, four decades on from when it was designed it remains a valuable fighter for several of the world's air forces.

PILOT'S VERDICT

"The F-5 handles so very well that you can do almost anything with it that you can think of."

Col. Olivier 'Wasy' Spieth
16 Squadron Commander
Swiss Air Force

'The F-5E is a light supersonic fighter aircraft with a first-generation air-to-air-radar,' explains Colonel Olivier 'Wasy' Spieth, a Swiss Air Force F-5 instructor pilot (IP) with more than 1,600 hours in the jet. Intended as an affordable fighter that could be operated by the world's smaller air forces, the F-5 is, as retired US Air Force Colonel Paco Geisler explains, 'a simple fighter for a third world country. That means that it is not only easy to maintain and keep in the air, but it is also easy to fly. It is also very fast and, in the right hands, lethal.'

The F-5's ease of use certainly did not apply to many other fighters being designed and fielded in the 1950s. Spieth says that the F-5 'handles very well, and you can do almost anything with it that you can think of.

Of course, it uses a conventional control system that consists of mechanical and hydraulic links, rods and pulleys — there is no fly-

MAIN PHOTOGRAPH: Christened 'Freedom Fighter' at the height of the Cold War, and renamed Tiger II in its modernized F-5E/F form, the aircraft more closely resembles a shark, with its slender fuselage and straked wings and tail.

MAIN PHOTOGRAPH: The US Navy and US Air Force never operated the F-5E as a front-line fighter, since they were already investing in far more expensive and sophisticated alternatives like the F-15 Eagle and F-14 Tomcat; but they did recognize that the Tiger II made an excellent MiG-21 simulator, and both employed it as an Aggressor/Adversary trainer.

RIGHT: Without computer-driven flight controls, the F-5 has a reputation as being a real 'stick and rudder' fighter that requires the most highly-skilled pilots to take it to the edge of its flight envelope. Even so, it is a forgiving aircraft when those boundaries are exceeded.

BELOW: The cockpit is tight, but not cramped or cluttered: old-fashioned analogue dials are nicely positioned to make instrument flying easier, and the side consoles are easy to reach and visually scan.

by-wire, as found in most modern jet fighters.'

But make no mistake, the ease with which the jet can be manoeuvered does not belittle its potential to cause havoc in air combat, even when flown against some of the more modern designs in service today. Geisler explains why.

'The F-5's only real attribute against a hi-tech fighter with a high thrust-to-weight ratio, like the F-15 Eagle or F-16 Viper, is its small size. However, a well-flown F-5E in a knife fight with a F-15 or F-16 … could easily be won if the Eagle or Viper was poorly flown. In fact, the advantage in such a fight was normally held by the pilot with the most experience – not by the guy with the best aircraft. Against contemporary fighters like the F-4 Phantom II, the F-5 was a lethal

adversary in the slow-speed arena and could easily win that fight, but against something like the Navy's A-4 Skyhawk, it was a much closer competition in the slow-speed fight. In fact, below 200 knots [370km/h] airspeed, the two aircraft were almost identical in their manoeuvering potential.'

The F-5 has *g* limits of -3*g* to +7.33*g*, which is not competitive with the +9*g* of modern fighters, but was standard at the time of its introduction to service.

For all its potency up close and in the classic dogfight, the F-5 is also easy to fly for another reason: when the pilot departs controlled flight, the aircraft can easily be recovered.

EASY TO FLY

'Its departure characteristics are the same as the F-15,' says Geisler, a veteran fighter pilot who flew the F-15C Eagle after spending time as an F-5 Aggressor pilot. 'It just runs out of airspeed and "falls off" in a stall until flying speed is attained. In short, it's not at all a violent experience. The F-5 needs about 150 knots [277km/h] of airspeed to be considered flying for continued manoeuvering, and its handling characteristics are enhanced [its stall speed reduced] by leading-edge flaps that are activated by the pilot at speeds *below approximately 200 knots [370km/h]. The flaps switch is labelled "manoeuvering flaps" and is located on the throttle. It has two positions, "Out" and "In", and is easy and natural to use.'*

When the jet does depart controlled flight, recovery is foolproof, says Geisler. *'It is very easy to recover. You just let go of the stick and it will fly itself out of almost any out-of-control situation. That, combined with the fact that the indicators prior to it departing controlled flight are very positive, makes for an honest aircraft that offers no surprises.'*

STRENGTHS AND WEAKNESSES

Jet fighters that can turn well are usually referred to as 'angles' fighters, and these types usually avoid vertical manoeuvres which require lots of thrust. Conversely, those with a good thrust-to-weight ratio are often called 'energy' fighters, and these are best advised to use their excess

thrust to power into the vertical plane where their opponent cannot follow them. According to Geisler, the F-5 can be flown as either an 'energy' fighter or an 'angles' fighter, making it a very flexible aircraft.

'It can hold its own in either,' Geisler affirms. *'Its advantage in the energy fight is its small size: we bet on the adversary losing sight of it as we flew up into the sky. We enjoyed the knife fight as an angles fighter because the F-5 is*

easily controllable at speeds down to as slow as 90 knots [167km/h] … it can easily reduce anyone's total advantage in either the energy or angles fight.'

IN THE COCKPIT

The F-5 pilot is almost cocooned in the sleek jet. *'The cockpit is comfortable,'* says Spieth, *'but you feel like you are in a bathtub: the canopy starts quite high and some distance behind*

ABOVE: The 57th Fighter Wing, based at Nellis Air Force Base, Nevada, was home to two F-5 Aggressor squadrons in the 1980s. The F-5 was so small, especially head-on, that it could humble even the most technologically advanced, or most skilled and experienced, of opponents if they lost sight of it before they had 'killed' it.

[MISSION REPORT]

SKOSHI TIGERS

While the F-5 was intended as a jet fighter for export to foreign nations, some senior commanders in the US Air Force saw the Freedom Fighter's potential as a close support aircraft in Vietnam, and even went as far as ordering 200 examples. The Department of Defence promptly vetoed the order, but in the summer of 1965 (as an act of conciliation) permitted the USAF to conduct a combat evaluation of the F-5 in South East Asia.

The evaluation programme was given the code name 'Skoshi Tiger', and in October 1965 the USAF was assigned 12 F-5As from foreign supply stocks, which were assigned temporarily to the 4503rd Tactical Fighter Wing at Williams AFB, Arizona. Several modifications were made to the jets, including the installation of an in-flight refuelling probe, armour plate on the undersides of the fuselage, jettisonable pylons under the wings, and a lead-computing gun sight. The rudder travel limiter was removed, and the aircraft were camouflaged in tan and two-tone green, with light grey undersides. The single seat F-5C and two-seat F-5D had been born.

The same day that the aircraft arrived at their new home of Bien Hoa AB, Thailand, they flew their first combat mission. Over the next four months, the 12 F-5s flew 2,500 hours of close air support, interception, and reconnaissance missions over South Vietnam. When six more examples joined the Wing, the total strength climbed to 18 aircraft.

ABOVE: The addition of a fixed refuelling probe to the 12 Skoshi Tiger jets was just one of the modifications that were hastily applied after they departed for combat in South Vietnam. The probe was of the 'bolt-on' variety. Note the wingtip fuel tanks, which characterised the F-5A/B.

By now the Wing had been redesignated the 10th Fighter Commando Squadron.

Carrying up to 1,400kg (3,000lb) of ordnance per sortie, another 1,500 hours of combat time were logged over the course of more than a thousand sorties. in total, by the end of the trial just two aircraft had been lost in more than 4,000 combat hours and 3,500 combat sorties, making the F-5 statistically the least vulnerable tactical fighter in South Vietnam. Despite this, the Department of Defence rejected a second Air Force request for F-5C/Ds, and instead forced the Air Force to consider the US Navy's A-7 Corsair II as an alternative.

[MISSION REPORT]
++++++++++++++++++++++++++

SWISS TIGERS

The Swiss Air Force is a long-term operator of the improved F-5E/F Tiger II, and uses the little jet as a lead-in trainer for pilots destined to go to the much bigger and more complex F/A-18C/D Hornet.

These future Hornet pilots spend several years flying with Squadron 16 at Payerne Air Base, where they first learn how to fly the F-5E in a building-block approach that ends with them being taught air combat manoeuvring and dog fighting. Once that is accomplished, the young pilots, of whom there are only three or four per class, with one class per year, will remain on the squadron and fly support missions for the Hornets and Switzerland's extensive ground control intercept (GCI) radar network.

Supporting the Hornets can involve towing a target dart which is trailed behind the aircraft and shot at by the F/A-18's 20mm M61A1 Vulcan Gatling gun; but more excitingly, often involves playing 'Red Air' – the bad guys – in mock combat with the Hornets. Such sorties are inevitably stacked in the Hornet's favour, but they are essential training for the new

pilot and Hornet pilots alike. Some of Switzerland's two-seat F-5Fs have been modified to carry an electronic warfare pod and an electronic warfare instructor in the back seat, and this equipment is used to simulate a degraded electronic environment for both GCI and the Hornets.

With a few hundred hours and a couple of years of flying these missions week in, week out, the Swiss F-5 pilot will eventually get to move on to the large and complex Hornet.

ABOVE: The F-5 has limited endurance, so the Swiss Air Force uses external fuel tanks. The brightly coloured tank (and AIM-9 missile on wingtip), help pilots in a mock dogfight to identify 'friendly' and 'hostile' aircraft.

MAIN PHOTOGRAPH: Switzerland ranks as one of the smallest nations to have ever operated the F-5, but the country's neutrality means that there are precious few opportunities for the Swiss Tigers to train with other air forces or visit other countries.

your head, so visibility down and back is obscured. Compared to modern aircraft, the cockpit is cluttered and not at all ergonomic, but it represents the way that things were done at the time the F-5 was built.'

Geisler added that rear-view mirrors help alleviate some of the poor rearward vision, and that despite being somewhat vintage in appearance, the cockpit layout

meant that it was quite easy to fly during poor weather.

Dominating the centre of the cockpit console is the display scope for the F-5's small, primitive Emerson AN/APG-69

radar. In fact, this radar is unique to the F-5E, as the original F-5 had no radar at all. Geisler explains the planar array APG-69's operation and modes.

'The radar has no acquisition symbols for azimuth lock-on, and you cannot control the elevation of the radar dish in the nose. The scope Pulse echo of a target within search limits, approximately plus or minus 6,000 to 8,000 feet [1,800–2,500m] of your altitude, starts to be detected by the radar at around 20 miles [32km]. Of

course, it can also pick up electronic countermeasures "chaff" strips at the same distance, and there is no way of knowing what you are locked onto – a real target or a cloud of chaff.'

Actually using this basic set in combat reveals just how limited it is. Geisler goes on: *'The radar is best used in the "look-up" environment, because using it in a level or look-down scenario results in the ground returns creating false targets. The boresight acquisition mode of the radar only works inside 10 miles [16km], and requires you to have a visual on the adversary. It works simply: you place the fixed gun sight on the target, press an acquisition button on the stick, and once locked the gunsight provides range and a lead computation for gun attacks only.'*

BELOW: Thailand has operated the F-5B, F-5E and F-5E. It now operates its Israeli-modified F-5T Tigris in concert with its Lockheed Martin F-16s.

So primitive is the radar that Geisler never used it prior to the 'merge' (the point at which two opposing fighters pass each other and begin dogfighting). However, he frequently used the boresight mode when he managed to manoeuvre behind the wing line of his quarry and wanted to simulate a gun shot.

Geisler summarized the F-5 as follows. *'It is small, hard to see, and has two engines that are smokeless. Its disadvantages are that it poses no long-range threat because of its simple radar, has a small fuel load that means it has a restricted combat radius, and I don't think it could handle a lot of damage.'*

And while the Swiss Air Force's F-5E/Fs have been updated to include modern electronic extras like an Inertial Navigation System and a state-of-the-art Radar Warning System, Spieth believes that the F-5's main detractor is its lack of modern radar and modern air-to-air missiles.

Yet, despite these shortcomings, *'It's a typical pilot's airplane that does everything you ask of it and has no airs or graces: you just fly it! It seems easy to maintain and it has flown with the Swiss Air Force for more than 30 years. Even today, other Air Forces are very interested in buying used F-5s for Red Air* [to use as mock enemy aircraft in training]. *I think that says a lot about it.'*

ABOVE: The US Navy had five Adversary F-5 units: Navy Fighter Weapons School, VF-126, VF-127, VF-43, and VF-45. Today, it has just two, VFC-13 at NAS Fallon, Nevada; and VFC-111 at NAS Key West, Florida.

Flying the P-3 Orion

For more than four decades, since its service debut in 1962, the Lockheed P-3 Orion maritime surveillance and anti-submarine warfare (ASW) aircraft has patrolled the oceans of the world. Yet the Orion has been much more than NATO's guardian of the seaways; it also deserves credit for many other achievements.

MAIN PHOTOGRAPH: Indicative of the Orion's formidable air-to-surface capability, this US Navy P-3C is armed with four AGM-84A Harpoon missiles on its under-fuselage and wing stations, and two AIM-9 Sidewinders on its outer wing pylons.

The Orion carries a crew of 10 or 12, depending on its mission and which Service operates it. There are two, sometimes three, pilots; two flight engineers; a Tactical Co-ordinator (TACCO), Navigator/Communicator (NAVCOM), two acoustic sensor operators, a radar/MAD operator, and an In-Flight Technician, whose task it is to make any in-flight repairs to the aircraft's avionics.

The latter also assumes the duty of Ordnanceman; an extra crew member was previously carried for this task. Crews are unanimous in their praise for the Orion. For one thing, it has two and half times the floor area of the P2V Neptune, which it replaced. It has a pressurized cabin, air conditioning, electrically heated floor panels, and plenty of stand-up and walk-around space. Controllable, polarized lighting reduces eye strain, and comfortable adjustable chairs cut crew fatigue.

Captain Derek Squire, who flew the Canadian version, the CP-140 Aurora, with Nos 404, 405 and 415 Squadrons, and also the Maritime Proving and Evaluation Unit of the Canadian Armed Forces, had only one serious complaint, and that had nothing to do with flying or crew comfort:

'The walk around is painful. As you check the bomb bay and the nose wheel area, the noise of the 30,000rpm of the APU jet engine in the nose compartment blasts through the ear defenders to rattle your skull. It has been compared, by aircraft engine technicians, to the amount of ear-splitting noise that they have been subjected to while working on a running F-104 engine.'

POWERFUL ENGINES

The Orion's powerful engines are a key factor in the Orion's success as a maritime patrol aircraft, says Squire.

'In the late 1950s, when the Lockheed Electra airliner was being heavily modified to eventually become the P-3, a seven-foot [2.13m] section of the fuselage was removed, resulting in a tremendous weight saving. The T56 engines, as used in the Electra and the C-130 Hercules, were retained for the P-3. These huge turboprops provide the ideal combination of high speed cruise transit to the operating area, as well as low fuel consumption during the low-speed and low-altitude operations in the search area.

The four Allison T56 engines are capable of each supplying 4,600 shaft horsepower [3,430kW] to the 13-foot [4m] diameter Hamilton Standard paddle-bladed propellers. It will definitely get up and move when called upon. As a measure of the P-3 handling properties, many

[MISSION REPORT] ENDURANCE FLIGHTS

The P-3 is no stranger to record-breaking endurance flying in the line of duty. On 1 May, 1964, a P-3A Orion commanded by Captain P.L. Ruehrmund of Experimental Squadron VX-1 returned to NAS Key West after completing an 18-day round-the-world flight that covered 49,197km (26,550 nautical miles) in several stages. During the over-water stages of the flight the aircraft dropped explosive sound signals to assist Naval Ordnance Laboratory scientists studying the acoustic properties of the sea as a medium for sound transmission over long distances. Seven years later, on 22 January, 1971, an RP-3D Orion, a research conversion fitted with equipment for atmospheric sampling and magnetic survey and captained by Commander P.R. Hite, took off from Patuxent River, Maryland, to attempt the Class C Group II World Distance Record. Sixteen-and-a-half hours later, after flying to and from the North Pole via Hudson Bay, Canada, and Duluth, Minnesota, the Orion landed at Patuxent, having covered 10,061km (6253 miles).

LEFT: A P-3C Orion of Navy Patrol Squadron VP-22, NAS Barber's Point, Hawaii.

BELOW: The Magnetic Anomaly Detector (MAD), its 'sting' pictured here, was once a key element in anti-submarine warfare, but is not commonly used today.

pilots have completed rolls and loops in their flight simulators – none have admitted to doing so in the real aircraft. Since modern simulators are built to the performance capabilities of the real thing, it should in theory, be possible to do the same in the actual aircraft.'

SHORT TAKEOFF AND LANDING
One of the Orion's biggest attributes, in terms of performance, is its ability to get off the ground quickly and land in a relatively short distance, as Derek Squire explains. 'The aircraft can be described as excellent at short takeoff and landing. The engine start-up sequence is number 2 first, disconnect the power cart on the starboard side, then number 1 followed by numbers 3 and 4. Air for the start is supplied by the APU normally. The nose wheel steering is positive and effective until the rudder takes over directional control on the takeoff. Once the throttles are thrown forward, the P-3 accelerates briskly. A fully laden Orion needs roughly 4,500 or so feet [1,400m] of runway for takeoff. At high weights, it will break the ground at around 135 knots [250km/h] with takeoff flap setting – 35 per cent. At lower weights, as for an air show or a pilot trainer, the performance is really impressive, and the Allisons really put out some smash. The aircraft is inherently stable and flies well hands off when trimmed properly, much as you would expect from a military aircraft that was developed from an airliner.'

The Orion/CP-140's anti-submarine warfare operations over the Western Atlantic during the dangerous years of the Cold War came under the responsibility of NATO's Western Atlantic Command, which comprises a Submarine Force Western Atlantic Area; an Ocean Sub-Area; and the Bermuda, Azores and Greenland Island Commands. The share of the Canadian Armed Forces' Maritime Air Group in these operations is to conduct surveillance flights over the sea approaches to Canada, over coastal waters and over the Arctic archipelago, and also to provide an airborne anti-submarine force in support of North American and NATO defence commitments. Canada's CP-140s equipped four squadrons, Nos 404, 405, 407 and 415; fourteen aircraft were based on Greenwood, Nova Scotia, and the other four at CFB Comox, on the west coast.

EXTENDING ENDURANCE

'The P-3's engines have so much power that it is normal and a standard practice to shut down one or two in flight, to extend the on-station endurance,' says Derek Squire. 'Fuel burn is normally around 4,500 pounds [2,000kg] per hour, per engine. "Loiter Operations" extend the endurance by making the remaining operating engines work harder and thus more efficiently. When one is shut down – normally the left outer known as number 1, since that is the only one that does not have a generator incorporated – there are no restrictions to the handling or altitude limits. The only stipulation is that you are not allowed to enter icing conditions, due to the fact that ice would accumulate in the engines and the crew would not be able to restart that engine if required. Two-engine "loiter ops" can generally be carried out when the

RIGHT: Systems operators at work in the main cabin of the Orion. The P-3 has a roomy and well-insulated cabin which provides the crew with a comfortable working environment.

all-up weight of the aircraft has been reduced by fuel burn and stores expenditure to below 120,000 pounds [54,500kg]. In the Canadian air force, the altitude is restricted to a minimum of 1,000 feet [300m] above terrain or water with two engines shut down, to allow time for the crew to start up a loitered engine if one of the operating ones should develop a problem. Pilots and flight engineers practice the quick air start procedures often, and can get a loitered engine on line and developing power well within one minute. Depending on time to destination and alternate, the endurance can be increased from the normal of 11 hours to over 16 hours when engines are loitered in flight. A Royal New Zealand Air Force P-3 flight of 21.5 hours set the record for the type.'

Derek Squire enthuses about the Orion's handling characteristics.

'It is a joy to fly.

Whether in cruise mode at 31,000 feet [9,500m] and 420 knots [777km/h] TAS, or at 300 feet [90m] above sea level at 190 knots [350km/h] IAS in a 60-degree bank tactical manoeuvre, it is a predictable smooth flying machine with very

ABOVE: US Navy P-3C Orions on the flight line. By 2007, the Navy's considerable P-3 fleet was being gradually reduced.

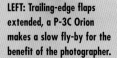

LEFT: Trailing-edge flaps extended, a P-3C Orion makes a slow fly-by for the benefit of the photographer.

ABOVE: A P-3C Orion of the Japanese Maritime Self-Defence Force formates with a counterpart from the US Navy during an exercise over the Pacific.

RIGHT: Crews are unanimous in their praise of the Orion's large and comfortable cockpit, with all its flight instruments and switches easily accessible.

BELOW: Hunter in the snow: Orion crews, who had to operate in all weathers, became all too familiar with conditions such as this in the North Atlantic.

few vices that might catch you unaware. The stated ceiling of the P-3 is 28,300 feet [8,625m], but there is so much power and controllability in the flight controls that I have had it up to 37,000 feet [11,250m] and only noticed a very slight mushing at that altitude. The problem becomes the cabin pressurization, which normally rises as the altitude of the aircraft increases. At anything over 35,000 feet [10,600m] altitude, the cabin is very close to 10,000 feet [3,000m] pressure, thus requiring supplemental oxygen for the crew.'

WINTER CONDITIONS

On the other side of the Atlantic, the P-3 crews of the Royal Norwegian Air Force (RNorAF), operating from the maritime air base at Andoya, sometimes had to cope with appalling weather conditions. During the winter months the runway at Andoya was usually covered in snow and ice, and conditions were at their worst when the weather became warmer and the snow and ice turned to slush. To compound the problems, pilots sometimes had to cope with crosswinds of up to 92km/h (50 knots), which could make take-offs and landings adventurous, to say the least.

During the Cold War, the task of the RNorAF crews of the Andoya-based No 333 Squadron formed the second line of defence against Soviet submarines slipping out of their ports in northern Russia, the first line of defence being the nuclear hunter-killer submarines of the USN and Royal Navy. The Norwegian Orions would aim to trap Soviet submarines before the latter reached one of two deep trenches which run between Greenland and Iceland and through the Iceland–Faeroes Gap. These

trenches run roughly north-east to south-west and permit submarines to dive deep while negotiating the Greenland–Iceland–Faeroes choke points. Russian submarine commanders aimed to reach these natural features as quickly as possible; in the case of a nuclear boat, this meant that the reactor cooling pump had to be kept running at full speed, with a consequent increase in the submarine's noise and radiation signatures.

As they approached the trenches, the submarines had to run the gauntlet of other Orions, operated by the United States Navy and the Royal Netherlands Navy (RNethN). At that time the Royal Netherlands Navy had

thirteen P-3Cs, operated by No 320 and 321 Squadrons based at NAS Valkenburg; detachments frequently went to Keflavik in Iceland, where they worked alongside USN P-3 units. No 2 Squadron, a maritime operational training unit, was also based on Valkenburg. The RNethN deactivated its two P-3 Squadrons in 2005.

It was a move that many crewmen regretted.

'We were very enthusiastic about the Orion,' commented one navigator. 'It proved very successful against submarines during NATO exercises under operational conditions and was far more reliable from the safety aspect than the Breguet Atlantic, which it replaced.'

ABOVE: At the height of the Cold War, Orions accounted for around 80 per cent of the maritime patrol aircraft available to the West.

[MISSION REPORT]
+ +
# HOSTILE ACTION

In the Pacific, P-3 crews often had to face the threat of possible hostile action, as these extracts from an aircraft log in 1965 reveal.

'Position 43.24N 136.40E. Two Russian Frescoes (MiG-17s) intercepted QA-3 which was heading 045 at 180 knots. The Frescoes initially passed abeam to port, heading 235 degrees T, then orbited aft of the P-3 and passed again abeam to port. The Frescoes then crossed the bow and ascended from 1500 to 2500ft. During all the passes, abeam, forward and aft, distance was approximately 1000 yards. During the intercept, QA-3 maintained 1500 ft, course 045, speed 180 knots. The total time held was eleven minutes.

Position 42.32N 135.40E. Two Russian Frescoes intercepted QA-8 while rigging (identifying and photographing) the Russian freighter Uman. The P-3 was at 200ft, course/airspeed 051/160 knots. The Frescoes passed 1000 yards abeam to starboard at 250 ft, then crossed the bow at 1500 yards, then abeam to port approx 1400 yards climbing to 2500 ft. During the intercept, QA-8 ascended to 12500 ft and altered heading to

LEFT: A satellite picture of the US Navy EP-3A Orion after its forced landing on Hainan Island after colliding with a Chinese fighter in April 2001.

071 degrees T. The total time held was ten minutes.

Position 44.27N 138.10E. Two Russian Frescoes (side numbers 31 and 51) intercepted QA-2. QA-2 was tracking a Russian freighter. The Frescoes were in a loose tail chase formation approx eight miles apart. No 31 passed 100 yards to starboard at 200 ft above the P-3, then orbited 2500 yards to starboard then to port. No 51 passed abeam to port at approx one mile. During the intercept, QA-3 completed the rig and proceeded on track. The total time held was eight minutes.

In April 2001, a Chinese J-8 fighter collided with the EP-3A Orion it was 'buzzing' off Hainan Island. The J-8 crashed, killing its pilot; the EP-3 made an emergency landing on Hainan (above), the aircraft and crew being detained by the Chinese authorities. The crew were later released.

Flying the E-2

With its fuel-efficient turboprop engines – which give rise to the nickname 'Hummer' – the E-2C can fly missions of up to five and a half hours. The Hawkeye is usually first off and last back to the carrier deck.

MAIN PHOTOGRAPH: The E-2s of VAW-123 'Screwtops' have the most distinctively painted rotodomes in the US fleet.

Using their powerful radar, the current E-2 versions can monitor six million cubic miles of airspace and more than 380,000km² (150,000 square miles) of land or sea surface simultaneously. Hawkeye crews consider themselves 'the eyes and ears of the fleet'.

The crew of a Hawkeye consists of five members. As well as two pilots in the cockpit, there are three Naval Flight Officers (NFOs) in the main compartment. As C-2 pilot 'Bunky' recommends to prospective NFOs unsure of which career path to take: *'If you want a view of what's going on outside, go jets. If you want a view of everything going on outside* [displayed on a screen], *go Hawkeyes.'*

OPERATOR INTERFACE

The interface between the operator and the display screens has varied over the years. On the Hawkeye 2000, it is a trackball, whereas most earlier models used a light pen to select objects of interest. The designers of the new E-2D considered using touch-screen technology, but decided against it, because fingerprints can make the screens, particularly those in the cockpit, unreadable due to reflected light.

According to unofficial sources, the Hawkeye's AN/APS-145 radar can detect airborne targets up to 400km (250 miles) away and track over 2,000 targets simultaneously, while the airborne controllers can control up to 40 interceptions at once. Opposite the radar consoles are three small portholes, one for each seat. They provide the only direct outside view for the mission crew, albeit to the starboard side only. For both catapult launches and arrested landings on an aircraft carrier, as well as land take-offs and landings, the three cabin seats swivel to face forwards. This pushes the crew backwards in their seats during acceleration and throws them against their harnesses on landing. Conversely, the passengers on the C-2 transport variant face backwards in fixed seats.

The E-2's seats are not particularly comfortable. A long mission is *'like sitting on a cinder block for 5.5 (hours),'* says 'Goober', an E-2 NFO. *'A lot of us have those small roll-up stadium seat cushions for some kind of insulation from the seat, otherwise your back hurts like hell when you finally climb out.'*

TOP: The E-2D is the newest Hawkye, and to a pilot or NFO it is very different from previous versions.

ABOVE: Today's Hawkeyes can detect and track targets at ranges that are several orders of magnitude greater than early models such as the E-2Bs seen here.

BELOW: The whirring propellers of the E-2 demand a lot of respect from personnel working on the flight deck.

Hawkeye crews have parachutes, unlike those on the C-2 Greyhound. *'E-2 guys hook into their parachutes* [attached to the seat]. *Since it would be bad form for the pilots of a C-2 to wear parachutes* [and the passengers without], *we're not allowed to wear 'chutes unless we're on a functional check flight'*, explains one C-2 pilot.

All the electronics in the Hawkeye require a lot of cooling. Each new variant of the E-2 has had a more powerful cooling system than its predecessor. The cooling system is measured in weight, but it is not clear exactly how. The

Hawkeye 2000 has a '12-ton' cooling system, for example, which either cools 12 tons of air in an hour or makes 12 tons of ice in a day, depending on who you ask. Whatever the truth, the system works efficiently and the E-2's cabin is quite cold when flying on station, despite all the high-powered computers whirring away.

FLYING THE HAWKEYE

The E-2 and C-2 have certain characteristics that make them unique in the world of carrier aviation. Most importantly, they are propeller-driven, which produces a considerable safety hazard to flight deck personnel.

'The E-2 doesn't have the nickname of the "Veg-O-Matic" for nothing. A moving prop has taken more than its fair share of lives in the last 30 years,' says NFO Lt (jg) Gabriel Helms. The E-2 and C-2 also have the longest wingspans (28m/80ft 7in) and heaviest weights of any current carrier aircraft. A fully loaded E-2C weighs 23,850kg (53,000lb) and a C-2A 25,650kg (60,000lb).

The large wingspan and wide spacing of the engines make carrier landings particularly challenging. Changes in throttle setting on approach produce significant amounts of yaw, requiring fancy footwork on the rudder pedals to keep the fuselage of the aircraft aligned with the carrier landing area.

Instructor pilot Lt Tim Slentz says, *'The most difficult thing for students in the E-2 and C-2 is controlling the aircraft's tendency to yaw left and right a bit, especially on power adjustments. To counteract this tendency, you have to add rudder, so your hands and feet are always moving as you*

try to maintain directional control. Also, the landing area of a Nimitz-class carrier is 90 feet [27.4m] *wide. The E-2's wingspan is about 81 feet* [24.7m], *so a landing approach that is only a few feet off centreline can present a potential hazard to personnel and parked aircraft. We train the pilots of the E-2/C-2 to a very strict tolerance on line-up.'*

The E-2 and C-2 have notable differences in flying characteristics. The E-2's rotodome is adjustable in height to fit in the carrier hangar deck, but also is set in flight at a positive angle of incidence to provide enough lift to handle its own weight. Nonetheless, it offers a large surface for gusts to act on, counteracted somewhat by the more powerful engines. Lt Slentz explained that he found *'the C-2 to be more stable in maintaining landing attitude compared to the E-2, but the power difference is a large factor in worst-case scenarios like a single-engine catapult shot in a humid environment, such as typical operations in the Arabian Gulf. You have a higher probability of staying out of trouble with the more powerful E-2 engines, even if you lost one on the catapult shot.'*

The four tailfins have only three rudder surfaces, but *'anyone who has flown an E-2 knows the importance of rudders,'* remarks pilot Lt (jg) Eric Frostad. During the mission, this configuration allows smooth, no-bank 'bat turns', which aid the operators in maintaining a stable radar picture.

MULTIPLE ROLES

It is often assumed that the Hawkeye's task is only airborne early warning for protection of the carrier group, but its role is much wider than that, as NFO Lt Nathan Greenwood says, and includes, *'Managing air strikes, managing air traffic in a US- or Coalition-controlled area, managing and directing aircraft in support of close air support missions in support of troops on the ground, communication relay between operatives and warfare commanders, controlling air-to-*

[MISSION REPORT]
+++++++++++++++++++++++++++++++

HAWKEYES OVER NEW ORLEANS

Hurricane Katrina, which struck the US Gulf Coast in August 2005, destroyed much of the area's communications infrastructure, including its air traffic control systems. Elements of three squadrons of E-2s and one of C-2s were deployed to assist with the relief effort.

The E-2's radar and communications suite were used to monitor airspace, locate stranded victims, direct rescues, locate standing buildings, identify space for safe landings and provide direction for aircraft activity in the area. In these missions the Hawkeyes were directing a form of close air support over New Orleans using the same grid and keypad code system to direct helicopters to survivors on rooftops as they use for fighters with bombs in wartime. At times E-2s were controlling up to 80 helicopters while communicating with agencies on the ground. On one occasion an E-2 located a helicopter equipped with a hoist and directed it to a nursing home where it rescued 60 stranded residents and staff. Helicopter pilots reportedly much preferred the Hawkeye to the E-3 Sentry that operated some of the time over New Orleans because the Navy crews were more used to

RIGHT: US Navy E-2s such as this Hawkeye 2000 acted as airborne air traffic control stations after the Hurricane Katrina catastrophe in 2005.

operating with helicopters, which fly slower and lower than fixed-wing aircraft and can hover. They also needed quick decisions about entering particular airspace. As one NFO put it, compared to an E-3:

'There's no committee, no time-lag...one guy turns to the centre seat and says: "I need to do this with this guy in order to do X. You good with that?" Centre seat makes the call and says run with it. Bottom line, each platform has its pros and cons. There's definitely been days in the Hawkeye where I would've killed to have 15 more people with me, and days I can't stand having just two. But I think if you ask any jet pilot out there, they'll tell you they'd much rather have a Hawkeye watching their back any day of the week.'

air engagement and contributing directly in visual identification [of unknown aircraft and ships]'.

Compared to a USAF E-3 Sentry, the E-2's crew work hard: 'The three-man crew of the E-2 has the same job to perform as roughly 16 to 18 people in the E-3. While the E-3 benefits from having 3 to 4 controllers, each benefiting from an assistant at times, the E-2 only has one person doing all that work.

In general, each member of the E-2 crew has much more to do,' admits Greenwood.

FUTURE DEVELOPMENTS
Although outwardly similar, the E-2D will add significant new capabilities and extend the already considerable mission endurance of the Hawkeye. Although the prototypes are not yet equipped, the E-2D will be

fitted in service with a fixed inflight refuelling (IFR) probe. It is likely to be retrofitted to US E-2Cs before the E-2D fully replaces them. According to Lt Greenwood: *'Air refuelling will better enable the E-2 to have uninterrupted periods of coverage for the Carrier Strike Group in addition to alleviating operational restrictions pertaining to such missions as controlling overland strikes'.* As Capt. Randy Mahr of the Naval Air Systems Command (NAVAIR) E-2/C-2

MAIN PHOTOGRAPH: With 13 examples in use, Japan is the largest Hawkeye operator outside the US.

like to see that probe go away quickly. As for the "D" model, from a NFO perspective, it's going to be really awesome. We'll get brand-new everything. Now, if only they could give us better cushions on the seats…'

Several issues need to be dealt with before the IFR system enters service, including establishing the best positioning of the probe to avoid adversely affecting the handling qualities of the aircraft and the pilots' field of view. Another potential problem is that the jet exhaust of a 'buddy' tanker aircraft such as the F/A-18E/F Super Hornet may damage the rotodome by overheating the composite skins or causing flexing.

NEW PROPS

All US Navy E-2s and some foreign aircraft now have the eight-bladed Hamilton Standard NP2000 propellers. These replace the Hamilton Standard electro-mechanical, steel spar, four-bladed propeller units.

programme office says, 'there comes a point when the aircraft out-endures the aircrew, but IFR will give us a couple of extra hours [of useful mission time]'. The ability of the E-2D to fly extended missions is not welcomed by all. One E-2 NFO says: 'I can speak from everyone in my squadron…we would

The main reason for the change is that the old units are no longer in production, but NP2000 also provides better efficiency, less vibration and lower noise. They also allow individual blades to be changed, unlike the old props, which had to be removed as a complete unit for blade changes. The new electronically controlled, hydraulically actuated unit is considerably lighter and has a one-piece steel hub and blades with a graphite spar and Kevlar shells. Crews appreciate the reduced internal noise and vibration and have nicknamed them 'Ginsu' propellers, because they resemble a fan of the Japanese ginsu steak knives frequently advertised on American TV.

Hawkeye NFO 'Goober' says: 'the new props help a lot – significantly less vibration and noise. Doesn't even require a prop synchrophaser any more'. The synchrophaser is a device fitted to the T56 engine that

ABOVE: A Hawkeye 2000 is catapulted from a US supercarrier. E-2s are usually the first to launch, and fly the longest missions of any aircraft in the air wing.

[MISSION REPORT]
++++++++++++++++++++++++++++++++

E-2 CARRIER OPERATIONS

Lt Cdr Przemyslaw Kaczynski of VAW-116 'Sun Kings' describes the powerful sensations of day and night carrier operations and recovery in the E-2.

'During our catapult launches it is a great rush to accelerate from 0 to 150 knots [0–240km/h] and hear the entire crew scream with joy across the intercom. At night, with a lack of a discernable horizon, all the joy is stamped out by the lack of physical orientation and the need to only rely on and trust the gauges during the rapid launch.

'Landings during the day are a fun challenge that is always gratifying. Sometimes, marginal weather will cause the visibility to decrease and the deck to pitch. This is when pilots rely on the trusting words of the LSOs [Landing Signal Officers] to guide the aircraft safely onto the glidepath and centreline of the pitching deck. At night, the whole idea of fun and healthy challenge is quickly tossed out the back of the plane with the exhaust. No matter how difficult or long the mission, the most

trying aspect of flying the Hawkeye is recovering back to the boat at night. Imagine locking yourself in a dark unlit closet, strap four other souls and $85 million to your back, and look forward to only see a small pinhole of light the size of a faint star floating in a black ocean which keeps looking smaller as you get closer to it, all due to the anticipation of landing.

'As the distance closes on the carrier, the corrections to stay on speed, on glide path, and on centreline become smaller and more rapid. Typically within the last three-quarters of a mile [1.2km] the pilot's pulse is at its peak as this is the point where he completely adjusts his instrument scan to viewing the outside. Inside this distance, the pilot has approximately 15 seconds to make his last corrections. The shadowy outline of the boat and the landing area come into view and the LSO will make any last-second calls to the pilot as he closes on the ramp and the wires. Upon touchdown the pilot must assume he has not caught any wires and be prepared to go around one more time and attempt another landing. Ultimately, once the aircraft violently decelerates to a stop the pilot and the whole crew usually breathes a large sigh of relief for yet another successful approach to the carrier.'

synchronizes the propeller rotation between the two engines. On older Hawkeyes it must be engaged shortly after take-off.

With the E-2D, the Hawkeye is becoming much better electronically integrated with other air and sea platforms in the US Navy inventory. For the air defence mission alone, the E-2D will share information with the SPY-1 surface radar, the Standard surface-to-air missile

and vessels and aircraft equipped with Cooperative Engagement Capability (CEC), sharing information about threats and targets over an area much greater than the E-2's radar range alone. The E-2D will act as naval aviation's 'server in the sky', according to Northrop Grumman. Other aircraft and UAVs will 'take off and log on'. Other catchphrases include 'plug and play', with the advanced Hawkeye being 'a node in a

network-centric battlespace'. One way of describing network-centric platforms is to look at them *'as if each cockpit was its own webpage, from which a crew can upload and download information from all the other pages'* says James D'Arcy of NAVAIR.

AT WAR AND PEACE

Since its debut in the 1960s, the Hawkeye has changed relatively little in appearance, and its core role of extending the radar range of the surface fleet remains, but since then it has taken on many other duties and has been deployed far beyond the carrier decks. E-2s have been deployed to land-locked Afghanistan to help coordinate air support and other missions there. They also played a significant role in the rescue efforts following Hurricane Katrina in 2005.

Lt Nathan Greenwood sums up the Hawkeye's importance: *'The E-2 has taken a greater role in every facet of warfighting over the past 30 years. These days, there isn't a mission the E-2 isn't involved in.'*

ABOVE: This colourful E-2C belongs to VAW-115 'Liberty Bells', based in Japan with the US Navy's Carrier Air Wing Five (CVW-5).

LEFT: Sometimes a carrier returns to port with some aircraft still on board, and a crane is the only way to get them off. The new NP2000 propellers can be clearly seen in this view.

BELOW: Like many Grumman carrier aircraft, the Hawkeye has wings that fold back against the fuselage for stowage.

Flying the F-111

The General Dynamics F-111 was extremely fast, could fly through mountainous and rolling terrain as low as 60m (200ft) above the ground, and could then deliver a killer blow of conventional or nuclear munitions. For many years, the F-111 was the sharpest of all the US Air Force's Cold War spears.

MAIN PHOTOGRAPH: The elongated nose of all but the ill-fated F-111B gave the Aardvark a slender look that belied its true size.

The F-111 spent nearly all of its time in service as a conventional and nuclear medium-range bomber, although a dedicated strategic nuclear variant, the FB-111A Switchblade, and an electronic warfare derivative, the EF-111A Raven, were also used to great effect.

ABORTIVE NAVY ROLE

The aircraft entered service with the US Air Force (USAF) as the F-111A in 1967, but it was also originally intended for use by the US Navy as a fleet defender and interceptor. The Navy was never entirely happy with its F-111B variant, and cancelled its participation in the programme in 1968, after only seven examples had been delivered. The Navy's participation explains the F-111's beefy undercarriage – the two-wheeled nose gear and chunky main landing gear with oversized wheels was intended to absorb the impact of a carrier landing.

A key feature of the F-111 that makes it different from most other tactical jet fighters is its variable geometry, 'swing-wing' design. The Aardvark's wings sweep back in stages to offer the best handling characteristics and manoeuvrability at different speeds.

'For take-off and landing the wings were swept to the full forward position. Once we were airborne and at a faster speed, the pilot would sweep the wings back to around 45 degrees. For really fast speeds, he'd sweep the wings all the way back to 72 degrees. This was done via a manual lever on the left side of the cockpit, and the wings themselves were moved hydraulically,' said Lt. Col. Ned 'Mob' Linch, who flew the F-111 from the right seat as the Weapons Systems Officer (WSO) before becoming an F-16 pilot.

Former F-111 pilot Major Craig 'Quizmo' Brown enjoyed flying the F-111. *'Due to the fact that it was one of the first aircraft with triple-redundant fly-by-wire – well, almost fly-by-wire, because it was decided to keep a traditional hydro-mechanical system, driven by flight computers – with*

complete stability augmentation ... what that meant was there was no traditional "feel" through the stick, the stick produced a rate of roll or pitch. Except for a change in angle of attack as you raised or lowered the nose, there was not a big difference on the stick in how the jet handled.'

So, was it easy to make the F-111 depart controlled flight? *'No, because of the way the flight controls worked: the stick could be held full aft while the airspeed bled-off and the nose would just lower to maintain a critical AoA*

ABOVE: The F-111 was deployed to the 1991 Gulf War. The F-model, equipped with Pave Tack, became statistically the most successful bomber of the campaign.

RIGHT: Australia anticipates that it will be using the F-111 for at least another decade, supplemented by the F/A-18E/F Super Hornet.

BELOW: the 48th TFW, based at RAF Lakenheath, England, deployed two squadrons of F-111Fs for Operation Desert Storm. Here an EF-111A Raven from RAF Upper Heyford joins a trio of Lakenheath jets over southern Iraq.

[angle of attack – the angle at which the oncoming air flow strikes the leading edge of the wing]. *However, after they lost a jet at Edwards doing spin testing, we were never allowed to get close to stalls, let alone departures.'* That's not to say the F-111 was easy to fly, Brown cautioned: *'I didn't realize how challenging it was to fly until I went on to fly the F-15E. There was nothing automated about the aircraft, you were always doing something and Emergency Procedures were complicated.'*

SMOOTH RIDE
Although the F-111 had a 19m (63ft) wingspan, it still had a relatively small wing area for its total weight. *'That meant that it was smooth as a Cadillac down low.*

You couldn't see out of it, but it sure was smooth!' Brown quipped.

'For landing, you'd drive the aircraft into the ground like a carrier landing... you didn't flare as you do in the Viper,' says Linch. *'I*

landed it twice as a WSO and was confident that if the pilot took a bird through the canopy, I could land it. The landing gear would take a beating and the landings were actually fairly smooth because of that beefy gear.'

THE WSO AND THE CAPSULE
Another highly noticeable characteristic of the F-111 was the arrangement of side-by-side seating inside a capsule that would rocket the two men to safety in the event of ejection, and which could float on the water. While the capsule allowed the crew to fly without wearing bulky exposure suits or life preservers, the side-by-side seating was essential if the crew were to master the complexities

[MISSION REPORT]

++++++++++++++++++++++++++++++++

WEAPONS DELIVERY

The F-111 was cleared to carry most of the USAF's conventional and nuclear freefall and retarded weapons.

'For conventional deliveries, the pilot could fly a pop pattern and drop from either a 10 degree or 20 degree Low Angle, Low Drag delivery,' Linch said, adding, 'But our bread-and-butter mission was nukes and the primary delivery would have been from a "level laydown" – basically, flying over the target at 200 feet [60m] and dropping it. We also practiced dive-toss manoeuvres as well, where you'd pull up a pre-determined distance from the target, drop the bomb and then roll inverted, pull down and then exit the area after flying over the target. The bombs had a parachute and would take longer to fall than conventional bombs. In a nuclear war, we'd have the cockpit [flash reflector] shields

up, wear an eye patch on one eye and do a radar delivery. It would not have been pretty and most of us expected to die. If lucky, some of us might have reached some remote safe area in the Alps.'

Brown agreed: 'The "special" mission! We were going to go deep, and while we were slated to land at an airfield with 100lb [45kg] of gas, I think we all knew that there wouldn't be anything to come back to anyway, so what the hell, let's go!'

The F-111 could also be fitted with the 20mm M61A1 Gatling gun to allow it to strafe targets. 'I had strafed many times in the F-4, but from the backseat. From the right seat of the F-111, the ground rush from doing a 10 degree dive from about 1,000 feet [300m] was a real attention-getter. The F-111 was a great strafing platform. It was very stable and the cannon did not shake the gunsight like an F-4. We felt a very faint buzz or vibration when the gun was going off. You heard it more than felt it. After one of our people shot a hole in his own wing from a ricochet, we got very aggressive about our pull-offs!' recalled Watson.

LEFT: Loaded up with 24 227kg (500lb) Mk.82 general purpose bombs, this F-111A from Mountain Home AFB, Idaho, descends below the surrounding ridgelines in anticipation of a low level attack on the target.

of the F-111's complicated and extensive avionics suite.

Two key systems, an attack radar and a terrain following radar (TFR) gave the F-111 its accuracy and low-level capability, and running both was the WSO's responsibility. Brown explains: 'Forget today's beautiful computer-driven radars, the "Vark-a-saurus" had three radars, one main attack air-to-ground radar and two TFR radars. The air-to-ground radar was operated solely by the WSO, and was not visible to the pilot. But we did have the "E Scope", a TFR scope situated high on the centre of the instrument panel so that both could see it easily.

'During TFR flight we navigated using the radar and we used it to monitor terrain clearance. The pilot worked more with the E Scope and we verbally compared answers,' said Lt.Col. Dennis Watson, another ex-F-111 WSO. Linch added, 'For TFR, we had a very active exchange of information between the two of us. We flew a lot in mountainous terrain such as the

LEFT: When the 48th TFW's F-111Fs departed Lakenheath and arrived at their new home, Cannon AFB, New Mexico, they were repainted in a one-tone mid-grey.

TFR IN DETAIL

ABOVE: NB tail codes identify this F-111A as being based at Nellis AFB, Nevada. Nellis was home to the earliest F-111 operations, including trials of its TFR.

The lowest height at which the terrain-following radar was used was 60m (200ft). *'This was used in peacetime very infrequently. We were only legal down to 400 feet [120m] for many of my years, although I was checked out to 200 feet [120m] in the early 1980s when the Army wanted to do simulated tests with their new surface-to-air missile. It was nerve-racking to fly 200-foot night TFR in the Rocky Mountains, especially during long turns. I guess after a while we just gave up and realized that if anything went wrong, we would probably die before we knew it,'* Watson recalled.

'We also developed a strong trust in the TFR and there were very few un-forewarned TFR failures through my years [1977–91]. The thing that really bothered me most was flying low at night in the mountains with a bright moon over snow. The view out the window was very disorientating. Mountains appeared visually much closer than they actually were, but this was only an optical illusion. In 1979 we received the "beeps and squeaks", or "talking TFRs", mode that added a digital TFR

computer to the F-111A and F-111E. The beeps and squeaks were aural tones in our helmets that were generated from somewhere besides the displayed climb/dive commands. This meant that they gave us a comparison between what we heard in the cockpit, what we saw on the TFR and E Scope, and what the aircraft was actually doing. It was helpful, although we kept the volume low so that they occupied the background. Prior to that, we had analogue TFRs and we could only safely use 10 degrees of bank in the turns, but we eventually got a TFR radar that could "look into the turn," and after that we could use 30 degrees of bank.'*

Scottish Highlands. The lowest we'd go at night in that area of the UK was 400 feet [120m]. When the weather was good and the moon was out, you could see ridge lines going right by your wing tips. It was a very demanding job flying TFR at night in the weather and in the mountains. But, it was a true all-weather aircraft, unlike other aircraft that make that claim.

You'd never do that in the F-16 at low altitude.'

ATTACK CAPABILITIES

Each successive variant of the F-111 featured different capabilities and levels of improvement, with the F-111D boasting a digital cockpit that was much improved over previous (and subsequent)

Aardvarks, and included a Heads Up Display (HUD) for both pilot and WSO; the F-111E, similar to the F-111D minus the 'glass cockpit'; and the F-111F, the most accurate on account of its AN/AVQ-26 Pave Tack FLIR (forward looking infrared) pod.

The F-model required the WSO to look down a rubber hood into what was called the Virtual Image Display (VID) that used a lens to allow the WSO to view two small screens behind it. Watson explained: *'The VID was an "over and under" display. Normally we kept the radar on top and the Pave Tack's low-light TV (LLTV) on the bottom. By using optics, they could enlarge the upper display, but keep a smaller, secondary display, on the bottom. Using a switch under our left hand, we could flip-flop the displays so that you have the Pave Tack imagery enlarged on top and radar picture on the bottom, or vice-versa. It was something like looking into a 1970s video game.*

'The right seat HUD in the D was glorious! We had a real good indicator of where the radar cursor was by looking through the HUD. As they say, "One peek is

BELOW: With its undercarriage extended, the F-111 lost much of its grace and good looks. You can just make out the partially-stowed Pave Tack pod behind the nose landing gear of this Lakenheath F-111F.

ABOVE: The F-111 could be refuelled in-flight via a receptacle aft of the cockpit and parallel with the pilot in the left seat.

worth a thousand sweeps." Unlike all other F-111s, we did not have a LCOS [lead-computing optical sight] *but rather a CCIP* [constantly computing impact point] *sight. This was more of a "death-dot" type thing where the bomb was going to impact where the dot in the HUD was. This was how we could roll up into about 90 degrees of bank, pull 3–4 gs, and drag the pipper though the target. When the pipper got to the target, [we'd press the] pickle, and "sling" the bomb sideways. And it worked! In the F-111F we would use the radar to get close to the target and then use Pave Tack to fine tune the aim point,'* concluded Watson.

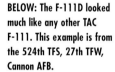

LEFT: Leading-edge slats on the wing deploy forward to reveal red-painted surfaces underneath. Noteworthy are the articulated leading edges of the fuselage, which were required to pivot upward to allow the slats to extend.

BELOW: The F-111D looked much like any other TAC F-111. This example is from the 524th TFS, 27th TFW, Cannon AFB.

Flying the SR-71

The Lockheed SR-71 Blackbird was a remarkable spy plane, capable of operating at Mach 3.3 at 26,000m (85,000ft). It was developed by the legendary Lockheed 'Skunk Works', a division of Lockheed involved with the U.S. government's most classified projects. In an operational history spanning 17 years with the 9th Strategic Reconnaissance Wing, the 'Sled' or 'Habu', as its crews referred to it, would spend 11,008 hours spying on foreign nations.

Many facets of the legendary but enigmatic Blackbird are a source of fascination, but few more so than its top speed and incredible cruising altitude. Rich Graham, an SR-71 pilot and 9th SRW Wing Commander, recalled: *'Cruising at Mach 3.2 at 85,000 feet [26,000m], you had a tremendous view of the world. Some of the sights were unbelievable. To be able to see stars out in the daytime, and a* dark sky above you, was a strange sight to adjust to. At night, stars and planets seemed three dimensional… as if you could reach out and touch them. The atmosphere was so pure and clear at that altitude.'

SPEED AND ALTITUDE

But the Blackbird's speed and altitude capabilities were more than a luxury; they were a necessity. They gave the unarmed Blackbird its best form of defence against attempts by the enemy to shoot it down.

Walter Watson, an SR-71 Reconnaissance Systems Officer, detailed why that speed was life for the Blackbird crews. Using the example of the mission that he and his pilot, Brian Shul, flew over Libya in April 1986 following the U.S. bombings of terrorist camps. He explained: '*We both knew that our best defence was altitude, speed and a turn if needed. The Libyans had the MiG-25, so the air threat had to be considered. [But] I always felt that if something was going to get us, it would be a surface-to-air missile. Brian knew that if I called for a defensive turn, it meant I was getting some pretty serious signals, and every nanosecond counted at that point. Changing our heading by only two degrees could destroy the missile's solution at the speeds we would be flying.*'

Pilot Brian Shul said of the Blackbird's performance, '*The SR-71 definitely had two distinct personalities; subsonic and supersonic. The first was quite predictable and stable; the latter always a bit of an adventure.*'

MAIN PHOTOGRAPH: The Blackbird very rarely took off with a full load of fuel onboard. Usually, the SR-71 would depart with a light fuel load, accelerate to high subsonic speed to 'warm' the airframe to help seal the fuel cells and skin cracks, and then join up with a KC-135 or KC-10 tanker to take on a full load of gas.

PILOT'S VERDICT

"The SR-71 definitely had two distinct personalities; subsonic and supersonic. The first was quite predictable and stable; the latter always a bit of an adventure."

Brian Shul, SR-71 pilot

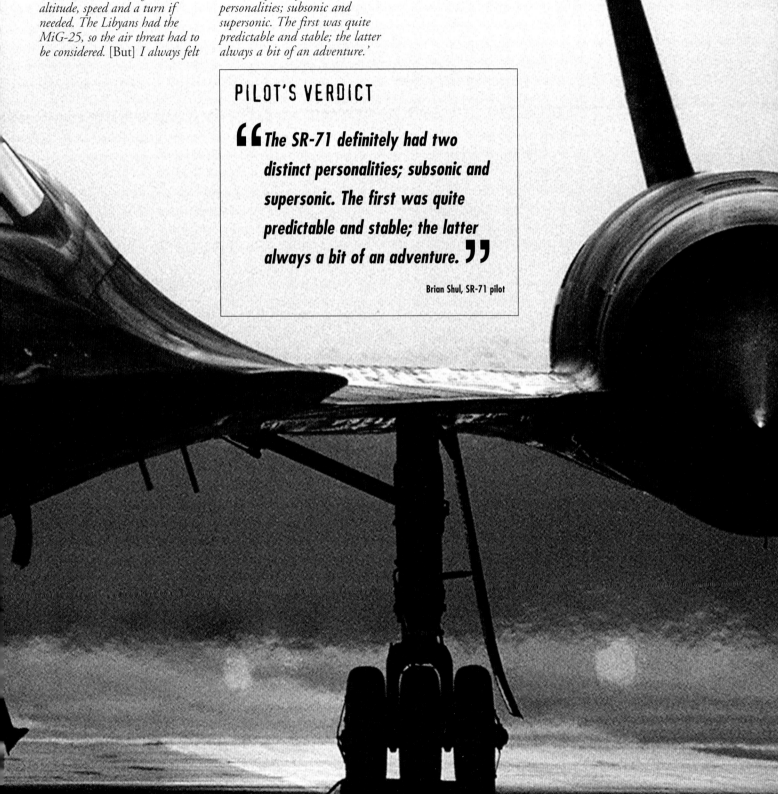

ABOVE: The SR-71's front cockpit was full of instrumentation, and did away with the tape gauges that had been used in previous incarnations of the A-12/YF-12 family. In the event that he lost communication with the RSO, the pilot could toggle a switch that illuminated a 'Prepare for Bailout' light in the rear cockpit.

BELOW: The aerodynamic shape of the SR-71 was subject to intense levels of heat. As the rarefied atmosphere at 26,000m (85,000ft) heated the Blackbird's titanium structure, the nose would reach 570°F (298°C), the windshield 622°F (327°C), and the engine nacelles up to 1,050°F (565°C).

The Blackbird used an automatic schedule to control the huge spikes that moved to govern the flow of air to the J58 motors' compressor blades as airspeed increased. Invariably, as the jet accelerated and climbed, the supersonic shockwave moving across the aircraft could play havoc with this schedule, and should an engine become unsettled an 'unstart' would occur and the motor would hiccup. Unstarts were violent, unpredictable and startling, and in the early days the SR pilot had to manually take control of the engine spikes to restore smooth airflow to the motor.

INCREDIBLE THRUST

The J58 produced an incredible 142kN (32,000lb) of thrust in afterburner, and was the first motor to be able to operate in afterburner for sustained periods of time. The conical spikes which regulated airflow to the motor were locked below 9,000m (30,000ft), but above that could travel as much as 66cm (26in) back and forth.

Starting the two engines required an AG330 engine starter cart; essentially, two Buick Wildcat V8 internal combustion engines with a common driveshaft attached. The cart would spin up the J58 to 3,200 rpm before the turbojet cycle could start, and this process could only be started once the jet's lubricants had been warmed up – at normal sea level temperatures they turned to solids!

PRESSURE SUIT

Flying above 17,500m (58,000ft), the point at which human blood would boil in the earth's rarefied atmosphere, necessitated that the crew wore space suits. The SR-71's crews were each issued with a full pressure suit, not dissimilar to those worn by astronauts, which was manufactured by The David Clark Company. It added to the surreal experience of flying high and fast, as Graham explained: 'It was very quiet in the cockpit. With the pressure suit on, there was very little background noise. The only sound you could hear was the inhalation and exhalation of you breathing 100 per cent oxygen.'

Bob Antilla, who was the project leader for the space suit, recalled, 'we took about 60 measurements for each guy so that we could custom fit his suit.' Antilla and his team devised built-in flotation devices for the suit so that crew members could stay afloat if they landed in the ocean following ejection, and they also devised a urinary collection device that allowed the RSO and pilot to relieve themselves during flight. Since the space suit could not be removed without the assistance

LEFT: At the very rear of the SR-71's tail boom was a dump mast through which fuel could be dumped. Managing the aircraft's centre of gravity was a key responsibility of the pilot, and he controlled pumps in order to move fuel between the Blackbird's fuel cells.

of two other people (and certainly not in flight!), this device was crucial to the crews' comfort.

When a more serious call of nature occurred, the crew had little choice but to hold out. Such was the importance of each and every Blackbird sortie that one pilot, struck with stomach cramps without warning before he had even taken off, spent the entire duration of the sortie sitting in his own mess rather than cancel the mission. The space suit was an excellent garment, but there were some things that it just couldn't do!

THE RSO
While Lockheed's earliest member of the Blackbird family, the A-12, featured only one crewmember, the SR-71 accommodated two. Positioned only a metre or so behind the pilot, the Reconnaissance Systems Operator (RSO) worked the jet's navigation, self defence and reconnaissance devices.

Watson explained: 'The SR-71 was unique in that, as much of a cohesive unit as the two people inside it needed to be, the duties in each cockpit we're radically different. For the pilot,

[MISSION REPORT]
++++++++++++++++++++++++++++++++

INTERCEPTIONS

The Russians often attempted to intercept the SR-71 as it flew its intelligence gathering missions in international air space off the coast of the Russian mainland. It was not until the introduction of the MiG-31 Foxhound that they were truly in a position to threaten the SR-71, however.

The Foxhound's two-man crew would be ordered to scramble by means of a shrill bell that would sound in their alert quarters. A search radar located on the Rybachiy Peninsula would often make the first radar sighting of the Habu, but advance notice that came from communications interceptions often gave the Russians up to three hours' notice that the Blackbird was headed in their direction.

The Foxhound pilots had to launch precisely 16 minutes after the claxon sounding; a timing calculated down to the second to allow the Foxhound to intercept the Blackbird on an optimum trajectory for missile launch. Such was the importance of intercepting the SR-71, that they were punishable by court martial if they made so much as the smallest error. The same punishment awaited anyone in the direct chain that was needed to keep the snooping American aircraft on its toes, and that included the radar controllers and Ground Control Intercept controllers, too.

Within five minutes of take-off, the MiG would reach 16,000m (52,000ft), and its infrared search system would usually detect the SR's red hot skin and exhausts against the freezing high-altitude sky as far away as 100–120 km (62–75 miles). With Ground Control Intercept guiding the Foxhound until its onboard computers had locked onto the Habu's heat signature, the Foxhound climbed to its maximum operating altitude of 20,000m (65,000ft) and accelerated through Mach 2.5.

Only rarely would a Foxhound pilot make a visual sighting with the SR-71, but many of its pilots have maintained that they often got well within the firing parameters of their missiles. The Blackbird crews never penetrated Russian air space, and so the order to fire was never given by the ground controllers. In any event, the Foxhounds were scrambled not only as a means to attempt to down an SR-71 in the event of a violation of Russian airspace, but to show American commanders that they had the capability to do so. The cold war was one that was fought in the minds of world leaders, and this cat-and-mouse game was just one part of that process.

LEFT: The MiG-31 'Foxhound' was a vastly improved derivative of the MiG-25 'Foxbat' interceptor. It carried a better radar, an infra red sensor to track the SR-71 without emitting radar signals, a weapons systems officer in the back, and more powerful computing capabilities.

ABOVE: Low visibility was extremely important. Mounted in the pilot's canopy was a small periscope that he could extend to make sure he wasn't producing any tell-tale contrails.

ABOVE: The SR-71 was largely as
immune from enemy action in the day as it
was at night.

BELOW: The RSO sat behind
the pilot, and was cocooned
underneath a canopy that
allowed only limited
sideways visibility. He had a
downwards-looking video
camera with which he could
spot distinctive landmarks.

*each mission was essentially the
same concerning his primary
duties. Though the specific route
or refuelling points differed, his
job remained unchanged: fly the
airplane, get the gas, take off and
land safely.'*

By contrast, Watson
explained, the RSO was

challenged differently on each
mission, according to *'routing,
threats, sensors and
communications requirements.*

*'The cockpit itself could even
be different, depending upon
certain types of equipment,'* he
went on to add. *'Regardless of
the route or type or type of*

*mission we were flying, I always
considered my primary job in the
jet to back up the pilot in any
way he needed. So, for the guy in
the back, each mission was a
mental test, blending the
priorities of helping the pilot
with the jet and accomplishing
the varied actions required for
mission success in the back.'*

OKINAWA

Although 'home' for all
Blackbirds was Beale Air Force
Base, California, whose 9th
Strategic Reconnaissance Wing
was responsible for the black jets
no matter where they were
deployed to temporarily, the
SR-71 was at times deployed to
foreign air bases. The first of
these was the small American-
run Kadena Air Base on the
Japanese island of Okinawa,
which hosted the Blackbird
throughout its career, and was

LOSSES

Type:	A-12	M-21	YF-12A	SR-71A	SR-71B	SR-71C
Built:	13	2	3	29	2	1
Lost:	5	1	2	11	1	0

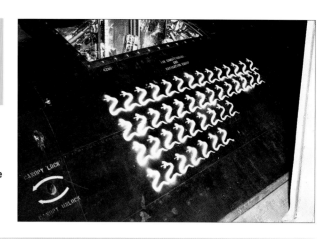

first referred to as Operating Location 8, and later as Detachment (Det) 1.

Det 1 proved crucial to the Blackbird's mission from the first moment that it was used. Initially, spy flights over North Vietnam formed the emphasis of the missions flown from the island, but as time progressed, it also provided a convenient operating location from which to overfly China, North Korea and parts of Russia.

It was at Kadena that the name 'Habu' was also born: some of the local Okinawans drew a comparison between the sinister, sleek black airplane and the dark coloured snake that could be found on the island in large quantities. It was not long before the Blackbird crews at Kadena picked up on the name: they liked it. So, they were soon wearing Habu patches on their flight suits, and their maintainers would paint discreet little Habu icons on the underside of the chines to denote each successful operational mission.

RIGHT: Habu symbols adorn a Kadena-based SR-71, each one denoting a successful spying mission flown from the small Japanese island of Okinawa. The 9th Strategic Reconnaissance Wing fell under the control of Strategic Air Command, which had a long running tradition of such artwork.

A-12, YF-12, M-21 AND SR-71 PRODUCTION

Serial number	Model	Serial number	Model	Serial number	Model
60-6924	A-12	60-6941	M-21	61-17965	SR-71A
60-6925	A-12	61-17950	SR-71A	61-17966	SR-71A
60-6926	A-12	61-17951	SR-71A	61-17967	SR-71A
60-6927	A-12B	/'60-6937'	/'YF-12C'	61-17968	SR-71A
60-6928	A-12	61-17952	SR-71A	61-17969	SR-71A
60-6929	A-12	61-17953	SR-71A	61-17970	SR-71A
60-6930	A-12	61-17954	SR-71A	61-17971	SR-71A
60-6931	A-12	61-17955	SR-71A	61-17972	SR-71A
60-6932	A-12	61-17956	SR-71B	61-17973	SR-71A
60-6933	A-12	61-17957	SR-71B	61-17974	SR-71A
60-6934	YF-12A	61-17958	SR-71A	61-17975	SR-71A
60-6935	YF-12A	61-17959	SR-71A	61-17976	SR-71A
60-6936	YF-12A	61-17960	SR-71A	61-17977	SR-71A
60-6937	A-12	61-17961	SR-71A	61-17978	SR-71A
60-6938	A-12	61-17962	SR-71A	61-17979	SR-71A
60-6939	A-12	61-17963	SR-71A	61-17980	SR-71A
60-6940	M-21	61-17964	SR-71A	61-17981	SR-71C

LEFT: RAF Mildenhall, situated in eastern England, was another haunt of the Blackbird. Like Kadena, there was often a detachment of this fascinating aircraft at Mildenhall, and as in Japan, the black jet captured the hearts and imaginations of the locals. For the SR crews, the typical British weather at Mildenhall often brought challenging flying conditions.

Flying the Harrier

The Harrier is one of the most unusual jet fighter designs ever to make it from the drawing board to front-line, operational squadrons. Able to operate in confined areas that were once the exclusive domain of the attack helicopter, the Harrier was a key tool in the West's arsenal during the Cold War, and continues to this day to be a stalwart participant in the global war on terror.

The Harrier's ability to take off and land in a clearing no bigger than itself is one of the most incredible achievements in aviation. But how is it done?

U.S. Marine Corps AV-8B Harrier II+ pilot, Major John Hicks, who has 1,500 hours in all American variants of the AV-8B, including a tour as an instructor flying the two seat TAV-8B, tells all:

'The Harrier has four exhaust nozzles that vector the thrust from the engine. The front two are called the "cold" nozzles: they are fed by the unheated air diverted from the low pressure compressor at the very front of the engine. At the rear are two so-called "hot" nozzles, which are fed heated air from the high-pressure compressor located in the turbine section at the back of the engine.

'Control of these four nozzles is maintained by a nozzle drive system connected to a lever in the cockpit next to the throttle. Pushing the lever all the way forward makes the nozzles face aft (zero degrees) and is used in forward flight. Pulling the lever rearwards commands the nozzles to rotate downwards, therefore deflecting the exhaust downwards. The pilot's nozzle control lever has a detent at 82 degrees that allows the jet to hover. This actually works by placing the exhaust nozzles at a 90 degree angle to the ground, but the pilot maintains a six-degree nose-up attitude, putting the engine slightly out of line with the pitch axis.

'Lifting the lever past this detent will allow the nozzles to be pointed forwards of the vertical plane to slow the aircraft very rapidly, such as on a high-speed landing. On the ground, this is known as "power nozzle braking" and is similar to the reverse thrusters on an airliner.'

'Control of the aircraft's attitude [pitch, yaw and bank] while in the hover is accomplished by high-pressure bleed air from the engine, routed to ducts on the wingtips, nose and tail.'

These ducts are sometimes called 'puffer jets', although the official collective term for these devices is the 'Reaction Control System'. They work by squirting high-pressure air out in response to the pilot's control stick and rudder pedal inputs. If he pushes the stick left to roll left, the puffer jet on the right wingtip opens and the air pushes the wingtip up. If he presses his right rudder pedal to yaw right, the puffer jet in the tail boom opens to allow air to shoot out from the left hand side, pivoting the jet to the right. And if he pulls the stick back to raise the Harrier's nose in the air, the puffer jet under the nose opens to push the nose up. Hicks says that 'It doesn't feel peculiar once it's done a few times. It's quite natural.'

JUST ADD WATER

Despite the Harrier's impressive V/STOL capability, the Harrier's weight can clearly not exceed the amount of thrust available,

A Royal Air Force Harrier GR.7 in two-tone green camouflage routes across the British countryside. In a war environment, the Harrier would transit at a much lower altitude to avoid threat systems.

ABOVE: The Royal Air Force regularly undertakes deployments to Norway to participate in cold-climate exercises. Here, two Harrier GR.5s demonstrate the temporary snow camouflage that is sported during such deployments.

downwards once sufficient speed is achieved for wing-borne flight. The sudden change of nozzle position helps propel the Harrier into the air as its stubby wings begin to generate lift and take grip, and helps the Harrier to arc into the sky at airspeeds that would normally be too slow for traditional jet fighters.

To help diminish the effects of altitude, ambient temperature and weight, the Harrier features a Water Injection System that enables the Pegasus engine's RPM (revolutions per minute) to be increased for a given turbine temperature, thus providing more power for V/STOL operations.

and so weapon and fuel loads sometimes have to be reduced in order to allow the jet to get airborne. Similarly, operating pressure, altitude and high ambient temperatures reduce the effectiveness of the Harrier's Rolls-Royce Pegasus engine (as they do on all turbofan and turbine engines), and can further limit the Harrier's permissible gross weight.

When a vertical take-off is not possible, a short take-off is usually the next best option, and this is normally initiated with the nozzles positioned fully aft and then swiftly rotated

MARINE HARRIERS

The U.S. Marine Corps is the most prolific Harrier user in the world, and has been instrumental in the development of the more advanced Harrier II design.

Hicks explains: *'The mission of the AV-8B in the Marine Corps is*

[MISSION REPORT]
+++++++++++++++++++++++++++++++

HOVERING HUD

The Harrier's unique hovering and V/STOL capabilities demand that the pilot be given some unique aids to help him fly the aircraft safely. While such assistance was sparse in early versions of the Harrier, advancements in computing, miniaturization and technology in general made it possible for the developers of the newer Harrier II (McDonnell Douglas and Hawker Siddeley/British Aerospace) to incorporate an enhanced Heads Up Display (HUD) to aid the pilot.

Hicks says that the HUD can display a great deal of information to assist with V/STOL flight. *'The HUD has a dedicated V/STOL Master Mode that displays information peculiar to the slow-speed landing environment that we enter at the start and end of every mission. These are the most notable examples: the sideslip "ball" indicator, which indicates whether the jet is yawing; a reading of the jet's airspeed down to 30 knots [55km/h]; a digital readout of its ground speed; the current Angle of Attack (AoA); a nose position indicator called the "witches hat", which tells me at what angle to pitch the nose at in order to attain the optimum hover attitude; a velocity vector that doubles as a vertical speed indicator (VSI) below 60 knots [111km/h]; and finally, a power margin indicator known as "the Hex" ... a growing hexagon around the letter J and another around*

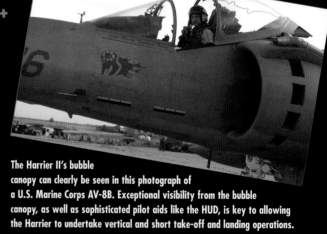

The Harrier II's bubble canopy can clearly be seen in this photograph of a U.S. Marine Corps AV-8B. Exceptional visibility from the bubble canopy, as well as sophisticated pilot aids like the HUD, is key to allowing the Harrier to undertake vertical and short take-off and landing operations.

the letter R. Each side of the hexagon, when filled in, represents a step closer to the maximum limits of the motor, and is a very effective visual cue as to how the engine is performing during the hover, and how many RPMs I have remaining at my disposal.'

In addition, either of the AV-8B's two colour multi-function displays (MFDs) can be used to display a V/STOL 'page' that lists the basic aircraft weight, water weight and basic drag index to allow the pilot to quickly assess the aircraft's performance limitations. For short take-off, another 'page' automatically calculates the nozzle rotation airspeed, take-off nozzle setting in degrees, the ground roll distance, and the distance required to clear a 15m (50ft) obstacle at the end of the runway.

to attack and destroy surface targets under day and night conditions and to escort helicopters … flying from naval shipping, forward bases, and tactically austere sites.' In the case of the austere sites, these are unprepared or minimally prepared locations such as forest clearings, or gaps in urban sites (such as between buildings).

At present, the Marines fly the AV-8B Harrier II Night Attack and the AV-8B Harrier II+ Radar Night Attack variants. 'The major difference is that the Radar variant has an APG-65 Radar in the nose while the Night Attack has a Dual Mode Tracker (DMT) in its nose,' Hicks explains, before adding, 'The DMT's combination of contrast camera and laser spot tracker uses the visual and laser spectrum to

find and lock onto targets.'

Although the Radar Night Attack Harrier lacks the DMT, it instead carries the AN/AAQ-28 Litening II targeting pod, which has an IR sensor, a laser spot tracker and an optical TV sensor to allow it to find, identify and engage enemy targets. The Litening II is also carried by the Night Attack Harrier to allow for even better targeting.

The Marines, like the Harrier's other operators – the British Royal Air Force (RAF), and the Spanish, Italian, Thai and Indian Navies – train to operate their Harriers from both landing strips

and ships. In the case of the latter, the Marines operate their own LHA-class and LHD-class assault ships, resembling small aircraft carriers, from which the AV-8Bs can take off and land.

Hicks admits that, 'Landing a Harrier on a ship can be both a

ABOVE: Harriers are designed to be able to operate from secondary taxiways and hardstands if an airfield's main runway is out of action but the danger of attack has passed.

ABOVE: Walking to his jet, this RAF Harrier pilot wears the standard garb: flight suit, boots and flying jacket, g-suit on the legs and lower torso, and survival vest with built-in life preserver.

real pleasure, and quite terrifying, depending on the circumstances. In the daytime and when there is good weather and calm seas, it is a real blast. But, at night time, and when the weather is bad, the sea is rough and the deck is

pitching all over the place, it is not fun at all.'

To assist the pilot in what can be a challenging event, the LHD and LHA amphibious assault ships employ 'cuers' that he can use as visual references, according to Hicks.

'We have a Hover Position Indicator (HPI), which is a lighted set of poles welded to the ship that, when centred [from the pilot's perspective], *will put you in a 50-foot* [15-m] *hover over spot number 7 on an LHD, or spot 7Π on an LHA,'* which are the aft-most landing spots on each of the two amphibious assault ships. *'Lateral placement is done by the "tram" line, which is a large yellow line painted down the centre of the ship.'*

Hicks further explains, *'We can land at any spot in the daytime using normal visual cues like the HPI and tram line, but darkness or poor weather has us use a Fresnel lens mounted on the ship's superstructure that brings us in on a three-degree glide slope. Following a radar approach, the pilot will "break out"* [visually acquire the LHA or LHD] *and use the lens to arrive at 50 feet* [15m] *over the deck'.*

Keeping an eye on proceedings throughout, whether day or night, is the LSO (Landing Signals Officer) positioned in a control tower on deck, Hicks points out. *'The LSO is an experienced Harrier pilot in the*

BELOW: Three U.S. Marine Corps AV-8B Harrier IIs en route to the bombing range. Each carries two Mk-82 227kg (500lb) bombs, the staple unguided 'dumb' bomb employed by U.S. aircraft that lacked a precision guidance capability of their own.

squadron who guides the aircraft in, ensures that the conditions – wind speed and direction, the surface of the deck, and the fuel remaining in the landing Harrier – are acceptable. In short, he ensures the safety of each pass. Also, each landing is graded by the LSO to determine the pilot's performance. The senior pilots of the squadron are usually the LSOs, and they take turns in the tower.'

THE AIR COMBAT TRICK

The U.S. Marine Corps' AV-8A Harrier pilots are widely credited with devising air combat manoeuvres in the Harrier that make use of the four nozzles to enhance manoeuvrability. One, known as Vectoring In Forward Flight – or, VIFFing – or officially Thrust Vectoring Control (TVC), according to Hicks, is 'a technique we use where we move the nozzle lever in the middle of a dogfight. As the nozzles rotate, we can achieve a faster turn rate or a decreased turn radius, and that can help us outmanoeuvre the bad guy. It makes the jet "bite" a little better, but does deplete the energy state of the jet [it slows down the aircraft].'

TVC is something of a last-ditch manoeuvre and a little bit of a gimmick, but the Harrier, and in particular the more modern Harrier IIs flown by America, Britain, Spain and

ABOVE: A Marine AV-8B unleashes a live AGM-65 Maverick missile against an unsuspecting target at the range. The aircraft also carries two inert Mk-82 bombs.

Italy, are anything but gimmicky. Hicks' summary of the USMC Harrier force is that, 'We are the ultimate in versatility: we can operate from a larger spectrum of sites than any other fixed-wing tactical fighter. Our latest upgrades have made us the most accurate and flexible attack aircraft in the world.'

Hicks has flown two combat tours in the AV-8B, and 'aside from the flight where I had to land in zero visibility on the boat at night when a dust storm out of nowhere descended over me, my most memorable mission was this one: I checked in with the FAC [Forward Air Controller], found out it was a buddy of mine from my last squadron, then dropped a GBU-16 [454kg/1,000lb laser-guided bomb] on an ammo bunker he talked me on to on the Al-Numinyah airfield. I scored a direct hit and huge secondary explosion followed. Coalition forces later captured the field and I wound up landing there two days after I bombed it. There were burned-out vehicles beside the runway and we were the only fixed-wing tactical jets that could land there. That was pretty fun, if you can call it that.'

ABOVE: The Harrier force that deployed to the Falkland Islands consisted of a mix of Royal Navy Sea Harrier FRS.1s (pictured) for air defence and escort work, and the Royal Air Force's air-to-ground specialized GR.3s.

HARRIER KILLS

The Royal Navy's early Sea Harrier FRS.1s provided the air cover for the Royal Air Force, British Army and Royal Navy's operations to liberate the Falkland Islands from invading Argentine forces in 1982. Freshly supplied with the very latest version of the AIM-9 Sidewinder heat-seeking air-to-air missile, and flown jointly by both Navy and Royal Air Force personnel, the 'Shar' excelled, killing the following without any losses to enemy fighters:

IAT Dagger A	9
A-4B Skyhawk	3
A-4C Skyhawk	2
FMA IA 58 Pucará	1
A-4Q Skyhawk Navy	3
Mirage IIIEA	1
B.Mk62 Canberra	1
C-130E Hercules	1

Flying the F-14

For over 30 years the Grumman F-14 Tomcat served as the longest defensive arm of the US fleet. Charged with the protection of the carrier battle group, the Tomcat was equally capable in a close-quarters dogfight as in combat at stand-off ranges. Latterly the F-14 was active in air-to-ground operations, a role in which it again excelled.

MAIN PHOTOGRAPH: The Tomcat was undoubtedly the most sought-after workplace among the US Navy's fighter pilot community. Here a USAF exchange pilot experiences a catapult launch in the back seat of a Tomcat.

*T*he F-14 is a Cadillac to fly…it's a quantum leap both in technology and pilot comfort. The aeroplane makes the pilot look good.'

After 36 years of service with the US Navy, the Grumman F-14 Tomcat was finally retired at Naval Air Station Oceana on 22 September 2006. In the preceding years the Tomcat had served both as an interceptor and subsequently as a 'Bombcat'.

In the latter role, Tomcats were delivering precision-guided weapons in action as recently as February 2006, when F-14Ds flying from the carrier USS *Theodore Roosevelt* undertook the aircraft's final combat missions during Operation Iraqi Freedom.

The Tomcat's original *raison d'etre* was the air defence of the carrier battle group, the cornerstone

of the US Navy's power-projection capability. This role is outlined here in the words of a Tomcat pilot:

'The F-14 was purpose-built for the air-to-air mission, to dominate massive volumes of airspace around the carrier and to engage and destroy enemy bombers or missileers way out... With our tactics, sensors and weapons, the enemy's going to be dead long before we can get close... It may not be so glamorous, but I can take him out before he even knows I'm there, and in wartime, that's exactly what I'll do.'

PILOT'S VERDICT

"We used to say it took a good pilot to fly an average Phantom sortie. But you can put an average pilot in an F-14 and he will fly a good Tomcat sortie."

'Flash'
F-14 Tomcat pilot
VF-101 'Grim Reapers'

For this exacting mission, the F-14 was manned by a crew of two, the pilot and the Radar Intercept Officer (RIO). The 'swing-wing' Tomcat was outfitted with the unique AWG-9 fire control system and long-range AIM-54 Phoenix air-to-air missiles.

The Tomcat first went to war at the tail end of the conflict in Vietnam, providing protection during the evacuation of Saigon in 1975. While F-14 crews never had the chance to engage the Soviet bombers that they had been trained to hunt, the Tomcat nevertheless proved itself during decisive air combats. In two separate confrontations against Libyan fighters over the Mediterranean in the 1980s, the Tomcat came out on top.

Tomcat crews may not have recorded any victories over fixed-wing aircraft during the 1991 Gulf War, but the F-14's weapons system did its job – keeping the Iraqi air force at bay, as this pilot recalls:

'The Iraqis definitely didn't want to fight – they wouldn't go anywhere near the powerful AWG-9 radar carried by our Tomcats – it was just too good. Ironically, that's a big part of the reason why the F-14 didn't get any Desert Storm kills.'

Towards the end of the Tomcat's career, the cockpit no longer represented cutting-edge technology, but its seats were still the most sought-after in the US Navy and the crew were notably well equipped for the demanding combat air patrol (CAP) mission, as this Tomcat 'driver' explains:

'The question of comfort is vitally important on long CAPs. You want to be comfortable; you don't want to be distracted. It's a large, spacious cockpit, and it's nicely air-conditioned. Even the seat is cooled. That comfort means that we can stay alert and efficient for a relatively long period, though we don't like to keep people up more than five hours. The longest mission I've flown was about six hours.'

DOGFIGHTING WITH THE 'CAT

The F-14's weapons system was optimized for suppressing incoming bombers before they could unleash their stand-off missiles. However, if called upon, the Tomcat also offered a potent dogfighting capability.

[MISSION REPORT]

+++++++++++++++++++++++++++++++++++++

OPERATION
DESERT STORM

At the time of the Iraqi invasion of Kuwait in 1990, the F-14 Tomcat had yet to be deployed in its advanced F-14D incarnation and was not routinely operated in the air-to-ground mission. As a result, the Tomcat-capable carriers that took the type to the Persian Gulf, the Red Sea and Mediterranean primarily relied upon the Tomcat for fleet defence and escort of both US Navy and USAF strike aircraft. A secondary reconnaissance mission was also undertaken with the under-fuselage TARPS pod as required.

AIR-TO-AIR LOAD-OUT
The typical weapons fit for the Tomcat during Operation Desert Storm comprised two AIM-54 Phoenix, two to four AIM-7 Sparrow and two AIM-9 Sidewinder missiles, plus onboard cannon. In a reflection of the strength of the US Navy's carrier air wings on station in the Gulf, it soon became clear that the Iraqi air force had little inclination to risk a confrontation with its opponents. The Tomcat was an especially respected adversary, the Iraqi pilots having been on the receiving end of Iranian F-14s during the Iran–Iraq War of the 1980s. In the first six months of that conflict alone, Iranian F-14 crews claimed over 50 Iraqi MiGs and Sukhois destroyed without loss. The Iraqis had evidently learnt their lesson, and contact with US Navy F-14s remained minimal; indeed, Iraqi aircraft would retreat as soon as the Tomcat's powerful AWG-9 radar was detected.

PHOTO-RECONNAISSANCE MISSION
During Desert Storm one of the two F-14 squadrons on each carrier was normally earmarked for the reconnaissance mission, with two or three aircraft modified for carriage of the TARPS pod. TARPS was subsequently used for various

ABOVE: Flight deck crew discuss a forthcoming mission with the pilot and RIO of a Tomcat onboard USS *Saratoga*, which hosted the F-14A+ interceptors of VF-74 'Bedevilers' and VF-103 'Sluggers' during Operation Desert Storm.

tactical reconnaissance duties, including target and mission photography, and the system was also used to monitor the burning oilfields that had been ignited by Iraqi troops during their retreat from Kuwait.

HELICOPTER SHOOT-DOWN
While Desert Storm CAPs were frequently delegated to USAF fighter crews, depriving the Tomcat a chance to take on Iraqi fixed-wing aircraft, a pair of VF-1 F-14As from the USS *Ranger* encountered a single Iraqi Mi-8 'Hip' on 6 February 1991, the helicopter being downed by the squadron's commanding officer and his RIO using an AIM-9. The US Navy recorded a single Tomcat loss during the conflict, an F-14A+ of VF-103 falling victim to an Iraqi SAM on 21 January 1991. Both crew ejected safely, although one became a PoW.

ABOVE: Flying over blazing Kuwaiti oilfields in the wake of Desert Storm, this Tomcat hails from VF-114 'Aardvarks'. Employed on a post-ceasefire CAP, the glove pylons on this aircraft mount both AIM-7 and AIM-9 missiles, and auxiliary fuel tanks are carried. By the early 1990s, the flamboyant squadron markings that characterized the F-14's initial period of service had given way to this subdued low-visibility colour scheme.

"West of Baghdad I spotted an SUV fleeing from the scene at about 120 mph along a nearby road... The driver quickly did a 180-degree turn when he saw us looming above him!"

Cdr Rick LeBranche
Commanding Officer, VF-31 'Tomcatters'

ABOVE: Vapour streams off the wings of a VF-103 'Jolly Rogers' F-14B as it makes a high-speed low-level pass. Despite its weight, a fully loaded Tomcat can still hit Mach 1.2 'on the deck'.

MAIN PHOTOGRAPH: A Tomcat pilot approaches the 'basket' during a refuelling operation. Carrier-based tanker aircraft or those equipped with 'buddy' pods kept Tomcats on round-the-clock CAPs when required.

Unlike the later-generation F-16 and F/A-18, which benefit from fly-by-wire flight control systems, the Tomcat was not specifically designed with a high degree of manoeuvrability in mind. In skilled hands the aircraft could more than hold its own against agile opponents, but it required an experienced pilot to keep the big interceptor under control during a dogfight. Cdr. Chip King, of VF-213 'Blacklions', explains:

'Despite its origins as a supersonic interceptor, the Tomcat is a very capable dogfighter. At its optimum manoeuvring speed of 320 knots, it would turn at over 16 degrees per second... At the slower speeds encountered during a dogfight, the Tomcat was quite a handful to control when operating at the edge of the manoeuvring envelope.'

As far as pilots and RIOs were concerned, the F-14 also compared very well with its contemporaries in the Air Force.

'We find that it is virtually an equal match for an F-16, and it is definitely superior to the F-15 series. Even the baseline F-14A is pretty much on a par with the F-15. They're pretty closely matched airplanes and the only thing the F-14A is lacking is the engines to go along with the proven airframe. The variable-geometry wing, the manoeuvring devices, all of that makes it a very good high-performance fighter airframe.'

With the end of the Cold War, the number of front-line US Navy F-14 squadrons was drastically reduced. Towards the end

of its career with the US Navy, the Tomcat turned increasingly to the precision air-to-ground role, in which it first became operational in 1992.

The 'Bombcat' delivered its first laser-guided bombs over Bosnia in 1995. Thereafter, LANTIRN targeting and guidance pods were added to the Tomcat's arsenal. These new items allowed RIOs to self-designate their own precision-guided weapons by day or night. During its final cruise, the F-14 began to use the highly accurate GPS-guided JDAM weapons. As such, the Tomcat continued to demonstrate that it was one of the most capable all-round assets available to the US Navy.

'As a Tomcat pilot I'm unbeatable air-to-air, I am shipboard recce (no one else does it), and now (with the Bombcat) I'm King Kong in the air-to-ground game also. Bomber pukes will always claim that fighters are fun, but that bombers are important – the Tomcat is both.'

RECCE EQUIPMENT

The F-14's significant all-weather reconnaissance capability was also increasingly utilized as combat air patrol missions and intercepts were reduced. The Tactical Air Reconnaissance Pod System (TARPS) provided the F-14 crew with two cameras and an infrared scanner. TARPS filled an important gap within the air wing, which otherwise lacked a recce-dedicated platform. The result of these developments was a true multi-role fighter of which its crews were rightly proud:

'Being in an F-14 squadron is unique to the Navy. We consider ourselves the pinnacle of naval aviation. The F-14 is the airplane that we consider to be the front-line navy fighter.'

Despite its continued success in the Middle Eastern theatre

TOMCAT UNITS IN THE PERSIAN GULF, 1990–91

Air Wing	Carrier	Squadrons	Variant
CVW-2	USS *Ranger*	VF-1, VF-2	F-14A
CVW-3	USS *John F. Kennedy*	VF-14, VF-32	F-14A
CVW-1	USS *America*	VF-33, VF-102	F-14A
CVW-8	USS *Theodore Roosevelt*	VF-41, VF-84	F-14A
CVW-14	USS *Independence*	VF-21	F-14A
CVW-17	USS *Saratoga*	VF-74, VF-103	F-14A+
CVW-7	USS *Eisenhower*	VF-142, VF-143	F-14A+

of operations, the days of the Tomcat in US Navy service were numbered. The type departed the carrier deck for the last time in early 2006, to be replaced by the shorter-ranged F/A-18E/F Super Hornet, as part of an ongoing rationalization of the carrier air wing component.

The Tomcat's front-line US Navy career came to an end on 8 February 2006, when a VF-213 aircraft caught the trap

aboard the USS *Theodore Roosevelt* in the Persian Gulf. Pilot for the final mission was Capt. William G. Sizemore II, commander of CVW-8:

'It's the end of an era and it just kind of worked out that I was the last trap. This is one of the best airplanes ever built, and it's sad to see it go away. It's just a beautiful airplane. It's powerful, it has presence, and it just looks like the ultimate fighter.'

[MISSION REPORT]

+++++++++++++++++++++++++++++++++

FIRST KILLS OVER THE MEDITERRANEAN

The Tomcat's baptism of fire came in 1981, while the carriers USS *Nimitz* and *Forrestal* were stationed in the Gulf of Sidra, off the Libyan coast. On 19 August 1981, two patrolling F-14s of VF-41 'Black Aces' were alerted by their AWG-9s to a pair of Libyan Su-22 'Fitters' that were being vectored towards them under ground-based radar control. Despite the Tomcats turning away from the approaching Sukhois, the Libyan fighters repeatedly selected a head-on course to the F-14s, and one of the navy pilots moved in closer to investigate their shadowers. The other Tomcat waited at higher altitude, and further behind, in order to protect his leader. As the two parallel formations became ever closer, the lead F-14 saw the leading Su-22 launch a heat-seeking missile, which failed to track either Tomcat. This, however, was the signal for the Americans to take action and, as the formations passed one another, the Libyan duo split, and the F-14s rapidly turned behind the

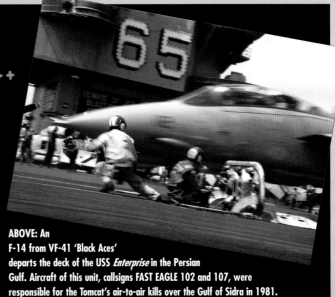

ABOVE: An F-14 from VF-41 'Black Aces' departs the deck of the USS *Enterprise* in the Persian Gulf. Aircraft of this unit, callsigns FAST EAGLE 102 and 107, were responsible for the Tomcat's air-to-air kills over the Gulf of Sidra in 1981.

Sukhois and received the order to fire. From the six o'clock position, the F-14 wingman launched an AIM-9L Sidewinder from around 800m (2,500 ft), destroying the lead Sukhoi. The Tomcat lead then took his turn to pull behind the remaining Su-22, waiting for the Libyan wingman to cross the sun before taking his turn to launch a heat-seeking Sidewinder, with the same devastating effect. The Tomcat had recorded its first air-to-air kills in what had been a very uneven contest.

Flying the A-10

The Fairchild Republic A-10 Thunderbolt II performs the Close Air Support (CAS) mission better than anything currently flying, boasting unequalled ordnance capability and endurance, and a remarkable ability to withstand battle damage.

MAIN PHOTOGRAPH: The A-10's large canopy affords the pilot excellent visibility, and the Heads Up Display (HUD) allows him to keep his eyes outside the cockpit as much as possible.

The A-10's snub-nosed fuselage, its proliferation of bumps, antennae and blade aerials, and the two massive turbofan engines mounted awkwardly between its stumpy tail fins, make for an aircraft whose unofficial nickname, 'Warthog', is perfectly suited. Indeed, it is this very ugliness that is a source of pride to those few fortunate enough to fly the 'Hog'.

There is no two-seat variant of the A-10 Thunderbolt II, meaning that a new pilot's first ever flight in the Hog is also his first-ever solo flight in the jet.

The lack of a two-seat trainer is easy to explain, says former A-10 pilot, retired U.S. Air Force Lieutenant Colonel, Andy Bush:

'Does the airplane have any flight envelope areas that are unusually challenging, such as out-of-control and departure characteristics? No. The flight envelope is relatively small and presents no unusual flight characteristics. The A-10's take-off and landing procedures and characteristics are benign, and the aircraft flies at relatively slow speeds. There are no unusual slow-speed vices like there are in many other fighters, and this is one of the main reasons why there was never a need for a two-seat trainer.

'The Hog's flight controls are powered and therefore do not require a lot of "muscle" to operate.

The stick loads are light, and the jet responds well to stick inputs throughout the flight envelope,' adds Bush, who flew the McDonnell F-4 Phantom II and the Lockheed F-104 Starfighter before moving to the A-10.

SLOW AND LOW

Boasting simple avionics, flight characteristics, and weapons systems, the A-10 gives the pilot a chance to expend more concentration on the mission at hand – usually killing enemy armour or protecting friendly infantry and armour in the CAS role.

To be truly effective in the anti-armour role, the A-10 pilot must fly close to the ground. This is not a good place to be, Bush confides:

'The modern battlefield is just too dangerous. Self-protection

PILOT'S VERDICT

"The A-10's mission has become more and more challenging... the A-10 pilot is flying an airplane that is 'easy-to-fly' but is having to deal with a mission that is not."

Lt. Col. Andy Bush
Retired A-10 pilot
U.S. Air Force

devices such as Electronic Counter Measure pods and flares are good, but it's best not to get shot at in the first place. But traditional CAS is hampered by high speed. The pilot just doesn't have the time to find the target, and this is especially true when the target's exact location is not known or if the pilot has to rely on map-reading to find the target. Trying to locate that green tank in a tree-line in Germany was very difficult, and the lower speed of the A-10 gave the pilot a little more time to locate the target. I have flown traditional CAS against comparable targets in

ABOVE: Today, the A-10 is the most crucial Close Air Support asset available to battlefield commanders in Afghanistan and Iraq. While many other aircraft types are also providing CAS to coalition troops, the A-10 is the first choice because it is so well suited to the role. This A-10 carries an AAQ-26 Litening II target pod under its right wing, and a 227kg (500lb) GBU-12 laser guided bomb on the inboard pylon of the left wing.

Europe in both the F-4 and A-10. Too often in the F-4, I overflew the target without seeing it…just going too fast to be able to do the job.'

Bush explains that while the jet is easy to fly, the already demanding mission can be made even more problematic as a result of flying in close proximity to the ground.

'Low-altitude operations are hazardous, and night operations are even more so. The A-10's mission has become more and more challenging as time has gone by; given the nature of today's high-tech battlefield, this results in the A-10 pilot flying an airplane that is "easy-to-fly" but having to deal with a mission that is not.

'Low level operations are much easier to fly in the A-10 than in the F-4 or the F-104… for the simple reason that the slower speed gives the A-10 pilot time to see what is going on around him. Visibility from the cockpit is outstanding, and the inertial navigation system, now integrated with GPS [Global Positioning System], helps reduce pilot workload and minimizes "heads-down" time that would otherwise have been needed for map reference or systems manipulation.

'But low altitude can be a killer. A moment's lack of concentration or complacency can result in bad things happening.

[MISSION REPORT]
++++++++++++++++++++++++
MAVERICK SHOT

ABOVE: An Air National Guard A-10 fires an AGM-65 Maverick missile during a weapons evaluation sortie. The AGM-65 is the Hog's only stand-off precision weapon.

Looking down into the cockpit at low altitude is a good way to die, according to Lt. Col. Andy Bush. So how does an A-10 pilot use the AGM-65 Maverick fire-and-forget missile without looking at the little TV screen in the cockpit?

'Analysis of the monitor is far too time-consuming to be done below 300 feet [90m] AGL, so in a traditional low-altitude environment – anti-armour in Germany – I would first have to know where the target was for certain. If that took a recce pass, so be it. Once the target location was known, I would fly a second attack at low altitude below the enemy line of sight. I would then "bump" up to 300 to 500 feet [60–150m] AGL, point the HUD [heads-up display] into the target area, and then go "heads down" into the monitor to see the target.

'Target acquisition and missile firing has to be done pretty quickly… we do not continue to fly towards the target while searching the area with the monitor to find the target. If I didn't get a tally and get the missile off in about 5–10 seconds, I would break hard away, exit from the target area and reassess what went wrong.'

The A-10 is no different than any other fighter in this regard. At 300 feet [90m] AGL [Above Ground Level], I was comfortable. At 200 feet [60m] AGL, I was paying attention to the ground. At 100 feet [30m], I was giving the ground almost my full attention. If I had to turn, look into the cockpit for any reason, I climbed up a little. Most of the time at 100 feet [30m], I was looking at 12 o'clock [straight ahead], since the time it took to fly into the ground from that height, even when flying as slowly as 300 knots [550km/h], was measured in seconds. It is no place to get distracted.'

SURVIVABILITY

While the A-10's ability to fly low and slow is a key reason for its success as a CAS fighter, the very fact that the jet is low enough to see and slow enough to visually track means that it is vulnerable to small-arms fire, radar-directed ground fire, radar-guided surface-to-air missiles (SAMs), but most of all, Infrared (IR) man-portable air defence missiles (MANPADs).

Accordingly, Fairchild Republic did its best to design the A-10 to absorb a huge amount of punishment and still get the pilot home.

One of these features is the titanium 'bathtub' that surrounds the pilot and is designed to protect him from shrapnel and even direct hits from anti-aircraft fire. When asked about the tub, Bush admitted that he gave it *'little thought'*, adding, *'I've always considered the bathtub talk to be mostly hype.'*

Against such threats as the Soviet-made ZSU-23-4 Shilka – a tank armed with four 23mm (0.9in) liquid-cooled cannons linked to a short-range radar director – Bush admitted that *'There are far too many other factors to be taken into consideration when facing this type of threat than feeling warm and fuzzy about some airplane armour! Instead, the idea is not to get shot in the first place. That's what I spent most of my time worrying about… making sure that I'd get the ZSU before it got me.'*

MANUAL REVERSION

There is a key system in the A-10 to which several pilots owe their lives: Manual Reversion (MR). Fairchild built the Hog's hydraulic-powered flight controls with a back-up mode – MR – that made it possible to

fly the Hog when in other aircraft the pilot would have no choice but to eject.

According to Bush, *'In normal operations, the A-10 uses hydraulic pressure to move the flight controls, with artificial feel built in to give the pilot a sense of typical control pressures. These hydraulic controls give the jet a sense of lightness on the controls and are very effective in providing a quick response to pilot inputs. This "lightness" and quick response goes away in the event of the loss of the hydraulic system. The manual reversion system is an emergency flight control back-up system designed to get the jet back home… and little else.*

'In MR, mechanical linkages are used to position the flight control surfaces. In the event of hydraulic pressure loss, the flight control system automatically

reverts to MR in pitch and yaw [elevator and rudder]. *The only trim available is in pitch. Reversion to MR roll control is not automatic… the pilot must actuate a switch to gain control over roll. This means that the jet is not controllable in bank with MR.*

'In MR, stick loads are much higher than normal. Roll control is done by the movement of the tabs on the ailerons, not the ailerons themselves, so roll effectiveness is reduced. Pitch loads are high and pitch trim must be used to provide the pilot with the "muscle power" to fly. Because of this, manoeuvring is best kept to a minimum.'

'THAT' GUN

Fairchild Republic built the Hog around its centrepiece GAU-8A

30mm (1.18in) cannon, which can fire Depleted Uranium, High Explosive Incendiary (HEI) and Armour- Piercing Incendiary (API) rounds that can shred 38mm (1.5in) armour from 1,000m (3,280ft) away.

'From a procedural point of view, using the GAU-8 in an air-to-ground attack is not that much different from the 20-mm [0.78-in] M61A1 Gatling gun I used in the F-4 and F-104,' Bush said. *'What is different is how the capabilities of the GAU-8 allow the pilot much greater flexibility in making these attacks.*

'The main advantages of the GAU-8 are its longer range, a flatter trajectory, and a tighter dispersion pattern. With the M61, we usually strafed at around 2,000 feet [600m] slant range, from a variety of dive angles. You can achieve reasonable results from as far out as 4,000 feet [1,200m] in a dive…

but the dispersion will be effective only against "area type" targets. With the GAU-8, we can accurately hit "point targets" out to 6,000 feet [1,800m] and have to demonstrate this on a yearly basis on flight check rides.

'The gun is actually useful out to as much as two nautical miles [3.7km]. I have fired at point targets at the Red Flag exercise at Nellis Air Base, Nevada, at two nautical miles and had good results. The 30mm [1.18in] round has much more capability to do damage than the 20mm [0.78in] …and the rate of fire really chews things up. The higher velocity at impact is noticeable in flight when firing at tactical "hard" targets even with training rounds. The inert rounds still "flash" when hitting something hard…from the heat produced by the velocity at impact.

'Oh!' adds Bush, almost as an afterthought, *'it was also awesome fun to fire!'*

FLYING THE HOG DURING THE COLD WAR

BELOW: A-10s wearing the three-tone European One camouflage are now just a dim and distant memory.

Lt. Col. Andy Bush accumulated more than 1,200 hours flying the Hog in Europe and the US between 1982 and 1988.

'The Cold War was still a reality and we flew missions designed to blunt a Warsaw Pact armour attack against West Germany. Our primary missions were anti-armour, anti-helo, and traditional CAS of ground troops. We flew this at low altitude – 300 feet [90m] and below. While stationed at RAF Bentwaters in the U.K., we deployed to our four detachments in Germany: Ahlhorn in the North German plain, Sembach and Norvenich in central Germany, and Leipheim in the south.

'Above all else back then, I liked the independence I had as an A-10 flight lead to plan my own missions. We pretty much went wherever we wanted, and went on a visual flight plan. In the U.K., I could start off with a two ship that was supposed to hit a U.K. gunnery range. If the weather was bad, I'd tell my wingman to bring his German maps to the briefing. I'd brief a simple U.K. mission, knowing that the weather probably would prevent that, and then I'd brief a more detailed mission in Germany.

'We'd take off from Bentwaters and switch to our own discrete radio frequency. We'd level at about 300 feet [90m] and motor up to the U.K. range. If the weather was sour, I'd turn east and take up a heading for Germany. We had to be at a minimum of 500 feet [150m] over water, so I'd climb to that altitude and head across the English Channel, not talking to anybody on the radio. We'd coast in over Holland and climb to 1,000 feet [300m] because of their low-fly rules, then once in Germany, we'd drop down to 250 feet [75m] minimum and start trolling around for something to do.

'That was usually two things: flying over to a German gunnery range and giving them a call to see if they had open time, or a "fence check". For the gunnery range, we'd expend our practice bombs and 30mm there. After leaving, we'd check out some of the NATO military training areas to see if any "tracks" were out in the field. If so, we'd run mock attacks on them ... again, not talking to anyone on the radios.

'For the fence check, we'd fly into the Buffer Zone [BZ] and fly along the East German fence just to annoy the communists. A-10s were the only NATO aircraft that could enter the BZ without radio clearance! When reaching bingo fuel, we'd head for the coast, climb to 5,000 feet [1,500m], coast in near Bentwaters and land. Nobody knew we had been in Germany... and nobody cared.

'The Hog has a good endurance and we could plan multiple mission elements: I could take off, let my wingman lead a practice low-level route that he had planned, have that route end up at the gunnery range where we would unload our practise ordnance, then I'd take the wingman out for some low-level mock tactical attacks against things I had found around the English countryside, like bridges and abandoned vehicles. There was even a monument that looked like a missile in firing position, so I used it as a make-believe SCUD! Finishing that, we could climb up into the air-to-air training area and fly some basic fighter manoeuvres, before finally going home.

'Low altitude visual flight rules operations took us away from much of the red tape and restrictions that the fast movers had to deal with on a daily basis. This aspect was probably the major defining point; a freedom of action that others simply couldn't match. In the U.K., we were issued a jet, two hours' of fuel, six practise bombs, 100 rounds of 30mm [1.18in], and told to go have fun. No flight plan, no, "go here and do that," just "be back by such and such time, and have fun!"'

Flying the F-15

Having entered service more than 32 years ago, the F-15 Eagle remains the most successful air superiority fighter ever. Although it is now surpassed in some aspects of its performance by the Lockheed Martin F-22A Raptor, it has staked its place in air combat history with a kill ratio of more than 105 enemy aircraft for not a single loss of its own.

MAIN PHOTOGRAPH: A self-portrait of a photographer in the back seat of a 67th Tactical Fighter Squadron F-15 Eagle. The aircraft is equipped with an AIM-9 Sidewinder missile.

'It's the most powerful air superiority fighter known to man. It's exceptionally easy to fly, as easy as a Cessna.' So says Colonel Doug 'Disco' Dildy (ret.), a USAF F-15 pilot, squadron commander and vice wing commander.

HANDLING CHARACTERISTICS
From the outset, the Eagle was designed to kill its foe from long distances and with awe-inspiring efficiency. To achieve this it had to be light, fast and agile, a combination that aircraft designers at the time had seldom been called upon to fulfil in a single aircraft.

When it first produced the F-15 in the late 1960s, McDonnell Douglas had to meet the requirements that the

United States Air Force had set for the the aircraft. It had to offer exceptional interceptor performance – fast acceleration and a superb climb capability – but also the ability to 'turn and burn', or dogfight, when at close range with the enemy.

The McDonnell Douglas design resulted in a large wing area that allowed good sustained turn capability, but which also offered a minimum of aerodynamic drag to let the Eagle accelerate beyond twice the speed of sound.

The Eagle's two F100 afterburning motors would enable rapid acceleration, and a computerized flight control system would allow the pilot to maintain control of the aircraft in scenarios where many fighter jets of the time would depart from controlled flight.

Although the computerized flight controls were not as sophisticated as today's fly-by-wire systems, they allowed the pilot relatively care-free handling during combat – a time when maximum brain

PILOT'S VERDICT

❝ The airplane is so stable that when you relax the controls it stays in the same position. This lets you work the radar, look for threats, and work the weapons system. ❞

Col. Doug 'Disco' Dildy (ret.),
USAF F-15 pilot

ABOVE: This frontal shot of an F-15E shows the contoured conformal fuel tanks of the Strike Eagle. These CFTs fit flush with the aircraft fuselage and contain 4432kg (9750lb) of additional fuel in each tank.

BELOW: The F-15E's cockpit allows the pilot and weapons system operator to view, operate and employ the aircraft's targeting and weapons systems with ease.

bytes should be expended on killing the enemy, and not on flying the jet.

'Disco' Dildy, who has 1500 hours of Eagle time, explained: '*The airplane is so stable that when you relax the controls it stays in the same position. This lets you work the radar, look for threats outside the jet, and work the weapons system. That's completely unlike the F-4, which required a pilot to fly the jet, and a second person to operate the radar and weapons. While the Eagle is stable, it's also able to generate a lot of*

lift because of the cambered wing. Accordingly, it can turn on a dime, and if you're overshooting behind a target, all you have to do is pull on the pole to come in behind the target and align fuselages for a kill.

'The airplane shudders a little bit as you bleed the airspeed, and this is the signal to let off the Gs or run out of airspeed. The airplane talks to you all the time; nothing abrupt or scary, but noticeable. There is an increase in noise below 250 knots and the vibrations tell you what the jet is

doing. We can either intimidate the enemy with our nose – there's no corner we can't turn – or keep our energy and get a shot a little later, saving energy for a possible defensive situation should other fighters enter the fight. Knowing what to do, and when to do it, is a case of practicing it over, and over again. So, the airplane responds to you when you lose your airspeed and you can let off the stick, or you can fly with your finger tips at the end of the stick and just "tickle" the Eagle into the turn.

ADVANCED STICK CONTROL

'With most fighters up until the F-15, the more you pulled the stick back the more resistance came from the artificial feel system. However, in the F-15 you can move the stick and pull gs, which generates turn rates, which lets you put the nose where you want it; but to get that finesse McDonnell Douglas built in a system that allows you to put the same amount of force on the stick to achieve the same g regardless of speed. So, if you want to do a hard bat turn at 450 knots, or a less abrupt turn at 250 knots, you pull on the stick the same amount for the same amount of g. That was a very advanced concept in 1974.'

The downside to the large, cambered wing and the thick fuselage containing twin

DOGFIGHT OVER
THE BEKA'A VALLEY

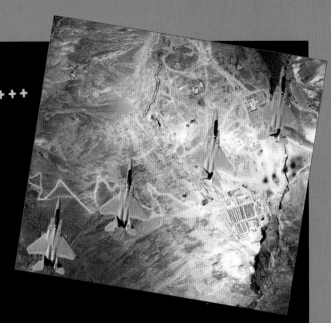

ABOVE: Israeli F-15s in fingertip formation over an arid backdrop. Israel's Eagles have been updated and modified to take advantage of indigenous avionics and weapons technologies.

LEFT: Map of Lebanon showing the Beka'a Valley area, the scene of vicious dogfighting between Israeli F-15s and Syrian fighters during June 1982.

The 1982 Lebanon War (Operation Peace for Galilee) began on 6 June 1982, when Israeli Defense Forces (IDF) units invaded southern Lebanon. The Israeli government approved the invasion in response to an assassination attempt against Israel's ambassador to the United Kingdom by a Palestinian terrorist organization. The operational objectives of the IDF were to push Palestinian militants back from the Israeli-Lebanese border, and the first move occurred when Israeli F-16s bombed Lebanese targets that were protected by Syrian anti-aircraft defences.

In the ensuing conflict, Syrian Air Force aircraft attempted to aid Lebanese forces, and to provide them with air cover against IDF attacks. However, the recently-acquired F-15s of the IDF were more than a match for the Syrians, and accounted for nearly half of the 86 Syrian kills claimed by the Israeli Air Force. Although Syria claims to have downed one F-15, and damaged another during two of these aerial engagements, the IAF maintains that it lost not a single aircraft to Syrian Air Force actions. Although many of the kills claimed in the short conflict came from medium-range AIM-7 Sparrow shots, there were several occasions where Eagles 'mixed it up' with Syrian MiGs. On these occasions the Eagle pilots used their superior manoeuvrability to position themselves behind their foe, and the Eagle's superior thrust and sustained turning capability allowed them to employ the AIM-9 Sidewinder in the heart of its envelope.

As the MiGs and Eagles twisted about the sky, each vying to shoot down the other in engagements that lasted mere minutes, the F-15's advanced radar modes came into play. Declassified HUD footage shows the moment one Syrian MiG flashed past the windshield of an Israeli Eagle as it fled the fight: the Eagle pilot activated his automatic acquisition radar mode and aggressively pulled in behind the MiG, which was too busy running away to notice. The Eagle's radar automatically detected and locked-on to the MiG, immediately giving the Eagle pilot an indication to shoot. In the dramatic seconds that followed, the Eagle pilot loosed off a single AIM-9, which snaked its way to the MiG's glowing tail pipe. In the Eagle's HUD the pilot switches to auto-guns mode as he closes in to finish the kill, but there's no need. The MiG descends quickly into a death spiral, engulfed in flames. These frantic 'knife fights' always turned out the same – the Eagles were being flown to their many strengths; the MiGs were outflown and outgunned.

ABOVE: The F-15I Ra'am (Thunder) – a version of the F-15E Strike Eagle sold to Israel – has become Israel's pre-eminent long-range strike fighter. Alongside the numerous F-16s also operated by the IAF, the F-15I has been at the forefront of recent IAF operations in southern Lebanon.

OPERATION IRAQI FREEDOM

Operation Iraqi Freedom began on the night of 19 March 2003. On the first full day of the war experienced Strike Eagle crews were tasked to launch AGM-130 strikes against key leadership targets. Four Strike Eagles each carried aloft a single AGM-130, as well as fuel and AIM-9 Sidewinders. Two were assigned to strike Republican Guard barracks in the vicinity of Baghdad International Airport, while the other two were to strike Saddam Hussein's Yacht club – both targets were chosen to make it harder for Saddam to flee the city in the coming hours. The mission yielded limited results due to technical problems, but the F-15E would go on to excel during the remainder of the war. The Iraqi Air Force offered up no resistance, and the light grey Eagles would eventually be sent home early when it became clear that Iraqi pilots had no intention of fighting. Sadly, one F-15E was lost in circumstances that remain unclear, killing both the pilot, Captain Eric 'Boot' Das, and weapons systems operator, Major Bill 'Salty' Watkins.

ABOVE: The Strike Eagle arrived at Al Udeid AB, Qatar in mid-January, 2003. Once the war kicked-off in March, they began flying kill box interdiction, close air support (KICAS) and strike coordination and reconnaissance (SCAR) sorties.

engines is that the Eagle is a huge fighter. That means that when the enemy approaches the merge (the point at which two opponents visually spot one another and cross paths) the Eagle can be spotted from as far away as 16km (10 miles), particularly if it has exposed its massive wing in a turn towards or away from its quarry.

BIG RADAR

'The mother of all radars!' was how 'Disco' Dildy characterized the APG-63 in the Eagle's nose. He added: *'The F-15 radar is 36 inches across, compared to 24 inches for the F-4, and this means it can throw out more power. The amount of power correlates directly to the distance you can see. The further the target can be detected, the better. From WWI onwards, the traditional fighter pilot rule was that the first to see the enemy would be victorious. Whether its Von Richthofen in his Dr.1 triplane, or someone in the F-15,*

PILOT'S VERDICT

❝ I thought the Eagle was a joy to fly: a super-modern jet with all the F-4's faults corrected. **❞**

Dick 'Lucky' Anderegg
F-4 and F-15 pilot and instructor

MAIN PHOTOGRAPH: As a maintainer inspects the wing surfaces of an F-15 prior to flight, he lends scale to the Eagle's massive size. The Eagle's large plan form can be seen as far as 16km (10 miles) away, requiring that Eagle drivers limit their manoeuvring once they close on their prey inside that distance.

the first to see the enemy has an advantage. Once you see the enemy, you can maneuver outside of your enemy's radar view, and this allows you to come in from the side, or from the stern. You want to make the enemy defenseless and then kill him like clubbing a baby seal.'

The Eagle's radar represented an advance in capabilities beyond the wildest expectations of fighter pilots in the mid-1970s, not only because it could detect contacts at much greater distances than had been possible in previous fighters, but because of the way in which it computed the raw radar returns and provided the pilot with a synthetic, computer-generated picture of what the radar saw.

HUD AND HOTAS

Alongside the radar, the Eagle boasts several other firsts in the age of modern jet combat. Two of the most important from a fighter pilot's perspective are the Heads Up Display (HUD), and the controls that incorporate switches and buttons known as Hands On Throttle And Stick (HOTAS). Dildy explains:

'The HUD allows you to see all of your flight information as part of your normal lookout outside the aircraft, but it will also allow you to see targeting information about your target. For a MiG-21-size target, the normal distance for a visual pick-up is about two miles, but the HUD and its target information consequently allow us to pick up a similar size target at four to five miles. That's a huge advantage.

'It takes about 200–250 hours of flying the airplane to get good at using the HOTAS. By then you were about getting good at working the radar and weapon system with HOTAS. It's simple enough for most guys to get the hang of it,

but to get good enough to employ in a demanding multi-bogey environment where you are shifting targets while you're closing fast, it takes repeated practice. Prior to that, guys can sometimes allow a target to fly through a weapons envelope while they got into a cluster with their HOTAS. You're constantly moving all of your fingers, in a specific

ABOVE: An F-15E of the 492nd Fighter Squadron, based at RAF Lakenheath in England, pops flares during a combat sortie in support of Operation Iraqi Freedom.

sequence, to work the radar or prosecute the threat. We want to fly through the merge and kill at least two guys, not counting the ones who died pre-merge from the fire-and-forget AMRAAMs. HOTAS, the HUD and the radar allow us to do that.'

MSIP II IMPROVEMENTS

In the early 1980s the F-15A/B/C/D were improved via updates known collectively as Multi Stage Improvement Program II (MSIP).

'There was a new display in the cockpit,' explains Dildy, 'that was introduced to show armament

information, but the real advantage of MSIP was that it gave us a digital computer that gave us a quantum leap in capability over the old analogue computer. Along with that came the AIM-120 AMRAAM missile and a new radar component that allows us to program a lot of new radar modes into the computer. The constant changes that these new modes brought about means that things are always changing. The AMRAAM is a great long range fire-and-forget weapon, but it's also a good point and shoot weapon.'

F-15 CONFIRMED KILLS

Dates	Location	Operation	Kills
27 July 1979	Southern Lebanon	N/A	5 Syrian Air Force
September 1979	Lebanon	N/A	4 Syrian Air Force
December 1980	Lebanon	N/A	3 Syrian Air Force
29 July–31 Aug 1981	Lebanon	N/A	3 Syrian Air Force
6 June–12 June 1982	Beka'a Valley, Lebanon	Peace for Galilee	40 Syrian Air Force
5 June 1984	Saudi Arabia	N/A	1 Iranian Air Force
30 October 1985	Lebanon	N/A	2 Syrian Air Force
17 Jan–22 Mar 1991	Kuwait, Iraq	Desert Storm	36 Iraqi Air Force
24 Mar–26 Mar 1999	Yugoslavia	Deny Flight	4 Yugoslav Air Force

Flying the F-16

The Lockheed Martin F-16 Fighting Falcon is one of the most prolific jet fighters in service today. World-renowned for its breathtaking manoeuvrability, the 'Viper' has matured from a simple point-defence fighter into a sophisticated, multi-role fighter-bomber.

The F-16's cockpit is well laid-out and very simple in comparison to previous fighter cockpits.

According to the U.S. Air Force, the F-16 is officially known as the Fighting Falcon, but through the years several more popular nicknames have evolved.

Lt. Col. Ned 'Mob' Linch, an F-16 pilot for 14 years, explained the genesis of its nicknames: *'The F-16 is the result of the Lightweight Fighter Program, a program to develop a true air superiority lightweight fighter, which started in 1972. The jet's first unofficial nickname was "Electric Jet" because of its fly-by-wire flight controls.'* However, the most popular name for the F-16, and the one used by its pilots and maintainers, is 'Viper'. *'When I think of a Viper, I think of a serpent that can strike and kill in a moment…much like the F-16. Most of us pilots will agree that Viper is a much cooler name than Fighting Falcon or Falcon. Historically, Viper originated from the movie* Battlestar Galactica, *which had a single-seat fighter spacecraft called the Viper.'*

FLY-BY-WIRE

One of the goals during the development of the F-16 was the ability of the pilot to have 'care-free' manoeuvring at the

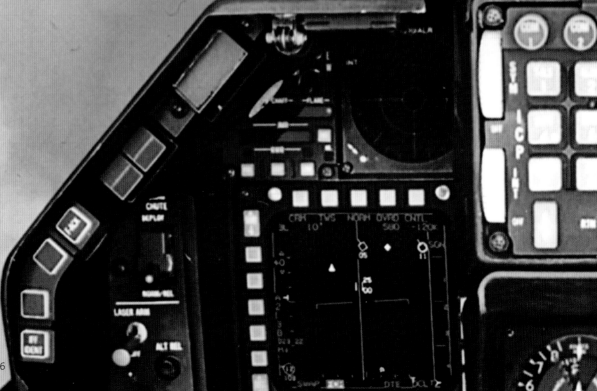

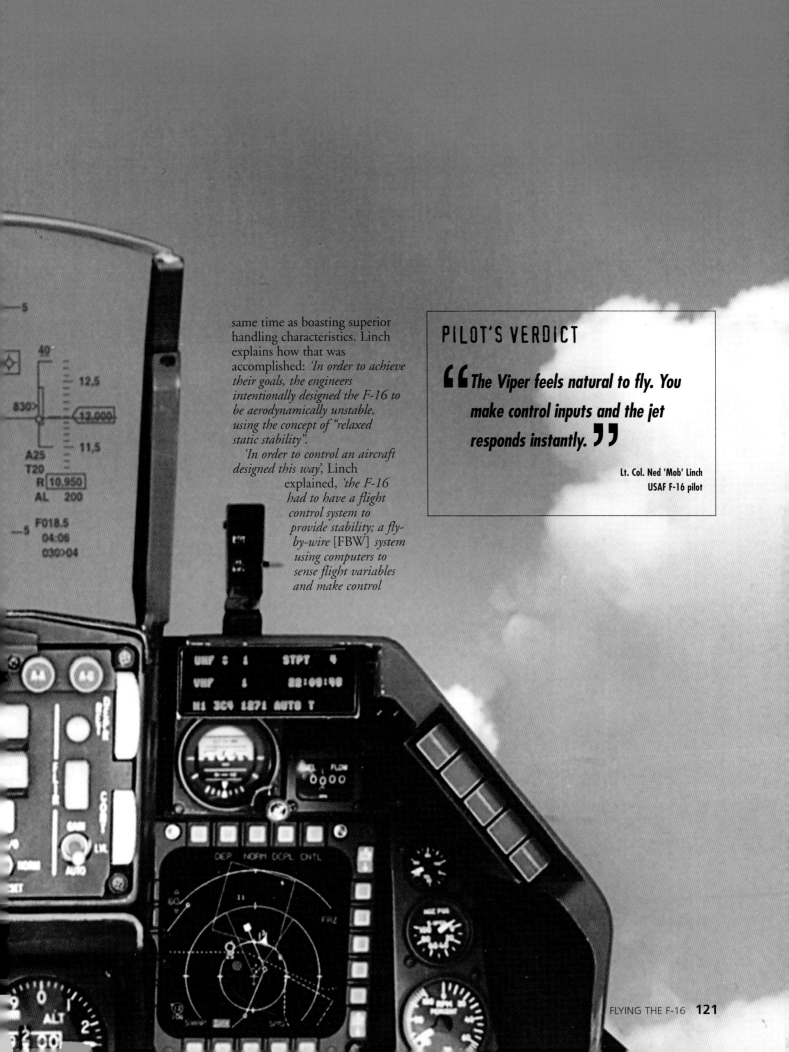

same time as boasting superior handling characteristics. Linch explains how that was accomplished: *'In order to achieve their goals, the engineers intentionally designed the F-16 to be aerodynamically unstable, using the concept of "relaxed static stability".*

'In order to control an aircraft designed this way', Linch explained, *'the F-16 had to have a flight control system to provide stability; a fly-by-wire* [FBW] *system using computers to sense flight variables and make control*

PILOT'S VERDICT

❝*The Viper feels natural to fly. You make control inputs and the jet responds instantly.***❞**

Lt. Col. Ned 'Mob' Linch
USAF F-16 pilot

RIGHT: The F-16 began life with one simple goal: to dominate airspace close to its home base during the day, and in periods when the weather was good. Over the years it has been developed and enhanced to make it multirole capable, at night as well as day, and in all kinds of weather.

BELOW: One of the by-products of reclining the F-16's ACES II ejection seat is that it improves pilot comfort over long distances, and also helps improve g tolerance.

inputs to stabilize the aircraft. Basically, without FBW, you would not be able to fly the jet.'

The FBW computer does a great job, Linch reports. 'The Viper feels natural to fly. You make control inputs on the stick and the jet responds instantly. The jet is always seeking 1g, so you don't have to trim the aircraft like most aircraft, which makes it very easy to fly. We have a Rudder Interconnect which means that the computer automatically feeds in rudder during rolls and turns, so you rarely use rudder in flight. The rudder pedals are really there for taxiing and for when you need some yaw to increase drag if you're about to overshoot a rejoin with your flight lead.'

To evaluate the F-16's handling, Linch even put his 14-year-old son in the simulator: 'He was able to maintain basic aircraft control and even land the jet. The natural ability to fly this jet gives the pilot the opportunity to effectively and tactically employ it as a single-seat, single-engine fighter.' It is in this tactical element that FBW helps the Viper to outperform other fighter jets in the close-in, dogfighting engagement.

'The "Corner Velocity" – where a jet can pull the maximum gs for the tightest turn with the best turn rate – of the F-16 is not a specific airspeed as in most fighters. Instead, our corner velocity is actually an airspeed range. This is the best advantage we have over non-FBW jets. The F-16 wing changes shape during different phases of flight: FBW, the leading edge flaps, flaperons, horizontal stabilizer and Rudder Interconnect all work in conjunction with each other to optimally provide the best performance.'

In doing so, the Viper constantly gives the pilot the best turn performance available at any given speed, giving him a decided advantage over his opponent as the dogfight progresses and airspeed decays during constant turning.

[MISSION REPORT]

++++++++++++++++++++++++++++++

DESERT STORM

On 17 January, 1991, the combined Coalition force led by the United States initiated offensive operations against Iraqi forces that had illegally occupied neighbouring Kuwait in August 1990. The operation, known as Desert Storm, made full use of no less than 249 U.S. Air Force (USAF) F-16s.

In total, the Vipers flew more than 13,000 combat sorties against Iraq personnel, armour and facilities –more than any other Coalition aircraft. Their targets included Iraqi equipment in Kuwait and southern Iraq, Scud missiles and launchers, and interdiction targets such as military production and support, chemical production facilities, and airfields.

The F-16 boasted a 95.2 per cent mission-capable rate – meaning that the 249 Vipers were almost always ready for combat, and rarely grounded due to maintenance issues – five per cent above its normal peacetime rate.

Seventy-two of the F-16s in theatre were capable of carrying the LANTIRN (Low Altitude Navigation, Targeting and Infra Red for Night) pods that would enable them to cut through the dark of night and speed towards their targets at extremely low level. And, although only the AAQ-13 Navigation pod was available (the full LANTIRN suite also includes the AAQ-14 IR target pod), these F-16s were a true

success story in their own right. Indeed, LANTIRN's mission-capable rate was over 98 per cent.

Five F-16s were lost in course of the 13,000 combat sorties: three to surface-to-air missiles (SAMs), one to a premature bomb detonation, and one to an engine fire.

In the decade that followed the ceasefire and the establishment of two No-Fly Zones over Iraq, the F-16 continued to patrol over Iraq and distinguished itself in numerous punitive air strikes. Then, in March 2003, the second Gulf War commenced, and the Viper was once again in the thick of things.

ABOVE: An F-16C refuels from a KC-135 Stratotanker in late January 1991. In the countdown to war, swarms of Vipers assembled behind Stratotankers to get their fuel before pushing into Iraq and Kuwait.

FBW has other, less obvious, advantages too. Linch gave one example:

'A cool feature is when you put the gear handle down for landing, the flaps come down automatically. One issue you have to be careful with on takeoff is putting your gear up too soon because the flaps retract as well... and on a hot day with a heavy bomb load, you need that extra lift so you delay retracting the gear for a few more seconds than normal.'

9G CAPABILITY

The F-16 was the first jet fighter ever to be built to sustain turns at 9g – or nine times the force of gravity. Linch says that this capability is *'important in a dogfight situation. You want to get to the enemy's turn circle as fast as possible, solve as many angles as possible by pulling high gs and get to a "control zone" behind him to employ ordnance as fast as possible.'* In essence, the more gs you can pull, the better

your chances of outmanoeuvring your opponent.

Pulling 9gs is *'an aggressive event,'* according to Linch. *'In your mind you're totally focused on flying the jet and employing it against the enemy. When you hit the turn circle in a BFM [Basic Fighter Manoeuvring] engagement, you pull for all the jet

will give you. Most of the time you know you're going to get at least 8gs and probably close to 9g.'*

Flying such physically demanding manoeuvres carries with it certain physiological symptoms, Linch adds. *'Looking at your arms after a flight where you've been pulling 9gs will reveal a ton of "Geasles". Geasles are*

BELOW: Perhaps the most obvious weakness of the F-16 is its relatively small weapons payload. Here, U.S. Air National Guard F-16s from New Mexico, Colorado and Montana fly formation, each carrying a 'heavy' load of two 907kg (2,000lb) GBU-31 JDAMs.

ABOVE: The versatility of the F-16 means that it can carry most of the munitions in the US Air Force's expansive arsenal. For targets that require a little stand-off distance to kill – particularly armoured personnel carriers and tanks supported by radar and IR guided SAMs – the AGM-65 Maverick missile is perfect.

broken blood vessels in your arms, or down the side of your body, and are small purple-coloured dots. Sometimes it might look like sunburn on your arms. There's no pain or anything, and the Geasles are gone within about 24 hours."

G-LOC

A more serious hazard for the F-16 pilot is the threat of *g*-Induced Loss Of Consciousness (*g-LOC*) that can come about from pulling even moderate amounts of *g*s, and which is especially a consideration at high *g*s. *'The F-16 has killed several pilots due to* g*-LOC. So, pulling high* g*s is an accepted risk and part of the business. All F-16 pilots have to pass a demanding 9*g *ride in the centrifuge prior to strapping on a real jet. The more you fly the jet and the more fit you are, the better tolerance your body has to high* g*-forces. So, diet and exercise is an important aspect of flying the Viper. Eating balanced meals (balance of protein and* complex carbs), plus weight training as well as cardio, has reduced g-LOC mishaps.'*

COMBAT EDGE

To help combat the threat imposed by *g-LOC*, the Viper pilot has two tools at his disposal – a straining exercise undertaken by the pilot when experiencing high *g*, and an advanced cockpit air system which actually reduces the risk of *g-LOC*. Linch explained them both.

[MISSION REPORT]
++++++++++++++++++++++++++++++++

F-16 KILLS

The F-16's first kills came courtesy of the Israeli Defence Force in 1981, when Israeli Air Force Vipers downed a Syrian Mi-8 helicopter and a Syrian Air Force MiG-21 Fishbed fighter. The Viper's kill tally continued to grow in 1982, when Israel engaged yet more Syrian Air Force aircraft during Operation Peace for Galilee, also known as the Lebanon War.

Between May 1986 and November 1988 – towards the end of the ten-year Soviet-Afghan war – Pakistani Air Force F-16s shot down between 8 and 10 Afghan Air Force and Soviet Air Force ground attack and transport aircraft that had wandered into sovereign Pakistani air space.

Although the F-16 did not down any Iraqi fighters during Operation Desert Storm in 1991, operations Southern Watch and Northern Watch to patrol the No-Fly Zones over Iraq did see the jet rack up its first two kills in U.S. service.

USAF F-16s were later were also employed by NATO during Bosnian peacekeeping operations in 1994–95, where two

ABOVE: Israel, the Netherlands, Pakistan and the U.S. have all scored kills with the F-16. In addition, the F-16 has been involved in a number of air-to-ground combat missions, making it one of the most versatile and successful multirole fighter jets of modern times.

Vipers claimed four Super Galeb attack jets. Five years later, Operation Allied Force yielded another USAF Viper kill, as well as the first F-16 kill for the Royal Netherlands Air Force, when an F-16A downed a Serb MiG-29 with an AIM-120 AMRAAM.

'The current USAF "L-1" g-straining manoeuvre combines a regular, three-second strain against a closed glottis, interrupted with a rapid exhalation and inhalation of less than half a second, with tensing of all major muscle groups of the abdomen, arms, and legs. To assist your L-1, the F-16 has "Combat Edge"; a system designed to increase g-tolerance, reduce fatigue and prevent g-LOC mishaps. The Combat Edge PBG [Pressure Breathing for g] forces high-pressure air via the oxygen mask into the pilot's lungs.

'The system does not replace a good g-straining manoeuvre; it just gives the pilot an extra edge, plus helps with fatigue. Just as the g-suit gives your muscles something to push against, the high-pressure air is the same type of force for your breathing, which is a three-second-cycle quick air exchange. The high-pressure air helps keep the air pressure higher in your lungs, which helps the heart pump blood to the eyes and brain while inhibiting the downward flow of blood.' It is this draining of blood, and thus oxygen, from the brain that actually causes g-LOC to occur.

HUD AND HOTAS

The F-16 uses a combination of switches on the throttle and side-stick controller known as HOTAS: Hands On Throttle and Stick. In addition to this, the layout of the Viper cockpit is exceptionally clear and well-thought-out.

Linch says: 'You "wear" the F-16 like a tight pair of jeans and in combat you're also wearing a survival vest and a g-suit packed to the gills. So, moving around in the jet at night to look for a tiny switch on a console panel is not desirable, nor is trying to find a switch at 9gs in a dogfight. So, HOTAS makes it quick and easier to employ the jet – especially at 9gs!'

'After taking off in the F-16, most switches used by the pilot are on the stick and throttle as well as the two MFDs (Multi Function Displays) and the Integrated Control Panel (ICP), which is the buttons below the HUD (Heads Up Display). The ergonomics of the F-16 are outstanding. I've

flown in both the F/A-18 and F-15 and you can't beat the user-friendly ergonomics of the Viper. User-friendly avionics and having switches in the right place for the right time has helped reduce mishaps. There is nothing worse than rolling in on a target to drop a bomb and realizing that you forgot to load the correct weapon into your weapons computer.'

MULTIROLE

Having long since shed its roots as a point interceptor, the F-16 has been steadily upgraded over the years to turn it into a capable fighter and bomber that can operate day or night, and in bad weather if so required.

Linch, as a seasoned Viper pilot and veteran of some very intense combat sorties in Iraq in March 2003, explains that, 'Flying the Viper in air-to-air and air-to-ground is demanding. As the years have gone by, we've gone from a day-, visual-flight-rules-fighter with heaters [short range, heat seeking AIM-9 Sidewinder missiles] and GP [General Purpose, unguided] bombs; to an all-weather, night fighter-bomber shooting heaters and Slammers [AIM-120 Advanced Medium Range Air-to-Air Missiles] utilizing

targeting pods to drop laser guided bombs. Plus, we now do this all while wearing NVGs.'

Being good at all the Viper's missions is a difficult challenge all of its own.

'It's a proficiency issue,' Linch continues. 'If all you do is drop bombs, then you get really good at it. Then, six months later, you go out to fly BFM and it takes a ride or two to get back to where you were when you were more proficient at that particular mission.'

ABOVE: Denmark is just one of several European operators using the F-16A/B. The European nations of Holland, Belgium, Denmark, Norway and Portugal joined forces to develop the Mid Life Upgrade (MLU), which updated their old Vipers to near Block 50 standard.

BELOW: Defensive systems on the F-16 include built-in chaff and flare dispensers in the fuselage booms.

Flying the Tornado

The Tornado may have been in front-line service for 25 years, but it is testament to its impressive capabilities that it remains very much at the sharp end of the air forces of its four operators, and is expected to serve for many more years to come.

With almost 1,000 examples built, the tri-national Tornado remains one of the most successful European warplanes of the post-war era. It has seen much combat and has spawned specialist defence suppression and air defence variants.

While the basic Tornado design was later adapted for air defence duties as a long-range 'bomber destroyer', its primary duty remains ground attack. Back in the Cold War days, it was envisaged that the Tornado IDS would be used to fly fast and low – ideally under the cover of adverse weather, or by night – hitting key enemy installations with accuracy and performing interdiction sorties over the rear areas of the battlefield. While its low-level, terrain-following ability remains arguably unmatched, the post-Cold War era has seen the Tornado IDS adopt new roles, including battlefield close air support (CAS) and stand-off precision attack from medium level, using a new generation of cruise missiles. New capabilities have been bestowed on the type via avionics and weapons upgrades, such as the RAF's latest GR.Mk 4 version.

After advanced training on the Hawk, Pete B. arrived with the

RAF's Tornado GR.Mk 4 community as a pilot in 2002 and flew the type operationally over Iraq with No. 31 Sqn. 'The first time I actually saw the Tornado GR.Mk 4 up close was at No. 15 Sqn where I was with the Operational Conversion Unit, and my first impressions were really that it was a massive jet compared to the Hawk,' he remembers. 'It's huge in comparison...The size is pretty noticeable when you first arrive in it. It's a much, much bigger aircraft; the cockpit is huge in comparison to the Hawk and there's a lot more systems in it – it's a lot more complicated...It's a lot more comfortable and feels a lot more solid than the Hawk at low-level.'

In terms of dimensions, the Tornado is actually smaller than the 'legacy' Hornet, but it has a bulkiness and brute force that are immediately striking. 'The first time I flew [the Tornado GR.Mk 4] properly on the OCU – my first solo, and my first solo with a trainee navigator as well – I can remember looking back and you have this huge intake right next to you, level with your shoulders, and then this huge wing out next to you, as opposed to the Hawk, which is really quite small. Flying it, it feels pretty big and nowhere near as manoeuvrable as the Hawk. It flies pretty much the way that it looks – it is pretty big and heavy. Unlike the Hawk, which is nimble, the Tornado tends to be a bit of a lumbering aircraft at low level, although it is very fast and feels pretty powerful.'

From the outset, the Tornado IDS was equipped with

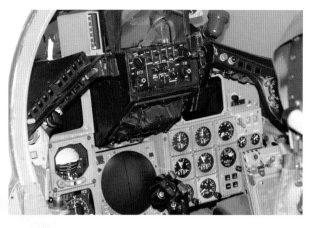

ABOVE: The GR.Mk 1's front cockpit was notably uncluttered; the central display is the moving map.

MAIN PHOTOGRAPH: A Luftwaffe Tornado ECR from the specialist JBG 32 unit at Lechfeld approaches the tanker with its refuelling probe deployed. In place of the RAF's Sky Shadow ECM pod, the German Tornado fleet mounts the Cerberus pod (carried here to port).

PILOT'S VERDICT

‟It looks and feels like a really solid aeroplane. Its nickname among a lot of us is "the armchair" because when you're flying it, it's like being in a big armchair.”

Pete B.
ex-Tornado pilot, No. 31 Squadron, RAF

learning curve – especially for Germany and Italy, whose front-line aircrew had little or no experience of flying with a back-seater. This German pilot recalls his conversion from the single-seat F-104G to the far more sophisticated Tornado: *'When you get trained in a single-seat aircraft you have to make all your decisions by yourself, there's nobody you can ask, and of course there's no crew concept. Even if you fly a trainer and you are with another buddy in the back, or even as a passenger, it is completely different. You have to do everything on your own, and in a Tornado all of a sudden everything changed. You could concentrate on flying and have the back-seater do all the weapons designation, do the radar and stuff like this. It was quite a change. Especially when you wanted to look at the radar…It was quite a change to have a second man in there and to develop a crew concept, and to have the crew work together making decisions together.'* Now a qualified flying instructor, Pete B. of the RAF agrees that having a back-seater demands a whole different way of flying and fighting: *'When you start flying with a navigator you've got someone there to help you, and once you get used to working as a team, it really affects the way you operate,'* he confirms.

In contrast to equivalent Western attack aircraft in its class, the Tornado IDS differs in its use of a variable-geometry, or 'swing' wing. Wing sweep is controlled by the pilot, with different positions selected by using what Pete B. describes as a *'big, pretty crude lever that you move backwards and forwards, depending where you want the wings.'* The pilot can move the wing all the way forward to 25 degrees for optimum low-speed handling, such as during take-off and landing, to an intermediate setting of 45 degrees, or all the way back to 67 degrees for high-speed flight. The pilot is also provided with HOTAS controls, and the throttle carries controls for the air brakes and flaps. According to Pete B., *'the whole time when*

ABOVE: An unarmed RAF Tornado F.Mk 3 manoeuvres at low level, with its wings at maximum 67-degree sweep for high speed.

RIGHT: An AMI Tornado displays a range of stores, including 27-mm Mauser cannon. The cannon port itself is also visible, just ahead of the aircraft's code.

advanced systems tailored to its demanding low-level attack role. While its terrain-following capability remains valuable, the RAF's Tornado GR.Mk 4 upgrade has added new systems for 21st century mission scenarios, including stand-off reconnaissance, and the upgrade has also provided the two-person crew with more modern cockpits.

MAIN PHOTOGRAPH: With wings at intermediate sweep, a Tornado F.Mk 3 of the RAF's No. 56 (Reserve) Squadron pulls into a climb.

'Again, it's quite a big cockpit,' explains Pete B. *'Up in front of you, on the main console you've got the basic instruments, they're all just "raw" instruments, there's no EFIS* [electronic flight information systems] *or anything like that. But what you have got is a large digital display, which has got a moving map on it, which is pretty high quality…You've also got the HUD obviously, and that's got all the information you need for flying when you're looking out of the cockpit. When you're flying, you're normally glancing between the HUD and the moving map down below…So again, compared to the Hawk, it's a massive step up; the systems are a lot more complex and you have a whole new element – having to operate all the various aircraft systems as well as flying and doing everything else.'*

AIRCREW COOPERATION

At the time of the Tornado's introduction, the two-man crew was something of a steep

[MISSION REPORT]
++++++++++++++++++++++++++++++++

BACK TO IRAQ

The RAF's Tornado fleet first saw combat use during the 1991 Gulf War – in Operations Desert Shield and Desert Storm – and both ground-attack, reconnaissance and interceptor variants remained in the region for the subsequent peacekeeping and policing duties over Iraq. By the time of Operation Iraqi Freedom, beginning in March 2003, the RAF was operating the newly upgraded Tornado GR.Mk 4/4A, and this type – together with F.Mk 3 interceptors – went back to war. The 2003 Iraqi missions were conducted under Operation Telic, as it was known to the UK forces, and among their Tornado GR.Mk 4 pilots was Pete B., who had only been posted to his first front-line unit a year earlier. The 24-year-old Flying Officer, at the time the RAF's youngest Tornado pilot, saw action even before Operation Telic had begun, as he recalls here:

'I'd only been combat-ready for about six months. The whole unit knew something was likely to happen. When we went out there [to Kuwait] in January 2003 we were initially doing the Operation Resonant role, which was policing the no-fly zone in the south. We were based at Ali Al Salem. We would fly missions over Iraq, a lot of the time just to see what was going on over there, and seeing at times how they would react to us being airborne. In those days, every now and then they'd launch an aircraft beyond the no-fly zone and they'd come down and again see how we'd react to that. We did that for a while, until March. We did actually do some bombing on Operation Resonant...One of the formation that was already airborne got fired at by some AAA, so we had what we called a "reaction option". If we got shot at then we would get told to go and bomb a pre-planned target. As the aircraft that were already airborne had run out of fuel, I was tasked to get

airborne and in the end I went across the border for the first time and dropped on an air defence target in southern Iraq... At that time, some people had done three or four tours out there already on Operation Resonant, but had never actually dropped, whereas I ended up getting airborne, going across the border on my first trip and dropping on a target in southern Iraq – the opportunity was quite rare.'

Thereafter, Pete B. remained in theatre and flew his first Telic mission on 16 January – a night sortie of around six hours, twice taking on fuel from tankers – against a target located in the northwest of Iraq, although no bombs were dropped on this occasion. Pete B. flew a number of missions in a reconnaissance role using the Raptor stand-off pod, and Alarm defence-suppression sorties. He also went on to fly missions in the CAS role, attacking targets of opportunity within designated 'kill boxes' and providing on-call firepower for ground forces. This he remembers as *'quite difficult and stressful'*, and it involved him working together with other Coalition ground forces; often remaining over the target for long periods, there was a serious a risk of running low on fuel. *'One particular mission we did was CAS with some US Marines, not too far from Basra. There was a line of tanks and APCs and we got essentially a visual talk-on, from a Marine forward air controller on the ground, and then we prosecuted various targets. We started with a visual call up at height – to reduce the threat from any SAMs – and then, to actually release the weapons, we dived down, in order to expose ourselves for the minimum amount of time.'*

BELOW: Refuelling from a USAF KC-10 tanker over the Iraqi desert, this RAF Tornado GR.Mk 4 displays a typical Telic warload of a pair of Paveway series laser-guided bombs under the fuselage, 'Hindenburger' large-capacity fuel tanks and Sky Shadow and BOZ series pods. As well as carrying chaff and flare decoys, the BOZ pod can also be adapted to mount the Ariel towed radar decoy.

LEFT: This RAF Tornado GR.Mk 4 wears the markings of No. 14 Squadron, now based at Lossiemouth. Originally part of the considerable Tornado GR.Mk 1 force within RAF Germany, No. 14 Squadron moved to its current Scottish base in January 2001.

you're flying, you're constantly manually selecting manoeuvre flaps to increase the lift on the wings, so whenever you turn, you have to remember to deploy. With the HOTAS you have all the weapons selections and you've got the ability to access the navigation equipment through the stick as well. You've also got on the left-hand side two big twin throttles, one for each engine.'

Whether flying at low or medium level, the IDS can call upon a wide array of weaponry to suit all mission profiles. The RAF continues to issue its GR.Mk 4 units with advanced new weaponry, including the

[MISSION REPORT]
++++++++++++++++++++++++++++++
WEAPONS DISPENSERS

The realities of the Cold War were such that NATO forces would have found themselves outnumbered on the ground and in the air, had war ever broken out between East and West on Europe's Central Front. As a reaction to their smaller numbers in the field, NATO planners made efforts to exploit technology in an attempt to turn the tables on their opposition. Illustrating this trend were two of the weapons developed for use by the Tornado IDS in the Cold War: the RAF's JP233 and West Germany's MW-1 area-denial stores – saturation weapons that were to allow small numbers of aircraft to inflict high levels of damage.

The JP233 was intended for deployment during low-level missions over Warsaw Pact airbases, destruction of which would have been vital if NATO's smaller number of tactical aircraft were to have a chance in a potential Central Front air war. The MW-1, meanwhile, was designed to counter the Warsaw Pact's numerical supremacy in terms of troops and armour, and was to be used against columns of tanks, infantry fighting vehicles, troops and materiel. Designed and built by Hunting, the JP233 took the form of two 2,335kg

(5,148lb) sub-munitions dispensers mounted side-by-side under the Tornado GR.Mk 1's fuselage. Each dispenser contained 30 parachute-retarded sub-munitions designed to detonate below the surface of the runway. These were accompanied by 215 free-fall area-denial mines that would disrupt any attempts to repair the cratered runway. The mission profile with the JP233 included a 60m (200ft) run-in to the target, flown at 500 knots (925km/h), with the two types of sub-munition being dispensed automatically in one of two aircrew-selected patterns, dependant on approach.

West Germany's MBB *Mehrzweckwaffe*-1 (multi-purpose weapon, or MW-1) comprised four jettisonable stores carriers that ejected sub-munitions to the left and right. Again mounted under the fuselage, the MW-1 could carry up to 224 sub-munitions: a combination of fragmentation bomblets that would detonate on impact, and passive minelets. As well as attacking mechanized forces and troop concentrations – typically those of the follow-on formations, behind the front lines – the MW-1 was envisaged as a weapon for Germany navy Tornados, for defence against amphibious landings.

While the MW-1 never saw combat use, among the first missions flown by RAF Tornado GR.Mk 1s in Operation Desert Storm in 1991 were strikes on Iraqi airfields using JP233 weapons. The relatively high losses incurred to Iraqi defences went some way to show what a high-risk mission this would have been, if it had ever been flown in anger against the Warsaw Pact. Both JP233 and MW-1 were withdrawn from the inventories after the collapse of the Warsaw Pact.

LEFT: Seen during MW-1 release trials, this *Marineflieger* Tornado IDS was assigned to the German defence ministry's trials unit, WTD 61 at Manching.

LEFT: After dispensing its sub-munitions in one of two pre-programmed modes, the JP233's two empty containers would be automatically jettisoned.

Storm Shadow stand-off weapon that saw its first combat use over Iraq in 2003, and the Brimstone anti-armour missile. Other Tornado operators are keeping pace, and Germany has introduced the Taurus stand-off weapon, with capabilities similar to Storm Shadow. While weapons delivery has traditionally been the role of the navigator, or WSO, in the back seat, Pete B. reveals that for certain weapons the pilot can acquire the target in his or her HUD: *'You can move a target mark using the navigation controller. To mark a target you can do this with your left hand, using another controller behind the throttle.'*

AIR DEFENCE TRAINING

The Tornado IDS is equipped with a comprehensive electronic warfare suite. However, underwing stations are provided for self-defence missiles, meaning that the 'mud-moving' Tornado IDS can even tangle with enemy aircraft if required. *'Every year, we flew out to Cyprus for three weeks of air combat training,'* recalls Pete B. *'In these periods we would fly one-versus-one, two-versus-one, or two-versus-two missions, predominantly using the Sidewinder. During most of our training we'd have an element of air-to-air, more in the defensive role – if someone was bouncing up at low level we'd be able to counter them with Sidewinder.'*

In addition to being equipped with one of the first production fly-by-wire flight control systems, the terrain-following radar (TFR) function remains a key to the Tornado's capabilities. Despite a shift in emphasis towards medium-level operations, aircrew continue to train for low-level flying. While the 'under-the-radar' mission may be best associated with Cold War-era tactics, such is the efficacy of the Tornado's TFR and navigation systems that it remains a vital component of current training and still has an important place at the operational level. *'We still do have that*

capability,' Pete B. confirms. *'With the Tornado, originally the whole concept was to be able to fly at ultra-low level underneath any enemy radar in any weather. The TFR on the radar is pretty impressive – you can fly down to 200ft [60m] at over 600mph [965km/h] in any weather over mountainous terrain and it does that in a completely reliable way…The low-level role – we use it a lot, and the kit in the Tornado is brilliant for it.'* Flying at such low level brings its own demands on the Tornado's aircrew, however, and can be as physically taxing as

executing high-*g* manoeuvres. *'During training, at a standard height of 250ft [75m], it's pretty comfortable,'* recalls Pete. B. However, once on the front line Tornado GR.Mk 4 aircrew will be expected to work down to as low as 30m (100ft) as they gain experience. *'At 100ft and at top speed, that is pretty demanding flying,'* reports Pete B. *'The pilot*

concentrates on flying a really aggressive route, and looks out directly ahead, while the navigator can start looking out around the rest of the aircraft. That's quite demanding, and takes a lot of the capacity of the pilot.'*

Although some of its roles will be taken over by the Eurofighter Typhoon, both the RAF and Luftwaffe envisage retaining the Tornado IDS until an appropriate UCAV becomes available, with the capacity to undertake the more demanding roles that can currently only be prosecuted by a manned warplane. The pilots themselves

are, according to Pete B. *'pretty fond of* [the Tornado]. *It's an aircraft that, once you get to know, you definitely feel confident to go to war, and to go on operations in. It's really robust, and feels really solid to fly. Although it's relatively old it's still very capable. If a pilot has to choose an aircraft to go to war with, they'd probably choose the Tornado.'*

BELOW: The first front-line Luftwaffe operator of the Tornado IDS was *Jagdbombergeschwader* (JBG, or fighter-bomber wing) 31, based at Nörvenich. The unit carries the honorific name 'Boelcke', after the World War I fighter ace, and is today a specialist in the delivery of LGBs.

BELOW: The Tornado's twin engines are Turbo Union RB.199 turbofans. In order to reduce landing distance, each engine is fitted with a 'clamshell' thrust reverser, to deflect jet thrust, obviating the need for a brake parachute.

Flying the B-1B

Few modern warplanes have undergone such a radical transformation in mission profile as the USAF's Rockwell B-1B Lancer. Initially serving as a low-level nuclear penetrator, the swing-wing bomber is now spearheading the Coalition effort in the Global War on Terror.

MAIN PHOTOGRAPH: Assigned to the 34th Bomb Squadron of the 28th Bomb Wing, a B-1B prepares to depart Ellsworth AFB on a training mission. Noteworthy is the 'fighter-style' one-piece stabilator, which can be used differentially to provide longitudinal control in the absence of ailerons.

Better known to its US Air Force crews as the 'Bone' (a contraction based on its military designation: *Bomber-One*), today's B-1B has its origins in the Mach 2.2-capable B-1A, which was designed as a Cold War-era replacement for Strategic Air Command's B-52 Stratofortress fleet. Although the B-1A was cancelled in 1977, the B-1B retains the salient features and some of the performance qualities of its predecessor, together with a weapons payload that is unmatched by any aircraft in the USAF inventory. It is this combination of near fighter-like performance with the ability to carry some 34,000kg (75,000lb) of precision-guided munitions over an intercontinental range that confirms the continued importance of the B-1B, despite it having relinquished its nuclear role in 1991, following the end of the Cold War.

The B-1B trades the high-end performance of the original B-1A for a much-reduced radar cross-section and improved survivability in a high-threat environment, while retaining a still respectable high-subsonic cruising speed.

FLIGHT CHARACTERISTICS

Although the B-1B may not possess the 'turning and

burning' characteristics of contemporary fighters, its crew are confident of the big bomber's acceleration and agility, and will even occasionally turn the tables on more agile opposition during air combat exercises.

'Utah', a B-1B pilot and former WSO, has around nine years' experience on the 'Bone', and serves with the 28th Bomb Wing at Ellsworth AFB, South Dakota. In his opinion, the aircraft's performance compares well with those of the fighter 'jocks':

'The comparison would be [that] *down low the B-1 is an "energy maker", as we call it, and we have plenty of engine thrust*

PILOT'S VERDICT

"*I can guarantee that we are the most feared airframe out there* [*in Iraq*]*...there's no beating us.*"

'O'Doyle'
B-1B pilot
7th Bomb Wing
Dyess AFB

and airflow. We can get tight turns [but] we're limited to 3g with our wings fully swept back, which is a lot less than a fighter.'

In fact, from a handling and manoeuvring point of view, the main difference between the four-engined B-1B and a fighter is the limitations on the aircraft's turn radius. 'O'Doyle', a Lancer combat veteran of Operation

Enduring Freedom, now with the B-1B 'schoolhouse' of the 7th Bomb Wing at Dyess AFB, Texas, explains:

'As far as roll rate goes, meaning left and right, and how quickly the wing's moving, [the B-1B is] very agile. It has spoilers on top of the wing, but we've also got what we call a stabilator, which is exactly like a fighter. We don't have an elevator like a conventional aircraft, like the B-52 has. For us the whole tail

[MISSION REPORT]

+++++++++++++++++++++++++++++++

OPERATION ENDURING FREEDOM

The B-1B first saw combat in the US-led strikes on Iraq during Operation Desert Fox in 1998, and returned to action in Operation Allied Force over the former Yugoslavia in 1999. Following the events of 9/11, the 'Bone' has found itself taking an active role in the Global War on Terror, expressed through missions flown under the auspices of Operation Enduring Freedom over Afghanistan, and Operation Iraqi Freedom, the latter beginning in 2003. A veteran of the Enduring Freedom campaign, B-1B pilot 'O'Doyle' describes a typical close air support (CAS) mission over Afghanistan:

'Once we're close to the take-off time we taxi out, take-off and then climb out and, depending where we're flying out of, it takes anywhere from between two and six hours to get to where we're going. We get out and level off, cruise to where we're going. Sometimes we'll have a tanker in there if it's a longer distance to get to the theatre to which we are going to deploy.'

Prior to departing on the mission, the B-1B's four-person crew will have been briefed with a number of air strike requests – essentially target information that is provided by commanders on the ground. 'O'Doyle' explains:

'In Afghanistan right now, [the requests come] from the Coalition; we'll get requests from any number of different nationalities – the last time I was over there we did a lot of work with the British forces on the ground. They will put in requests to have air cover for various reasons, and the guys that run the show decide what airplane is best to support which strike request.'

Once in-country, the crew will 'check in' with the Coalition controlling agency, informing them of their position, their particular weapons load-out, and the nature of their air strike requests. *'They'll tell us "proceed as fragged", meaning to go do what you agreed to do, or something else has popped up – what we call a Troops in Contact [TIC] – if there's some sort of*

engagement going on. We'll either go and support our air strike request, or sometimes we'll just be "on call", which means we'll go to a bit of airspace and just orbit, and wait, to report immediately. Often that's what we're doing when we're called to a TIC. A TIC is any time where there's an engagement going on on the ground... They're not necessarily shooting at each other – they can just feel threatened or they have intelligence that the enemy is getting ready to attack, or if they feel like they need air cover, we'll go and do that...

'Normally, most of the units out there will have a JTAC [Joint Terminal Attack Controller] ...if they have intelligence that they may be attacked, they may call us in. We're not necessarily going to be releasing weapons, but they're calling us in and they want us to come and do a show of force: fly over the area at low level making a lot of noise and let the bad guys know, "hey we're in the area" Quite often, if things are not "hot", if they're not being shot at, that's what they would prefer to do, they're really interested in doing the dissuasive step first, like "hey, they're here, maybe you guys should go away, otherwise we could be making your lives very difficult"...a lot of the time that will cool things off.'

'O'Doyle' is in no doubt of the key role played by the 'Bone' in the Afghan theatre of operations, reflecting that *'The forward air controllers love us. It would be nicer if we had a [targeting] pod, but that's coming, but they like us because we're big and we're loud for shows of force, and we carry a lot of weapons... We are very good at what we do and the guys on the ground really appreciate that. I don't know how may times I've been very gratified by the fact that I was able to save our guys' lives on the ground... It really feels good. That's why we're there. They're very appreciative and it's an extremely gratifying feeling, especially in the Coalition environment, especially in Afghanistan.'*

surface moves, like an F-15 or F-16, and when we roll the jet, the computer integrates, and the tail moves to aid in the rolling, so we get fighter-like roll rates. I would say it's very agile in that respect. The big limiting factor for us is turn radius. We fly at speeds that are the same as the F-15 and the F-16. We fly at high airspeeds, but if they go straight into a turn they can do 7 to 9g – [it's] called nose rate, the rate at which the nose is cutting through that turn. Obviously pulling seven to nine times the force of gravity, that nose rate brings you into a really tight turn. Because the airplane is so large and we are g-limited, our turn rate is such that we don't get nearly the nose rate that those guys do. But in all the other respects of performance, we're comparable, and in acceleration we are superior.'

Although the cockpit may provide the 'feel' of a fighter, flying the B-1B also means taking into account certain limitations at high altitude – a hangover from the original B-1 design requirements that optimized low-level performance – as 'Utah' points out:

'As far as flying with the stick and the throttle, it's very similar [to the F-15 and F-16]. Again, you're not getting the turn performance you're looking for [in a fighter type]. High-altitude, however, we are what you'd call a "pig in space". We're very energy-limited at high altitude, we have to be cautious about our gross weight, depending on the altitude regime we're flying in. The B-1B was designed as a low-level penetrator, so the engine and the airflow to the engines are designed for that environment... So that's the more challenging aspect of flying the B-1: using your knowledge of the systems and airspace to employ it at high altitude, i.e. extreme envelopes.'

TURNING THE TABLES

Confirming the fact that the 'Bone' is no slouch when it comes to air combat manoeuvring, 'O'Doyle' remembers one particular Red Flag air combat exercise where the B-1B used its acceleration to its advantage:

'We had an adversary – a Red Air F-16 – turning on us, trying to get behind us for a heat-seeking missile shot, and we just pulled the afterburner and basically dusted him – he had no chance of catching us, so we accelerated away... We can really pour the coal to it, especially at lighter weight. Usually at Red Flag we are at a lighter weight and we have an excellent thrust-to-weight ratio. As far as our comparison with fighters in that respect, we're definitely better. And then the other big factor is fuel – we have a lot more gas. On an F-16 you'll pull afterburners for 30 seconds and you'll run out of fuel; it'll really reduce his combat radius.'

While the B-1B achieved initial operational capability in 1986, making it a close contemporary of warplanes such as the F/A-18, its cockpit may appear old-fashioned to a pilot or WSO stepping from an F-15 or F-16, for example. Indeed, 'O'Doyle' describes the B-1B's level of cockpit automation as 'probably about the same as what

ABOVE: A 7th Bomb Wing 'Bone' makes a high-speed flyby during a firepower demonstration, with an aft wing sweep setting selected for the high subsonic regime.

ABOVE LEFT: Under the power of its four afterburning General Electric F101 engines, a B-1B leaves RAF Fairford, England, for a mission in support of Allied Force in 1999. During this operation, a force of just six B-1Bs dropped over 20 per cent of the total ordnance expended by the Coalition.

MAIN PHOTOGRAPH: B-1Bs have also served with the Air National Guard, this four-ship being put up by the 116th Bomb Wing, Georgia ANG. In 2002, the unit was reconfigured as an Air Control Wing.

[MISSION REPORT]

++++++++++++++++++++++++++++++

'BONE' WEAPONS

ABOVE: The most important series of weapons in the B-1B's inventory is currently the JDAM. Here, a weapons loader delivers a GBU-31 JDAM (based on a BLU-109 907kg [2,000lb] penetration bomb) to a waiting 'Bone' prior to an Operation Enduring Freedom mission. The B-1B can carry 24 such weapons.

On entering service in the mid-1980s, the B-1B was intended for the nuclear warfighting scenario – carrying a load of nuclear-armed cruise missiles to attack high-value, well-protected enemy installations. The end of the Cold War saw the 'Bone' give up its nuclear strike role in 1991 and, for a while at least, observers might have considered its value to the Pentagon as limited. However, events in the Middle East and the former Yugoslavia would give the B-1B the chance to prove itself in a post-Cold War environment, while successive stages of a Conventional Munitions Upgrade Program (CMUP) have seen the bomber's weapons options – and flexibility – increase exponentially. After 9/11, the aircraft has further demonstrated its vital function at the heart of US power projection and has steadily deployed a range of new, 'near-precision conventional munitions' over Afghanistan and Iraq. While the B-1B went to war in Operation Allied Force in 1999 carrying payloads made up exclusively of Mk 82 227kg (500lb) 'dumb' bombs, the 'Bone' has since introduced a GPS-guided Joint Direct Attack Munition (JDAM) capability; a range of cluster weapons in the form of the CBU-87 Combined Effects Munition, CBU-89 Gator area denial munition, CBU-97 Sensor Fuzed Weapon and the Wind Corrected Munitions Dispenser (WCMD) family; and the AGM-154 Joint Standoff Weapon (JSOW). The introduction of further new and advanced weaponry continues, together with the integration of a targeting pod.

'Right now in the B-1 we carry all manner of GPS-aided munitions,' explains pilot 'O'Doyle'. 'What we are carrying over there [in Afghanistan] primarily are the 2,000 pound [907kg] GPS-guided weapon – the GBU-31; and the 500 pound [227kg] GPS-guided weapon – the GBU-38. Those are the CAS weapons of choice right now; extremely accurate and fairly easy for us to work with the guys on the ground, who give us the coordinates... We don't carry laser-guided weapons...we just don't have room in the bomb bay, because they have a seeker head on them; we could conceivably carry them, but we don't have the ability to laser-designate targets... That might come eventually. They're also working on improving the number of 500 pound weapons we can carry.'

Meanwhile, 'Utah' describes some of the further weapons systems upgrades currently on the horizon for the 'Bone' fleet: 'We're looking to get a targeting pod for the B-1. This would give us the infrared capability and the electro-optical capability that the fighters have now. Right now we are limited to using our radar to identify targets, and we rely on the JTACs [Joint Terminal Attack Controllers] – the troops on the ground – to give us good coordinates for a call-in. With the targeting pod we're able to visually ID targets that are called to us, to give more accurate targeting, as well as non-traditional surveillance of areas... Really the weapons are staying the same, we're just going to use these sensors to more accurately employ the weapons.'

One new guided weapon that will dramatically improve the B-1B's already impressive combat persistence is the 113kg (250lb) GPS-aided Small Diameter Bomb (SDB). 'It is in the test phase right now,' reports 'Utah'. 'That will be another asset as well, that we can use down the road, as well as the AGM-158 JASSM [Joint Air-to-Surface Standoff Missile] that we're working with now: the stand-off missile [will] give us the capability to remain out of harm's reach, basically. The SDB will be great for the suburban CAS scenario. [It has] a smaller warhead with GPS precision... If we're able to carry SDBs, we can carry up to 96. Typically, we won't carry that many as we can carry mixed loads in the B-1 – that's another key strength of ours, that we have three weapons bays: we can mix weapons on different launchers. We can carry a plethora of weapons based on whatever our air component commander's requirements are.'

MAIN PHOTOGRAPH: Four B-1B Lancers depart their base for another Enduring Freedom mission. The first six months of the operation saw B-1Bs deliver almost 40 per cent of the total Coalition ordnance.

you'd find on a B-52H. [The B-1B] *is not a highly automated aircraft to fly. You do have an autopilot that we use in high-altitude cruise, but you don't fly coupled approaches, you don't fly auto-throttle and things like that, [that] you'll find on, say, the C-17. We can't pull as many g as say an F-15 or F-16, but at the same time we don't have nearly as complex a flight computer as those airplanes do. They're a lot less inherently stable, so…there's a lot more input from the computer side of things for those fighters… In an F-16 the pilot cannot over-g that aircraft – he can't pull more g's than the airframe can take. In the B-1 we don't have that type of stuff. It's a very hands-on aircraft. We fly all of our approach work, all of our low-level stuff we fly hands-on, so I think it's probably comparable in a lot of ways, but it's a little lower-tech than a lot of the current stuff out there… certainly the newer stuff, the C-17, the B-2, are very automated, they have full-colour displays in the cockpit, there's probably a fair amount of ability to let the jet fly things for you. We don't have that ability on the airplane, which is fine with me – but it's great to fly.'*

'SWING WING'

The B-1B's variable geometry is another factor that makes it unique within the current US inventory, and is a feature that 'O'Doyle' describes as *'a cool thing that a lot of jets don't have.'* The wing sweep is also controlled conventionally from the cockpit: *'You've gotta select it. We have a big lever. There are two of them…on the left side of the cockpit [at the commander's seat], and one on the right side. They're interlocked so they move together, but that's how we select it…we control that completely.'*

Considering the B-1B's pedigree as a low-level nuclear penetrator, it has been a major shift that now sees it make its mark in combat as a close air support platform – with operational missions typically flown at medium level. 'Utah' is keen to outline the advantages of the bomber in such a role:

'Most of our [mission] *altitudes are medium-altitude, medium to high, based on the threat environments and employing …JDAMs – you need some altitude for those to work. For the missions we flew over in Southwest Asia, we calculated what altitude we could best employ based on the fuel load and weapon load we had, to be able to turn the jet around and actually hit the target. The missions* [we do] *right now are what we call unopposed close air support, in effect there's no ground threats to worry about, so we have*

a little more free rein as to what we do with the altitudes we fly at, and how we employ the B-1. We typically have flights at slower airspeeds to sustain fuel, but we do have the speed available to support troops in contact situations – troops under fire – or time-sensitive taskings that are passed down from higher headquarters.

'We have longer legs than some of the fighters; we require less refuelling assets … we can loiter unlimited, really. We've had missions as long as 20–21 hours in support of ground troops on call, with air refuelling support, of course. Also, with the four-man crew we are able to divide the duties and share our workload – in a single-seat fighter the guy is only as good for as long as he can perform. With two pilots and two WSOs we can share the duties and take a rest once in a while. So that's definitely an advantage.… Longer times, more weapons payload, and with upgrades coming down the road we'll be able to provide even more support.'

MAIN PHOTOGRAPH: Wings swept forward for efficient high-altitude cruise, a B-1B homes in on a tanker to top up its fuel load over the mountain ranges of Nevada and Utah. The refuelling marks applied to the B-1B's nose are used by the 'boomer' to guide the boom into the receptacle.

BELOW: In the words of one B-1B pilot: 'We have fairly – I won't say old – but somewhat dated technology up front.' While there may be more modern cockpits in the USAF inventory, 'Bone' crew are happy with their working environment, the capabilities of which are enhanced by periodic upgrades.

Flying the AH-64

Brutish and uncompromising, the AH-64 Apache was built during the Cold War to kill tanks and armoured vehicles on a conventional battlefield. Instantly recognizable and with an impressive following in popular culture, the AH-64 is the world's most lethal helicopter gunship.

Gene Garrett, a veteran helicopter pilot who flew UH-1 Huey helicopters in Vietnam, described learning to fly the AH-64 as one of the hardest things he'd ever had to do.

'The Apache is not an easy aircraft to fly, and in fact when I started to fly it a lot of pilots didn't finish the course.'

To hear an experienced helicopter pilot admit this is a real eye-opener to the complex world of Apache flying, particularly since Garrett went on to reveal that many of those pilots who did not complete the course 'were Master Aviators with thousands of flight hours.'

It is certainly not the mechanics of flying the Apache that is more difficult than any other helicopter – using the collective to increase and decrease pitch, and thus ascend or descend; the cyclic stick to effect roll and pitch; and the pedals to counter torque and create yaw. Indeed, flying basic manoeuvres in the daytime and in good weather is less complicated than it would be in most helicopters because the Apache has a responsive and reliable flight control system. Also, the Apache's twin General Electric T700 turboshaft motors are governed by a full-authority digital engine control that means they are self-tuning and require little input from the pilot other than to start and stop them.

The challenge comes instead from operating the Apache as a weapons platform. The sophisticated AH-64 has complex avionics and attack systems that require a tremendous amount of the pilot's mental capacity, despite the fact that the helicopter also carries a co-pilot/gunner (CPG) whose job is to run some of those weapons systems and carry out the attack.

TADS AND PNVS

Two main sensors dominate the Apache's ability to reach out into the battlefield and kill with

MAIN PHOTOGRAPH:
Bristling with weaponry, this AH-64 Apache hangs in the hot, dry air during an Operation Desert Shield sortie.

PILOT'S VERDICT

" Technologically, the Apache is far superior to any other helicopter gunship. There is not a helicopter in the world that can outfight it. "

CW4 Master Aviator (ret.)
Gene Garrett

ABOVE: The Apache was an important part of NATO's Implementation Force (IFOR) in Bosnia and Herzegovina during 1995–1996. Here a US Army AH-64 Apache of the 2nd Squadron, 6th Calvary, lands at Comanche Base, located near Tuzla, as part of the peacekeeping effort.

BELOW: Members of the 102nd Quartermasters Company refuel an AH-64 between missions during Operation Desert Storm in 1991, the closest the Apache has come to fighting in a conventional anti-armour battle. Note the AGM-114 Hellfire anti-tank missiles.

great accuracy and speed, and each competes with the other for the pilot or CPG's attention: The AN/ASQ-170 Target Acquisition and Designation Sight (TADS) and the AN/AAQ-11 Pilot Night Vision Sensor (PNVS).

Between them, these tools enable the AH-64 to fly at low altitude in total darkness and adverse weather, to see ground targets, and to destroy them at stand-off ranges. TADS and PNVS are housed on separate sides of a rotating turret on the nose of the Apache.

TADS, which is the bulky assembly on the underside of the turret, is used to find, identify and target the enemy. Magnets in each cockpit sense an

electrical field created by the crews' special flight helmets, and this lets either the pilot or CPG cue the TADS sensors by simply turning their heads and looking at the target. In doing so, they

bring to bear the TV camera, Infrared (IR) sensor, high power telescope, laser spot tracker, and laser designator/rangefinder that make up TADS.

PNVS, mounted in a small peanut-shaped fairing on the top of the turret, follows exclusively the head movements of the pilot, using the same technology as TADS, and employs an IR sensor to let him see in the dark or in dusty and smoky battlefield conditions.

INTEGRATED SIGHT SYSTEM

This is all simple enough, but where it gets complicated is in the way that the IR video from PNVS and TADS is presented to the crew. Each member wears a special monocle just in front of their right eye, onto which is projected not only the IR video (TADS for the CPG and PNVS for the pilot), but also flight and attack symbology such that found in a jet fighter's heads-up display. The helmet and monocle are known as the Integrated Helmet And Display Sight System (IHAADS).

ABOVE: The United Arab Emirates Air Force is just one of several foreign nations to have purchased the Apache. Only the wealthiest nations can afford to buy and operate it.

FOREIGN OPERATORS

Country	Variant	Number
Egypt	AH-64A, all later upgraded to AH-64D	36
	AH-64D, new	6
Greece	AH-64A	20
	AH-64D	12
Israel	AH-64A, 24 later upgraded to AH-64D	43
	AH-64D, new	9
Japan	AH-64D	60
Kuwait	AH-64D	16
Netherlands	AH-64D	30
Singapore	AH-64D	20
UAE	AH-64A	20
UK	WAH-64D	67

RIGHT: The large cap on the top of the rotor helps identify this Apache as an AH-64D. In fact, it would originally have been identified as an AH-64C: the improved Apache, minus the millimetre-wave Longbow radar.

On top of that, the AH-64A has a separate monitor in each cockpit: it serves as a repeater for TADS in the CPG's front cockpit, and gives the pilot situated behind the CPG a view of what the TADS is seeing. In the newer AH-64D things are even more complex as both crewmembers have the repeater *and* two large multi function displays that can also display a moving map, electronic threat information and so on. Add to all of this the newest Apache's millimetre-wave 'Longbow' fire control radar, and you have yet another attack sensor to bring complete mental saturation one step closer!

PILOT TRAINING

Garrett explained that when he converted to the Apache, new pilots first qualified to fly as the CPG before moving on to the rear cockpit and being cleared as pilot, providing a building-block approach that eased pilots into the Apache as gently as possible. Other building blocks, he said, included, *first training you to fly during the day in VFR* [visual flight rules] *conditions, then later on, under the training hood and using the PNVS at night.*' And it

ABOVE: A Texas Army National Guard private tweaks a 70mm (2.75in) rocket pod at Balad Air Base, Iraq, during Operation Iraqi Freedom. The Folding Fin Aerial Rocket system is an effective anti-personnel weapon that can also be used against lightly armoured targets.

MAIN PHOTOGRAPH: An AH-64A lifts into the hover carrying a standard load for 1991: four AGM-114 Hellfire missiles and a 19-round 70mm (2.75in) FFAR pod on each stub wing.

is the parallax error between where the pilot is sitting and the TADS/PNVS that now makes things difficult: *'All of your visual cues come from six feet [1.8m] in front and two feet [0.6m] down, where the [PNVS] system is located. Even simple manoeuvres, like making a pedal turn around the mast, are very tricky until your mind wraps itself around the concept of your "eyes" being out where the PNVS is at.'*

Now, imagine seeing this bright off-set FLIR image with dancing flight symbology just in front of your your right eye,

while your left eye looks out of the window into the pitch black or scans the cockpit consoles bathed in red light, or tries to read the information presented on one of the multipurpose displays. For those with a dominant right eye, the situation is far less tricky to adjust to than those with a dominant left eye.

MISSION EXECUTION

TADS and the Longbow radar are all geared to putting weapons on target. For the Apache, this means

the 30mm M230 chain gun that can be slaved to follow the pilot and CPG's IHAADS and head movements, or locked-on to a target being tracked by TADS. For other close-in attacks, the Hydra 70 general-purpose unguided 70mm (2.75in) rocket is used, and while the pylons on which the rocket pods are mounted do not traverse in azimuth, they do have some movement in elevation – the pilot can make small changes in pitch during his attack and the pylons will tilt up or down to keep the unguided rockets

ABOVE: In its most lethal anti-armour configuration, the AH-64 can carry up to sixteen AGM-114 Hellfires.

[MISSION REPORT]

+++++++++++++++++++++++++++

APACHE RESCUE

When US Army Chief Warrant Officers Steven Cianfrini and Mark Burrows were shot down in their OH-58D Kiowa scout helicopter over Iraq in May 2007, they hit the ground hard and skidded over an irrigation canal before coming to rest. The pair then managed to scramble free of the aircraft before fire consumed the wreckage.

Taking fire from as many as twenty insurgents just across the field, the two men clambered into the irrigation canal, but it soon became clear that it contained far deeper mud and water than had at first seemed the case. The water came up to their necks, and although Cianfrini thought he might drown as his feet sank deeper into the mud, it proved to be a stroke of luck. Intense withering fire peppered the water and reeds around them, and then an insurgent walked to the lip of the canal bank and peered over, AK-47 assault rifle shouldered and ready to fire. Unable to see the two men, he signalled the rest of his squad to move further down the river bank.

Meanwhile, two AH-64Ds of the 1-227 Attack Reconnaissance Battalion, 1st Cavalry Division, had been vectored to the downed flyers by a Predator drone overhead. The two engaged the insurgents with their 30mm cannons. Next, they came to the rescue of the two Kiowa pilots. One of the Apaches, flown by Chief Warrant Officer Allan Davison, landed next to the canal and the two downed flyers approached. Noticing that Cianfrini was a little worse for wear, the Apache's CPG, Chief Warrant Officer Micah Johnson, dismounted the front cockpit and ushered the filthy wet Kiowa pilot to take his place. He then strapped himself to one of the fuselage hand grips above the stub wing pylon, while the Kiowa co-pilot, Burrows, did the same the other side. Davison lifted-off and flew all four back to the safety of their base.

This impromptu rescue reinforced the Apache's excellent extraction capabilities, as it was actually the second of its

kind in Iraq: the first occurring only a month before when Apaches from 1st Battalion, 36th Combat Aviation Brigade and 2nd Battalion, 12th Combat Aviation Brigade, engaged extremists and saved a critically-wounded soldier, Specialist Jeffrey Jamaleldine, during a firefight. When a dedicated Medical Evacuation helicopter had been not arrived to collect the casualty, the Apaches had stepped in. With Chief Warrant Officer Kevin Purtee at the controls, CPG Chief Warrant Officer Allen Crist took continuous fire as he jumped out and strapped Jamaleldine into his seat. He then took position on the stuff pylon as the helicopter lifted-off.

These kinds of rescues hark back to the days of the Vietnam War, when AH-1 Cobra gunship crews performed similar of daring and rescue, but the technique has been anything but formally endorsed. Today, that has all changed, and all helicopter aviators sent to Iraq and Afghanistan are given hands-on instruction on the correct way of attaching themselves to the hand grips on the Apache's fuselage.

aimed at the target. Typically, though, it will be the anti-armour AGM-114 Hellfire missile that the Apache will employ, using the relative sanctuary that can be found by hovering behind a hill or similar masking feature.

NAP-OF-THE-EARTH FLYING

Getting into and out of the target area unseen and unscathed requires low-flying skills that hug the contours of the terrain, and is called nap-of-the-earth flying (NOE).

'Each mission is planned with the terrain, weather, distance, enemy locations and weapons systems we expect to encounter in mind, and tailored to give us the maximum advantage and flexibility in determining the route and the type of flight. NOE is very intense and wears a pilot out much faster than typical straight and level flight, so we would save it for when it was necessary. Flying with the PNVS is difficult, as I mentioned, but experience with it makes all the difference,' Garrett said, but the PNVS can be essential for completion of the mission, he added. *'Flying PNVS and NOE is about as stressful as it gets. If we had a PNVS failure at night,* [the decision to continue the mission] *would depend the ambient light and the distance to travel. Flying the AH-64 on a dark night with no PNVS and near to the ground is not conducive to your continued good health!'*

LEFT: The metal-bonded rotor blades of the Apache were designed to take significant combat damage and still get the crew home. In recent years the US Army has tasked Boeing with the development of an even better composite blade that features stainless steel leading edges, and offers improved hover and forward flight performance.

BELOW: US Army AH-64D Apache Longbows of the 101st Aviation Battalion sit at sunrise on the flight line at Udaire Airfield, Iraq.

Flying the E-3 Sentry

The role of the E-3 Sentry has traditionally been to provide airborne early warning of air attack and control of fighter aircraft, but has more recently taken on new missions under the banner of ISTAR (Intelligence, Surveillance, Target Acquisition and Reconnaissance).

MAIN PHOTOGRAPH: Britain's Royal Air Force operates seven E-3Ds with the UK designation Sentry AEW.1. The aircraft are pooled between 8 Sqn and 23 Sqn, based at RAF Waddington, Lincolnshire.

These include supporting close air support missions, attacks on time-sensitive targets, and Special Forces operations on the ground.

The E-3s used by the USAF, NATO, France, Saudi Arabia and the United Kingdom all differ in their systems, internal layout and crew roles, as well as in the missions they perform. NATO's E-3As for example had a crew of 17, but this has been reduced to 16 following a major upgrade programme. The normal RAF E-3D crew complement is 18, although up to 30 can be carried on training missions.

The RAF Sentry's cockpit crew consists of two pilots, a navigator and a flight engineer. The mission crew is commanded by the Tactical Director, and includes: three Weapons Controllers; a Fighter Allocator; a Surveillance Controller and two Surveillance Operators; a Datalink Manager, a Communications Operator and an Electronic Support Measures (ESM) Operator. Supporting these, as a sort of airborne IT department, are three Airborne Technicians, one of each being responsible for data, radar and communications.

The basic task of the E-3 is to create and contribute to the Recognised Air Picture (RAP) and Recognised Surface Picture (RSP), made up of inputs from air, land and sea-based radars and sensors in the theatre. The onboard controllers then direct allied aircraft towards their targets and warn them of threats.

BIG WING ON TOP

E-3 pilots will typically learn how to handle a multi-engine aircraft on a small turboprop such as the Beech King Air, before moving to a light jet such as the Hawker Siddeley HS.125 Dominie or the Beech T-1 Jayhawk. Simulators are heavily used for converting pilots onto the E-3, as well as training mission crews. The interior of an E-3 cabin is recreated on the ground and whole missions can be 'flown' using data fed into the system by instructors in another room.

When it comes to flying the actual E-3, says pilot Squadron Leader James Radley of No 8 Squadron RAF, it is much the same as a standard 707 *'with a big wing on top'*, referring to the rotodome. The RAF's E-3D has more power compared to the E-3A. *'We have better performance. Even heavy after aerial refuelling we have the climb performance to get to our best operating heights in the low 30s* [thousands of feet] *whereas the E-3As have to burn some fuel off after refuelling to get to 27–29* [thousand feet]. *On a mission over Afghanistan the E-3A needs to refuel twice and the E-3A only once.'*

FLYING MANUALLY

'The rotodome is lift/drag neutral in level flight – they say. If you move away from level flight it will have an effect. The aircraft is quite reluctant to roll until 40 degrees angle of bank, then it affects the roll rate quite strongly. There are high break-out forces then the weight exacerbates the roll. Like all 707s, the only powered flight control surface is

RIGHT: Although the main cabin is full of sophisticated avionics, the cockpit instrumentation of the E-3 is very similar to that of the Boeing 707 airliner on which it is based, an aircraft which was designed in the 1950s.

[MISSION REPORT]
++++++++++++++++++++++++++++

E-3D MISSIONS

In peacetime, missions are a mixture of supporting exercises and training for other units, and training for the Sentry crews themselves. Flight Lieutenant Ben Russell of the RAF's No 23 Squadron explains:

'A typical mission consists of: take-off – on station – off station – potential for some air-to-air refuelling – PMRP [Post Mission Rectification Process] – and then any pilot training. Off station is when we are no longer declared to the CAOC [Combined Air Operations Centre] and are under normal air traffic control. We tend to do practise emergencies every other mission, as long as there's no weather issue or time constraint about getting back. Safety of the aircraft is paramount, so we won't do it if there's any doubt at all about recovering to base. 'We have 72 hours maximum duration with air-to-air refuelling. The limitation is crew

ABOVE: As part of Operation Telic, RAF E-3s flew many missions over Iraq during the 2003 war, based at airfields on the Persian Gulf.

fatigue so you need to have augmented crews. There are six crew rest bunks down the back. It could happen if we needed it to – if, for example, the recovery airfield is in extremis, in danger, in wartime.

One of the major issues we have is pilot currency, because [the pilots mainly] take off, fly around in an orbit and land. We either have dedicated pilot training sorties or wind up doing several approaches at the end of a mission. A lot of our extra flying time is pilot training, including aerial refuelling.'

BELOW: Distinctive features of the E-3D include the wingtip ESM pods, large CFM-56 engines and refuelling probe.

the rudder, so it's quite heavy on the controls. The autopilot is quite old-fashioned, so everywhere except the cruise we tend to fly it manually. There is no flight management system and no altitude capture. Modern navigation equipment such as dual GPS and INS feeds into an analogue autopilot. Colour displays were added since purchase, mainly because the supply of analogue instruments had dried up. The new displays just represent the old instruments and don't add any new functions.

'We still have a Flight Engineer because of the complexity of the systems. Engineering him out of the loop would require a replacement front end [to the aircraft]. The Navigator would be easier to engineer out. He "owns" the GPS and INS and produces all the waypoints and cross-checks with radio aids. If we were to lose navigators overnight we have no form of picture display of where we are. The other argument is that he can provide a tactical link with the mission crew. He can liaise with the Comms Manager to organize orbits. The Captain

also does this – liaising with the TD [Tactical Director] – making sure [the flightpath] is safe and makes the most effective use of the sensors. On operations we would ideally fly a figure-of-eight with most turns being over the [ground] threat. In the UK we tend to fly in a circle. ESM benefits from being on a straight leg such as on a racetrack or figure eight pattern.'

In recent years, operations have much more involved working with ground units, performing tasks such as close air support and time-sensitive targeting. These increasingly require crossing the front line. Flying has had to be much more tactical, moving away from the traditional stand-off radar platform role 200–300 miles (320–480km) away.

Radley continues: 'We now go to the orbit point when the fighters are marshalling. When the fighters push [towards the target] we go in with them. It all depends on the threat. We have been fortunate that Iran and Afghanistan have no air threat. We try and avoid making contrails as much as possible. Some days the contrails start at 28,000 feet [8,500m] and we sometimes have to compromise.

It comes back to risk management, balancing the task versus the threat.'

The E-3D currently has no anti-missile defence system, and the biggest threat today in a theatre like Afghanistan is from man-portable surface-to-air missiles, which could reach the E-3's altitude if fired from a mountaintop. Although RAF E-3 crews would like a defensive electronics system, there is currently no money budgeted for this. NATO aircraft, however will soon receive a system called Large Aircraft Infrared Counter Measures, which uses sensors and a laser to detect and destroy enemy missiles.

CHALLENGING

On piloting the E-3 versus other large RAF aircraft, Radley says, *'We do things slightly differently to the transport world and are qualified to fly in either* [left or right] *seat. There is not the same huge transition from one seat to the other. One difference is that the nosewheel steering control is only on the left hand side. It's a challenging aircraft to fly because it's old fashioned. It's the only RAF aircraft that does*

both types of aerial refuelling [boom and hose-and-drogue]. *Being captain is a big man-management challenge, but also great fun taking that many people away on trips.'*

Squadron Leader Lynn Johnson, a Standards Officer for No 8 Squadron, describes what it's like in the main cabin: *'Sitting down the back during refuelling, particularly right at the back, you do feel the aircraft snaking from side to side. Unless you see the pilots in the cockpit,*

you don't realise how physical it is, moving the control wheel back and forth to get the aircraft in position. I don't even want to think about night refuelling, when you have two large aircraft so close together and you can see – what outside?'

The mission crew all have specialist roles, which differ in some ways from those assigned to Sentry crews in other air forces. *'My one job encompasses two jobs on a US aircraft,'* says Weapons Controller Ben Russell. Tactical Director Sqn

ABOVE: The E-3 has similar flying characteristics to the 707 airliner, but landing can be more difficult in a crosswind due to the effect of the rotodome.

BELOW: The USAF operates 33 E-3B and C aircraft. One was lost in a crash in Alaska in 1995.

out who to talk to, including the ground crew and the captain, to make it all happen. When faced with decisions in the air – is this a decision that I have to make in ten seconds or an hour? If it's an hour, don't make it in ten seconds. It's the least button-pushing of all the jobs [on board]. If you are pushing a lot of buttons you are doing it wrong. What you must keep in mind at all times is the mission tasking.

'We work with everyone – Army, Navy, Special Forces, etc, and partly get into the political decision-making as well. Very often the TD is talking to the general on the ground at the HQ. He can tell us the objective but some things he has to leave to us to prioritize. Sometimes the [Weapons or Fighter] Controller has to step back. In a one-versus-one engagement he can give everyone all the info they need, but in a multi-versus-multi he has to step back and just make sure everyone knows the basics and let them get on with it.'

BELOW: The APY-2 radar is the heart of the current E-3 models. It rotates at a speed of six revolutions per minute.

ABOVE: The E-3D can be refuelled by the probe-and-drogue method or using the USAF boom-and-receptacle method. The refuelling door for the latter can be seen on the crown of the fuselage.

BELOW: The E-3 can cover gaps in land-based radar coverage. Three E-3s by themselves can provide radar cover over the whole of western Europe.

Ldr Ian Green says: 'The fighters have their training objectives. In peacetime it's almost as if they are controlling us. On operations it turns around and we are definitely controlling them.'

DECISION-MAKING ROLE

Tactical Director Flt Lt Hamish Montgomerie says: 'Tactical Director is an executive position in the true sense of the word. The busier it gets, the more hands off it should be, it's not something you can do by rote. The job is to tie all of the ends together, to work

Weapons Controller Flight Lieutenant Ben Russell of No 23 Squadron describes his mission: *'The Weapons Controller is the interface between the E-3 and all the assets it is controlling. He takes the Recognised Air Picture and calls out things in reference to "Bullseye" [an agreed reference point]. Targets are classified as unknown, friendly or hostile. If you send a fighter sweep towards unknowns it could be a feint and you lose coverage of your strike package. You must decide the best course of action within the rules as set out by the mission commander.'*

INTENSE ENVIRONMENT

Fighter Controller Sergeant Stu Rock adds that in his job, *'We can go from tracking maybe four aircraft fighting each other to an "intense weapons environment" over central Europe following hundreds of tracks.'*

Ben Russell continues: *'For a time-sensitive target, we get a nine-line brief passed from the CAOC (Combined Air Operations Centre), then you choose what assets to use, what platforms, what weapons. We keep an eye on missile ranges and engagement zones, all fuel and weapons states and shots fired. Between the time the first fighter aircraft checks on station and the last one checks off 2–3 hours later, you are mentally exhausted. You don't know where the time's gone at all.'*

[MISSION REPORT]
+++

'AIRBORNE I.T. DEPARTMENT'

Keeping all of the sophisticated communications equipment and electronics operating correctly is not something that can be left to maintenance teams on the ground when a whole battle can depend on the air picture and the information passed to friendly forces.

Chief Technician David Smith is one of three onboard an E-3D as part of the mission crew. They each have different specializations within the Air Technician (AT) rank – Radar AT, Communications AT and Computer and Display AT. The latter does the screens and the software, the Radar Technician does the radar and the Comms Technician works side by side with the Comms Operator.

'There is no crossover between them and each will stay on that specification for a five-year standard tour on the E-3, although may retrain afterwards for a different discipline,' Smith says. As for the E-3's communications equipment, *'the radios are quite old by today's technology. New ones have been needed in some cases and others changed for ones that work better. There are slightly different [electronic] fits within the [E-3D] fleet. It's just a matter of remembering which aircraft you are on, nothing complex. A common misconception is that we break open radios and carry lots of spares. There's quite a lot of redundancy and there are ways to change the systems around. It's not all about opening cabinets and swapping boxes in and out. I've never had to do that in the air.'*

The last phase of a Sentry flight is the Post-Mission Rectification

ABOVE: Keeping the fighter controllers working and maintaining a continuous view of the battlespace is an important job aboard the E-3.

Period (PMRP). *'All the systems are handed back to us [technicians] for additional fault-finding. Our actual job is to go out first and prep the aircraft before it is powered up. We confirm that the cooling system is up and running and then apply power to all the systems, including the main computer and radar, then hand it to the crew for the mission. From then until the PRMP, the computer and radar technicians won't be doing a huge lot unless things break down. The Comms Technician does more – retuning radios and rejigging the comms system. He is also responsible for the Link 16 JTIDS datalink. The Communications Operator is responsible for the Link 11.'*

COMFORTABLE ENVIRONMENT

'The E-3 is a great environment to work in. The crew camaraderie is really good. It's a very nice way to fly – very comfortable. It's not an aircraft that makes you air sick, not at the altitudes we fly at. You could be in a submarine for all you'd know.

'The radar generates an awful lot of RF [radio frequency] radiation. They can run it on the ground, but it generates a huge amount of heat, so cooling considerations mean there are very tight restrictions on ground running. It's best to test it in the environment it was designed for.

'The radios cover all the major frequency bandwidths and satellite communications. The transmitting aerials tend to be at one end of the airframe and receivers at the other to avoid breakthrough [of transmissions into reception].'

Summing up the Sentry compared to its predecessor, Smith concludes: *'It's a lot more than just an AEW platform. As far as the RAF goes, it was a quantum leap from the old Shackleton, God bless it.'*

Flying the Su-27

Ever since its public debut in the late 1980s, the carefree handling of the Su-27 and its derivatives has astonished Western observers, including seasoned fighter pilots.

BELOW: The cockpit of the baseline Su-27 features 1970s technology, with dial-type instruments rather than multi-function display screens.

PILOT'S VERDICT

"It's like flying a dream."

Vikram Gaur
Wing Commander
Indian Air Force

The aerodynamic qualities of those early aircraft has been enhanced by extra control surfaces, thrust-vectoring engines and modern weapons and systems on the latest models, many of which are finding homes with export customers, particularly in the Far East.

The ability to beat a notional 'evolved Flanker' has become the yardstick by which Western fighter manufacturers judge the capabilities of their designs. The operation or potential acquisition of Su-27 variants by an enemy or potentially unfriendly nation is regularly used by politicians and defence chiefs as a means of justifying purchase or extra development of modern fighters.

The commercial debut of the Su-27 was at the 1989 Paris Air Show at Le Bourget. Not only was the aircraft new to the public and the press, but several of its manoeuvres were demonstrated for the first time. One in particular was named 'Pugachev's Cobra' after Sukhoi test pilot Viktor Pugachev. Performing the Cobra involves pulling back on the stick until the nose goes up to and then beyond the vertical, while the aircraft continues forward at a constant altitude. Pugachev created the Cobra while developing a display routine in the run-up to the show, the first at which Sukhoi participated. He says that the most difficult aspect was *'to execute all this at a low altitude, because right up to then I had been executing the figure at high altitudes. For two months we were actively doing the Cobra* [until] *28 April 1989, when I executed this regime over the airfield in Zhukovsky for the first time before the general designer and our whole Sukhoi team.'*

UNIQUE MANOEUVRES

British Harrier test pilot John Farley was one of those who was deeply impressed by the Su-27 at Le Bourget, not least by its horizontal turning circle.

'I will never forget the first display flight of the Su-27 in Paris. Viktor Pugachev was turning his Su-27 360 degrees in ten seconds, the average rate of turn was 36 degrees a second. At that time we could only hope that our next-generation fighter could achieve 25 degrees a second. This is the kind of speed at which a pilot should be able to turn his plane to have the entire weapons suite ready for an attack. If we imagine that our new plane encountered an Su-27 in combat, after ten seconds all it

MAIN PHOTOGRAPH: The size, power and noise of a Flanker display never fails to impress both public and aviation professionals alike.

ABOVE: India's initial Su-30MKs, distinguishable by their blue colour scheme, were little more than refurbished Su-27UB trainers and suitable only for air superiority missions.

BELOW: The Su-37 prototype with thrust-vectoring nozzles was displayed in a sand-brown splinter camouflage in 1995.

the angle of attack (AoA) they can sustain for more than a moment or two, but the Su-27 family seems heedless of these restrictions.

Some observers question the utility of manoeuvres that rapidly bleed off energy, saying that they leave the Flanker in a sitting duck position. Others argue that the ability to point the nose, and thus the weapons, at the enemy across the circle of a dogfight (whether horizontal or vertical) is invaluable, even if only achieved momentarily. At longer ranges, an apparent stop in forward motion by a targeted aircraft can be enough to break the lock of pulse-Doppler airborne radars and defeat certain missiles.

THRUST-VECTORING

Early generation Su-27s were essentially a 1970s design. Since then, Sukhoi has exploited advances in engine technology, aerodynamics and flight control systems to create even more manoeuvrable 'Flankers', a remarkable achievement considering the aircraft was and remains one of the largest and heaviest fighter aircraft ever built.

The Su-30MKI, MKK and other 'Super Flanker' variants ,whose engine thrust can be vectored by special nozzles on the jet exhausts, can remain controllable at sustained angles of attack over 60 degrees and

transient AoA of as much as 180 degrees, recovering safely to normal flight.

Allied with this are great advances in avionics and combat systems. Using helmet-mounted sights and both forward and rearward radars, the crew can theoretically track and engage a threat coming from any aspect. This includes enemy missiles, which, if certain claims are to be believed, can be tracked by the NIIP N011M Bars ('Panther') pulse-Doppler phased-array radar and destroyed by a counter-shot of an R-77 'Amraamski' missile at medium range or evaded by out-of-plane manoeuvres using thrust-vectoring at close range. The N011M radar can theoretically track up to 15 targets simultaneously. As well as the main dish in the massive forward radome, there is a small rear facing radar installed in the tailcone to give unparalled rear aspect warning capability and situational awareness in a dogfight.

Indian Air Force Su-30MKI pilot Squadron Leader P. Lall had this to say about the new possibilities of TVC:

'With regard to thrust-vectoring, you can never say that you have learned it all.' He disagrees that thrust-vectoring is all very well for airshows but has limited combat use. *'Thrust-vectoring has phenomenal combat utility, but of course it has to be tempered by the type of combat you are engaged in. It is a good aid when used intelligently.'*

John Farley sums up the advantages of super manoeuvrability as offered by the Sukhoi 'Flankers', at least in particular circumstances:

'If your only wish is to win in every guns dogfight that you find yourself in, then you do need extremely good agility, aerodynamic departure resistance, an ability to disconnect the flight path vector from the attitude of the aircraft – which makes it harder for the enemy to anticipate what you are up to and so to plan their tactics – and either a lot of fuel or a low fuel consumption at full throttle so that you will not be the first to break out of the scrap.

would be able to do is to lower the gear and land, if it was lucky.'

Some of the more spectacular manoeuvres such as tailslides and the Cobra are not especially hard to enter for a modern combat aircraft, but to exit them while remaining in control is the tricky part. The secret appears to be in part the ability of the Lyulka AL-31F turbofan engines, with their large, widely-spaced intakes, to absorb the rapid changes in volume and direction of airflow without causing compressor stalls. Most Western engines are limited in

In those circumstances a suitably skilled pilot (most important) with a Harrier or a thrust-vectoring variant of the Su-27/Su-30 family should not get shot down and may even shoot the other guy down.'

BVR AND STEALTH

Of course, with its powerful radar and battery of missiles, the Flanker is just as effective at beyond-visual-range (BVR) combat. The leaked results of classified simulations conducted by the USAF show that in a notional encounter between an F-15 and an Su-30, a well-trained and sneaky Flanker pilot could use thrust-vectoring and the limitations of the F-15's radar to get into a position to fire off two missiles and escape before the Eagle pilot could respond.

One thing the Flanker lacks compared to competitors such as the F-22, and to a lesser degree, the Typhoon, is stealth, having a large radar cross section (RCS). This increases detection range, allowing a potential adversary to acquire, target and launch against the Sukhoi before its own sensors detect its opponent. Some refinements such as reshaped intakes and the use of radar-absorbent material (RAM) in certain areas have helped reduce the RCS of some Flankers, notably the Chinese two-seat version, the J-11B. Reports that an Su-27 has been used in Russia as a testbed for a type of 'plasma stealth' using a generator of ionized gases remain unproven.

ABOVE: This Su-30MKI wears special markings to commemorate the 75th Anniversary of the Indian Air Force in 2007.

[MISSION REPORT]
++++++++++++++++++++++++++
SU-30 MK1 CONTROL SYSTEMS

ABOVE: Vapour can be seen streaming from the canard foreplanes of this Su-30 as they work to pull it into a tight turn.

LEFT: When at rest, the thrust-vectoring nozzles of the Su-30MKI droop downwards. They can swivel in the same direction in the horizontal axis and together or in opposition in the vertical axis.

Unlike the Harrier, with its separate nozzle control lever, the Su-30MKI has a conventional throttle and stick control system. TVC is initiated by flicking a switch to the pilot's right, which engages the full capability of the quadruple-redundant fly-by-wire flight control system. The FCS computers determine the mix and degree of aerodynamic surface (flaperons, tailplane, canards) and nozzle deflection to achieve the manoeuvre desired by the pilot. No individual control input is needed to move the canards or nozzles. Like the Typhoon, the Su-30MKI has an incredible climb rate and can be at several thousand feet altitude well inside the airfield boundary. With its wing, canard foreplane and large tailplane, the Su-30MKI has enormous lifting capability and control authority even without considering the TVC nozzles. This three-surface configuration has sometimes been called a 'triplane' layout.

In the 1990s, Sukhoi test pilot Yevgeny Frolov added some new manoeuvres to the Flanker's repertoire, using the first model to be equipped with TVC, the Su-37 demonstrator, which was displayed at Farnborough and other trade shows. Frolov said the Cobra manoeuvre was really quite easy to perform. 'You just push a button and pull back on the stick. The fly-by-wire is very responsive.' His new party trick was the 'Kulbit' (circle). This begins like the Cobra, but instead of letting the nose drop forward after a few seconds beyond the vertical, it is rotated backwards to complete a full somersault with little loss of height. The single-seat Su-37 did not sell on the export market, but led directly to the development of the two-seat canard-equipped Su-35 and on to the Su-30MKI for India and related versions for China and Malaysia.

ABOVE: A standard Su-27 fighter in landing configuration shows off its large ventral airbrake. The full-span leading-edge flaps can also be seen.

The current export Flankers differ from the baseline Su-27 in many ways, not least of which are that the most sophisticated versions are multi-role two-seat Su-30s. The differences from the single-seat interceptor that was the Su-27 and dual-control Su-27UB trainer warranted a different designation. With the Russian Air Force buying no new fighter designs during the 1990s, it fell to the Indian Air Force to be the first air arm in the world to induct a non-VTOL fighter with thrust-vectoring control (TVC) into service. On the Indian Su-30MKI and Malaysian MKK, the engine exhaust nozzles of the AL-31FP turbofans can vector in two planes. Each can be directed horizontally 32 degrees and 15 degrees up or down in the vertical plane. Directing one nozzle up and the other down causes a 'corkscrew' effect that a conventional opponent cannot match.

NEXT GENERATION

Internally, the Su-30MKI is a generation or more ahead of the Su-27 as fielded by Russia and most export users, which for the most part rely on 1980s Soviet technology and conventional dial instruments.

'We have multi-functional displays, it's almost a glass cockpit as far as we are concerned,' says Squadron Leader Lall. 'We use the conventional instruments for standby only.' As regards the MKI versus the initial IAF Flanker version, he adds: 'The Su-30MK has conventional nozzles. The nozzles are just one part of [the advantage of the MKI]. The major difference lies just in the confidence in the equipment we have on board. The electronic equipment is quite a bit different and compared to the Su-30MK is really modern, it is really state of the art.'

It has been said that it's easier for a pilot to transition from the MiG-29 to the Su-30 than the Su-30 to the MKI because it represents such a jump in technology. 'We do not need to learn Russian to operate this aeroplane. The Su-30MKI has a lot of components from many countries. Many of the avionics are not Russian, but the commonality between them is English,' says Lall.

Non-Russian equipment in the MKI includes a number of French Thales Avionics components, including the six colour LCD multi-function displays in the two cockpits, and the holographic HUD. An Indian-designed Identification Friend or Foe (IFF) transponder is integrated with the radar and weapons control system, Indian mission computers and display processors, and RWR. Much else is sourced from Israel including the Elta 8222 jamming pod, and the Rafael Litening target designator pod.

Speaking of the aerodynamics and systems of the MKI,

[MISSION REPORT]
+++++++++++++++++++++++++
FLANKER OPERATORS

SUKHOI 'FLANKER' CUSTOMERS

SOVIET/RUSSIAN AIR FORCES:
Approximately 680 Su-27s delivered and 400 still in service. Upgrades planned.

OTHER CIS MEMBER STATES:
Belarus c.25
Ukraine c.65
Kazakhstan c.42
Uzbekistan 25

ANGOLA:
8 Su-27s

PEOPLE'S REPUBLIC OF CHINA:
48 Su-27s, c.200 to be licence-manufactured by Shenyang as the J-11; 78 Su-30MKK; 48 Su-33 for the Navy on order

ETHIOPIA:
Operated 10 Su-27s

INDIA:
8 Su-30K, 10 Su-30MK and 50 Su-30MKI supplied by

Russia and 150 being built under licence by Hindustan Aeronautics

INDONESIA:
2 Su-27SK and 2 Su-30MK with further orders expected

MALAYSIA:
18 Su-30MKM with thrust vectoring on order

USA:
believed to operate at least two Su-27s for evaluation purposes

ABOVE: China has acquired a large fleet of Flankers and is building the type under licence. The two-seat trainer version is known as the J-11B in PLAAF service.

VENEZUELA:
24 Su-30MKV2

VIETNAM:
12 Su-27SK with 24 more on order

LEFT: The Su-33 supplies air defence for Russia's only fleet carrier, the *Admiral Kuznetsov.* Here an Su-33 makes a hook-up pass during carrier suitability trials.

well trained and given adequate flying hours, the same cannot be said for most Russian and CIS pilots over recent years. The outcome of a notional dogfight between an F-15 and an Su-27 or -30 would depend as much on pilot training and skill as on the quality of the equipment.

The Sukhoi demands a much higher workload of the pilot to get the best of his or her systems in the few seconds that mean the difference between life or death in air combat. On the other hand, some of the features of the latest Flankers, such as TVC, helmet-mounted sights, infrared detection and tail radar are the envy of pilots flying the majority of Western fighters such as the F-16, F/A-18 and Mirage 2000. The increasing proliferation of 'evolved Flankers' does provide some justification for the F-22, which despite its enormous price tag, (all else being equal) beats even the latest Su-30 models in every respect, at least on paper.

BELOW: The primary armament of current Flankers is the Vympel R-77 (AA-10 'Adder') medium-range AAM. It is Russia's equivalent of the AIM-120 and sometimes called 'AMRAAMSKI', although very different in design.

another Indian pilot, Wing Commander Vikram Gaur says: *'It is like flying a dream.'* Gaur, who previously flew the MiG-21 and Mirage 2000, says, *'The aircraft is an amalgamation of all the qualities of the MiG and Mirage. I can't choose between them,'* he added. *'It's like choosing between your children. The MiG-21 demands a lot of your flying skills and the Mirage 2000 teaches you system handling. The Su-30MKI requires both.'*

TWO-SEAT FIGHTER

The Indians are coming to grips with operating their first two-seat fighter aircraft, moving towards the pilot and weapons systems operator (WSO) concept used by air forces such as the RAF and USAF.

'The Su-30 is operated either with two pilots or a pilot and a Weapons Systems Operator. It's basically the same concept as the Tornado F.3.' Says Lall. *' There are some differences, however, as the IAF has limited experience with two-seat multi-role aircraft. Currently, the IAF is putting its junior pilots new to the squadron in the back seats to work the*

radars and run the mission. They spend a year in the back seat before becoming front seat pilots.

'The RAF WSO programme has been established for a very long time, but we are just establishing ours. It will take some years to reach the same state as the RAF. We have some pilots who have just come from ab initio *training flying the MKI who have not come from another combat type. Otherwise we have a mixture of pilots from different fleets – we don't really believe in the Indian Air Force in selecting MKI pilots from a particular fleet. We have a mixture of Jaguar, MiG-29 and Mirage 2000 pilots. Almost all the fleets have some representation.'*

While the Indian pilots are

BELOW: An Su-27 uses its dual cruciform braking parachutes to slow down after landing.

Flying the MiG-29 Fulcrum

Appearances of the MiG-29 'Fulcrum' at international air shows from the late 1980s onwards impressed western civilian and military observers alike. In contrast to previous Soviet fighters, which were designed for speed and climb performance while under strict ground control, the MiG-29 and Sukhoi Su-27 designs emphasised manoeuvrability and presented the pilot with the information with which he could make his own decisions in combat.

Nonetheless, the airshow displays' tight turns, tailslides and 'Cobras' performed by experienced test pilots gave little indication of how these new fighters would perform in real world combat in the hands of average squadron pilots.

The aftermath of the fall of the Berlin Wall put the MiG-29 in the hands of Nato air forces, initially the united Germany's Luftwaffe. Nato itself soon expanded to incorporate Fulcrum operators in the Czech Republic, Slovakia, Hungary and Poland, so the secrets of at least the early model Fulcrums, hereafter referred to as MiG-29As, were soon revealed to the west.

In time, western pilots, now well acquainted with its strengths and weaknesses encountered it over the former Yugoslavia and Iraq and in every combat engagement to date have emerged victorious, somewhat denting its reputation.

Actual documented combat victories for the MiG-29 are few, but have most recently included an unmanned Georgian drone. A notorious incident in the mid-1990s saw unarmed light aircraft shot down by the Cuban air force.

IN THE COCKPIT

Although the MiG-29A's cockpit, with its dial instruments and single CRT display screen, were at least half a generation behind contemporary western fighters, the MiG-29 had some innovations that helped counter this disadvantage. A helmet-mounted sight (HMS) was a standard feature on the MiG-29 before it was widely adopted in the west. In fact it was not until 2003 that the US Air Force and Navy introduced an equivalent system. The MiG's HMS allowed the pilot to cue his missiles to a target 45° either side of the aircraft's heading, giving a significant advantage in a close-in dogfight. The HMS can be used to designate visually-acquired targets for the radar, IRST and the IR seekers on the missiles.

The early model MiG-29's cockpit is primitive by modern standards, owing more to the previous generation of MiGs like the MiG-21 and -23 than western contemporaries such as the F-16 and F/A-18. The MiG-29A's instrument panel featured only one small monochrome radar display screen, rather than the multi-function displays (MFDs) of the

LEFT: The MiG-29A's cockpit panel is old-fashioned by today's standards, with traditional 'clockwork' instruments and individual warning lights for each aircraft system.

MAIN PHOTOGRAPH: This shot of a MiG-29SM clearly shows one of the 'Fulcrum's unique features, the intake shutters that close when the aircraft is on the ground, protecting the low-slung engines from foreign objects sucked up from the airfield surface.

PILOT'S VERDICT

❝❝Against the F-16 at close range, I think we have the advantage. ❞❞

Captain Peter Baca
MiG-29AS pilot
Slovak Air Force

ABOVE: The two-seat MiG-29UB 'Fulcrum-B' lacks radar but has a short range air-to-air combat capability using the infra-red search-and-track (IRST) system and the R-73 (AA-11 'Archer' missile.

F-16A and F/A-18A. The Hands on Throttle and Stick (HoTaS) controls have limited functions in comparison with their Western counterparts.

During the life of the MiG-29 design, various cockpit upgrades have been proposed and implemented to bring the systems up to modern standards and in some cases make them Nato compatible. On the MiG-29M, the HoTaS system was improved, and two monochrome CRT-type displays installed. There were several MiG-29S programmes, dating from 1985 onwards, that offered improved radar and avionics. The MiG-29SD is believed to have been the basis for Malaysia's MiG-29Ns with a single LCD screen added to the cockpit.

The MiG-29SMT, which came along later, introduced two flat-screen 15x20cm (6 x 8in) colour LCD panels in place of the two CRTs, but also added another couple of CRTs. The HoTaS system was further improved, and an advanced navigation system was installed.

In all cases, the he single-seater Fulcrums had better visibility to the front, above and and sides than their Soviet predecessors, although the rear view was poorer than modern western types. The two-seat trainer versions have a low-profile canopy and require a periscope to give a forward view to the instructor in the rear seat. This is usually deployed during take-off and landing.

One Dutch F-16 pilot who was able to fly the MiG-29 in a squadron exchange with the Hungarian Air Force praised the MiG's turn rate, which he said was comparable with the F-16's, but criticised its cockpit layout, which had poorly placed switches and a view that was very restricted beyond the '3-9' line (i.e. behind the pilot's shoulder line). The MiG's endurance was low, and keeping it in a dogfight beyond five minutes was enough to use up its fuel, but he cautioned that if you got low and slow with a MiG-29, *'it would kick your ass.'*

THE MANUFACTURERS' VIEWS

Vladimir Barkovsky, Deputy Director General of Russian Aircraft company (RAC) MiG,

[MISSION REPORT]
+++++++++++++++++++++++++++++++++
UNIQUE FEATURES

The basic aerodynamics are essentially the same in all production MiG-29s, the most major variations coming with the canard-equipped MiG-35 and the MiG-29 OVT with thrust-vectoring engines, which have yet to see service. The wing and fuselage are integrated to create an overall aerofoil shape, giving considerable lift, particularly at high angles of attack.

In normal operation the thrust-to-weight ratio of a MiG-29A was usually greater than one, enabling high velocities, high rates of acceleration and high turn rates. The wing has leading edge flaps, trailing edge slotted flaps and ailerons. The tail surfaces include small inset rudders on each vertical fin and large tailerons that give both pitch and roll control.

One of the unique features of the Fulcrum is its intake guard system. When weight is on the landing gear, doors close to prevent objects being sucked into the low-slung intakes. Airflow enters the engines through louvres on top of the intake trunks instead. The transition between the different modes is said to be unnoticeable. The Klimov RD-33's variable inlet ramps and variable stator vanes on the first two stages of the high speed compressor allow optimum engine performance over a wide part of the flight envelope.

In common with all recent Russian fighter and attack aircraft, the MiG-29 is fitted with a rocket-powered Zvezda K-36 ejection system, which provides zero-zero capability. This has proved effective at low level and low speed as demonstrated at several international air shows.

ABOVE: With folding wings and tailplanes and an arrestor hook, the MiG-29KUB is designed for carrier operations, but is outwardly similar to the land-based versions. Training is its primary role, but the KUB can also perform the same combat missions as the single-seat MiG-29K.

the successor to the old Mikoyan-Gurevich design bureau, described the MiG-29's strengths at the 2008 Farnborough Air Show:
'The basic MiG-29 can be thought of as a soldier. Our trials prove that the aircraft can live for 40 years and 4,000 flying hours. We analysed battle damage found on aircraft used in North Africa and we can say that the MiG-29 can handle very heavy battle damage.

'The ex-Warsaw Pact nations rejected all sorts of ex-Soviet weapons but kept MiG-29s. They are making upgrades and taking decisions that will keep them in service until 2015–2020.'

The MiG-29SMT was the first production version to feature fly-by-wire controls, all previous models having conventional systems. Speaking in London in 2008, Mikhail Pogosyan, the General Director of MiG's arch-rival Sukhoi, took a dig at MiG's caution after describing the novel features of the Su-27, which had fly-by-wire from the outset.
'...meanwhile...,' he told an audience from the Royal Aeronautical Society *'...the other famous Soviet fighter design bureau decided to keep mechanical control systems in their contemporary fighter because they decided that fly-by-wire was too risky in engineering terms.'*

Others would say that achieving the level of manoeuvrability that the MiG-29 demonstrates with hydraulic controls actually demonstrates a considerable achievement, particularly when it can hold its own against the FBW F-16.

FULCRUM IN COMBAT
In the lead up to the 1991 Gulf War, Iraq's handful of MiG-29s

were regarded as the most formidable adversaries in Saddam Hussein's large air force. When it came to actual combat in Operation Desert Storm in January and February, the MiG-29 proved no match for the USAF's F-15C Eagles, which destroyed six – five of them with AIM-7 Sparrow missiles and one without firing a shot. In one of the few manoeuvering fights of the war, an F-15 flown by Captain Cesar A. Rodriguez encountered an Iraqi MiG-29 at close range at 2,500m (8,000ft).

'I had to get a visual ID on him,' Rodriguez said. *'It turned into a single circle type of fight.'* As is normal in such cases, the two aircraft descended as they turned, reaching about 100m (330ft) above the desert when the MiG pilot made a fatal mistake, rolling over and pulling a 'split-S' manoeuvre in an attempt to escape. Instead he

flew straight into the ground.

In the Kosovo conflict in 1999, the air force of the then Serbia and Montenegro was able to put up only a token response to the onslaught of Nato airpower employed in Operation Allied Force. Serbian fighters may have flown as few as 11 sorties during the bombing campaign, although the use of realistic airfield decoys, including model MiG-29s, convinced Nato that there were more fighters available than was really the

ABOVE: The MiG-29M2 is a fully combat-capable two-seat version, being marketed as the MRCA (multi-role combat aircraft).

BELOW: Western air forces have had many opportunities to exercise with the MiG-29s of the new Nato nations. F-16s of the Illinois Air National Guard went to Poland in 2005 for exercise Sentry White Falcon to fly with Poland's MiG-29As.

ABOVE: Poland supplemented its MiG-29s with aircraft from the Czech Republic and Germany when these nations retired their own 'Fulcrum's.

BELOW: The MiG-29K has been sold to India for use on the ex-Russian carrier *Admiral Gorshkov*, now known as INS *Vikramaditya*.

case, and bombs were wasted on wooden replicas. Battling unserviceable weapons, radar warning and navigation systems as well as the enemy, three of the five MiG-29s that took off on 24 March, the first night of the war, were shot down, one of them by a Dutch F-16, and one was badly damaged. One MiG-29 was the victim of now Lt Colonel Cesar Rodriguez,

one of the few pilots to score victories in jets in two separate wars. One part of the MiG-29s worked well, each of the shot-down pilots being able to escape death with his K-36 seat.

Two days later, one pilot's luck ran out when his MiG-29 was one of two to be brought down by AIM-120s fired by F-15s and he did not eject. Two more MiG-29s and another pilot were lost in aerial combat before the war's end. Four others were destroyed on the ground and one crashed on a test flight.

In 2008 RAC MiG announced that they had completed the first phase of a programme to return some of Serbia's five or so remaining Fulcrums to operational status.

FULCRUMS OVER AFRICA
The most extensive use of the MiG-29 in air-to-air combat was in the fighting between Eritrea and Ethiopia in 1999–2000. Both sides were equipped with fairly modern equipment from Russian and Ukranian sources. The Eritreans

ABOVE: MiG-29s were in service with the East German air force and the unified Luftwaffe from 1988 to 2004. During a visit to the USA in 2003, JG71 took the opportunity to fire AA-10 'Alamo' radar-guided AAMs over a Florida missile range.

acquired MiG-29As and UBs from Russia in late 1998 and encountered Ethiopian Su-27s for the first time on 25 February 1999. In an engagement that saw numerous missiles fired by both sides, the only known victim was a MiG-29 flown by the head of Eritrea's air force, who is believed to have been killed. The following day, a MiG-29UB was lost to an Su-27, which according to some reports was flown by a female pilot. Two more MiG-29s may have been lost in combat soon after, but the Eritrean Fulcrum pilots claimed to have shot down two Ethiopian MiG-21s and a MiG-23 in this period. Against the more powerful Su-27, the Eritreans had no such luck, two MiG-29s being lost in March 1999 and another two in May 2000, most of these to R-27R missiles from the Sukhois. In return, another two Ethiopian MiG-21s were claimed, one with cannon fire.

CONTROVERSIAL KILLS
Although the full details of losses and victories in these engagements may never be known, there are some widely documented incidents in which the MiG-29 emerged victorious, albeit against unarmed opponents. In February 1996, two Cessna 337 twin-engined light aircraft, flown by a group called Brothers to the Rescue, approached Cuban airspace from Florida. Their mission was to drop liferafts and supplies to fellow Cubans trying to make

[MISSION REPORT]
+++++++++++++++++++++++++++++

UPGRADING
THE FULCRUM

The MiG-29 airframe is solid and dependable, and modernizing it is the best option for many nations unable to afford new fighter aircraft. One air force upgrading its MiGs to extend their useful life is that of Slovakia, who currently operate 12 aircraft. The programme, which includes a new diagnostic system and changes to maintenance procedures, was carried out by RAC MiG, who say that it will increase the aircrafts' service life to 40 years or 10,000 hours. The modified aircraft, designated MiG-29AS for the single-seaters and MiG-29US for the two-seaters, were completed in February 2008. The main aim of the upgrade was to make Slovakia's MiGs compatible with Nato standards and western air traffic control systems and procedures.

The most obvious external change is the replacement of the traditional Russian 'Odd Rods' IFF aerials with an F-16ADF-style 'bird slicer' unit in front of the windscreen. Another new large aerial is mounted on the spine. In the cockpit the instruments have been replaced and changed to imperial rather than metric measurements to be compatible with Nato standards. A new MFD has been installed to the right of the HUD. The majority of instruments are of the conventional dial type.

Slovak Air Force pilot Captain Peter Baca says that the MiG-29's inherent strengths are its high power-to-weight ratio and good aerodynamic shape. With the upgrades the aircraft is now easier to operate and the pilot has more time to concentrate on dogfighting. *'You have more time to think and for tracking the target.'* The Nato- and civil-compatible avionics now allow them to fly anywhere in Europe or even the US if need be. *'We can now fly the whole world.'*

Flight information is downloaded from the squadron's office desktop computers and is then input to the aircraft using a familiar method. *'I just load the coordinates using an ordinary USB key,'* says Baca. *'It is a Russian product but it operates using Windows 2000 or Windows XP.'*

The new HUD and improved autopilot system makes the MiG-29SD much smoother to fly in bad weather, allowing landing approaches to be made with only the use of the trim controls on the joy stick. The combat potential has also improved. *'Against the F-16 at close range, I think we have the advantage,'* says Baca.

ABOVE: Under the company designation MiG-29SD, RAC MiG has developed an upgrade for the MiG-29s of Poland, Bulgaria and Slovakia incorporating new western and Russian avionics. This is a Slovak MiG-29AS, resplendent in its new 'digital or 'pixel' camouflage and sporting new aerials ahead of and behind the cockpit.

their way by sea to the USA. These flights had long annoyed Fidel Castro's government, which saw them as American interference that encouraged refugees. Two Cuban Air Force fighters, a MiG-29 and a MiG-23, intercepted them and brought them down with R-60 missiles, killing all four occupants.

In 2008 a Russian MiG-29 used an R-70 missile to bring down a Georgian drone over the disputed region of Abkhazia. Russia claimed they had no fighters in the air at the time and that an Abkhazian L-39 Albatros was responsible. Video shot by the Hermes 450 drone in the moments before its demise clearly show a twin-tailed MiG-29 launching the fatal missile, however.

To summarise the Fulcrum's combat record, the MiG-29 may be the best equipment that many nations can afford, but it does not make aces of poorly-trained and poorly-led pilots, particularly in the face of opponents equipped with AWACS aircraft and jamming systems.

LEFT: The Russian Air Force 'Swifts' aerobatic team uses MiG-29As and UBs, one of which is shown just before landing. The periscope used by the back-seater, usually an instructor, can be seen extended above the cockpit.

Flying the Mirage 2000

While its delta-wing configuration and sparkling performance confirm its Dassault heritage, the Mirage 2000 is a far more advanced aircraft than its classic predecessors, with fly-by-wire (FBW) flight controls and, in its later versions, a modern cockpit with multi-function displays and Hands On Throttle and Stick (HOTAS) controls.

In common with its forebears, the Mirage 2000 has been a major commercial success, and as well as forming the backbone of the *Armée de l'Air* (French air force), it has been selected by eight export customers in a variety of versions and configurations.

The Mirage 2000 has also proven supremely versatile. In addition to being developed to form a range of export adaptations, the *Armée de l'Air* operates the aircraft in five distinct forms fulfilling three primary roles: air defence, nuclear strike and low-level precision attack.

An experienced 'Deux Mille' pilot, 'Guss' joined the French air force in 1992, graduating as a fighter pilot after flying the Fouga Magister and Alpha Jet trainers. Having been ranked top of his class, he was given the choice between the first-generation Mirage 2000C in the air defence role, the conventional-attack Mirage 2000D and the Jaguar. His choice was not a difficult one:

'The Jag has never been a big hit in France. It was, at that time, about 20 years old – the aircraft was not very modern. I wanted a strike aircraft with a good attack and navigation system. I chose the Mirage 2000D because I wanted to be a mud-mover, basically; I wanted to do the strike mission.'

'Guss' spent six months at the type operational conversion unit (OCU) at Dijon before being posted to a front-line Mirage 2000D squadron – *Escadron de Chasse* (EC) 2/3 'Champagne' at Nancy – at the beginning of 1998. It was at the OCU that 'Guss' got his first experience on the Mirage 2000, and his initial impressions were of the relatively cramped cockpit, and the aircraft's excellent performance:

'The cockpit is really small, very tiny', explains 'Guss'. *'Because the aircraft is designed for speed, it's very thin, and quite small. So you've basically got no room to move your legs, and it's not easy to turn around.'*

For a sophisticated all-weather attack aircraft, the Mirage 2000D is also a relative 'lightweight', tipping the scales at around 16.5 tonnes (36,400lb) at maximum take-off weight, compared to the USAF's F-15E, which fulfils a similar role but has a maximum take-off weight of over 36 tonnes (80,000lb). Designed originally as a high-speed, lightweight interceptor, the Mirage 2000 retains a high degree of agility and an impressive thrust-to-weight ratio, as 'Guss' remembers from his first flight on the aircraft:

'When you taxi out, the thrust is not that high, compared to the F-16, but because the aircraft is quite light, the thrust is still quite impressive. So when you taxi, you always need to brake, because the aircraft accelerates all the time – so the take-off can be fun! The take-off is impressive – but most impressive is the rate of climb.

PILOT'S VERDICT

❝ The 2000D is a bit like a small Tornado... It carries less weapons, but is much more manoeuvrable. ❞

'Guss', Mirage 2000D pilot
ex-Escadron de Chasse 2/3 'Champagne'
Armée de l'Air

Basically, once the Mirage 2000 is flying at a speed of about 400 knots [740km/h] or Mach 0.85, it likes to climb. And it climbs very fast.'

The delta wing is a feature that the Mirage 2000 pilot needs to get used to, and at the time of its conception in the mid-1970s, Dassault's reversion to a 'classic' delta planform bucked the trends of contemporary fighter design; today, however, it is relatively commonplace.

According to 'Guss', the Mirage's aerodynamics mean that it *'likes to be in the high-speed area, above 500 knots [930km/h] or Mach 0.9… At high speeds it's very good, and the other advantage in combat is that it's got high wing loading, so your rate of turn is really high. But the problem is when you're pulling really hard with the delta wing. The rate of turn is great, but the drag also increases massively, so you're losing your energy fairly quickly. The idea is to be able to turn aggressively but not to lose too much energy, to continue the combat… After the first turn, if you lose too much energy, the idea is to unload – to get 0g, to decrease the drag as much as you can; to increase again, use the afterburner and continue the combat.'*

Although superficially similar to previous Dassault deltas, the Mirage 2000 allies the delta wing with an advanced fly-by-wire (FBW) flight control system and an inherently unstable aerodynamic configuration for improved manoeuvrability. Indeed, the Mirage 2000 was the first production warplane to combine an aerodynamically unstable configuration with mature FBW control technology. 'Guss' regards the FBW as *'basically excellent. You can try and over-stress the aircraft as much as you can… you always recover.'*

COCKPIT VARIATIONS

While FBW flight control is common across the family, the initial production Mirage 2000C air defence variant and its Mirage 2000B two-seat derivative are equipped with less-sophisticated, 1970s-era cockpits, as 'Guss' points out:

'The cockpit [of the Mirage 2000C and Mirage 2000B] is not that modern. It's quite old-fashioned. The Mirage 2000D version is much more modern. It entered service in 1993, with digital displays. You've also got a HOTAS concept and you've got a navigator. The navigation system has been updated with GPS. You've got a better EW system – including a jammer and warning system, and the jammer is designed for the strike mission.'

The weaponry available to the pilot differs widely according to variant and role. The original Mirage 2000C air defence model is primarily armed with Super 530F semi-active radar-guided air-to-air missiles (AAMs), while the improved Mirage 2000-5 adds active radar homing Mica AAMs. The two-seat Mirage 2000N is based around the ASMP stand-off nuclear missile, while the Mirage 2000D aircrew are trained to deliver a range of precision-guided conventional munitions. As the sharp end of the *Armée de l'Air*'s all-weather attack capability, the Mirage 2000D *'can carry pretty much every kind of GBU – laser-guided weapons – mainly 500lb and 2,000lb [227kg and 907kg] weapons,'* as well as specialist stand-off weapons.

'We've got also cruise missiles like the "French Storm Shadow" – it's called the Scalp. And the Apache missile – which is basically the same as the Scalp, but is designed for anti-runway

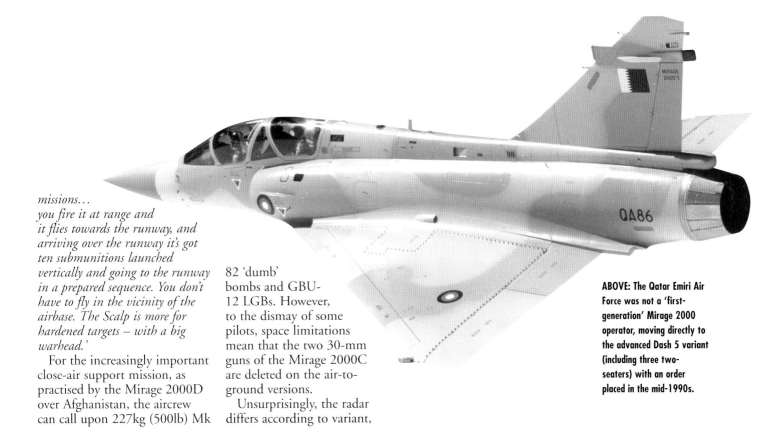

missions...
you fire it at range and
it flies towards the runway, and
arriving over the runway it's got
ten submunitions launched
vertically and going to the runway
in a prepared sequence. You don't
have to fly in the vicinity of the
airbase. The Scalp is more for
hardened targets – with a big
warhead.'

For the increasingly important
close-air support mission, as
practised by the Mirage 2000D
over Afghanistan, the aircrew
can call upon 227kg (500lb) Mk

82 'dumb'
bombs and GBU-
12 LGBs. However,
to the dismay of some
pilots, space limitations
mean that the two 30-mm
guns of the Mirage 2000C
are deleted on the air-to-
ground versions.

Unsurprisingly, the radar
differs according to variant,

ABOVE: The Qatar Emiri Air
Force was not a 'first-
generation' Mirage 2000
operator, moving directly to
the advanced Dash 5 variant
(including three two-
seaters) with an order
placed in the mid-1990s.

[MISSION REPORT]
++++++++++++++++++++++++++++

IN COMBAT

The Mirage 2000 has seen sustained combat operations with
three of its operators. The type's combat debut came during
Operation Daguet, the French contribution to Operation
Desert Storm in 1991, when *Armée de l'Air* Mirage 2000Cs
were deployed to Saudi Arabia, from where they flew in the
air defence role, but saw little or no action.

French Mirage 2000s played a more active role in missions
over the former Yugoslavia, with both Mirage 2000Cs and
Mirage 2000Ns delivering conventional munitions during
Operation Deliberate Force over Bosnia in the mid-1990s. The
loss of a Mirage 2000N to a shoulder-launched Strela missile
in August 1995 led to improvements being made to the type's
self-protection suite. Meanwhile, in the following month, the
Mirage 2000D made its combat debut over Yugoslavia,
introducing a valuable PGM capability.

French Mirage 2000C/Ds returned to action over the Balkans
during Operation Trident (the French mission in support of
Operation Allied Force) in 1999. On this occasion, Mirage
2000Ds performed precision-attack missions over Kosovo with
great accuracy, aided by the PDL-CT targeting pod, while
Mirage 2000Cs maintained defensive air patrols to cover
Coalition strike packages. As well as dropping conventional
free-fall ordnance, the Mirage 200Ds expended a number of
laser-guided AS.30L missiles, over 100 BGL laser-guided bombs,
and a smaller number of US-supplied 227kg (500lb) GBU-12
laser-guided bombs (LGBs). Mirage 2000Cs were also
called upon for offensive duties, but were limited
to the carriage of free-fall 'dumb' ordnance.

Since then, the Mirage 2000 has also played a part in
US-led anti-terror operations over Afghanistan, beginning in

2002 with deployments to bases in Kyrgyzstan and Tajikistan
under Operation Serpentaire. The Mirage 2000Ds have used
their targeting pods to 'buddy lase' for other French
warplanes, including air force Rafales. Mirage 2000Ds were
active during Operation Anaconda, a major anti-Taliban
initiative. In addition to the PDL-CT targeting pod, the
Mirage 2000D could also call upon the day-only ATLIS pod,
which proved useful for gathering high-quality TV imagery
during daytime missions. With aerial refuelling typically being
required four times for each mission, aircrew also found the
pods useful for coordinating with tankers, using sensors to
find a tanker by night, or in conditions of poor visibility.

The most notable combat use of the Mirage 2000 in Indian
hands came during the Kargil War of 1999. As well as
delivering 'dumb' bombs, the Indian Air Force used its two-
seat Mirages for the designation of precision-guided weapons,
with the ATLIS pod operating in conjunction with French-
supplied 1000kg (2,205lb) BGL and locally modified Paveway
II LGBs. Targets were mainly Pakistan military bases high in
the border area of the Himalayas.

Peru has also used its Mirage 2000s for air defence duties
during the border conflict against neighbouring Ecuador in
the mid-1990s. Their ability to make an impression in combat
was limited by the non-availability of Super 530 AAMs.

BELOW: India's Mirage fleet was blooded over the Kargil in 1999,
when the type was operated alongside MiG-29s. The Mirage has
the local name Vajra (Thunderbolt) and was delivered from
1985, initial batches being powered by the interim M53-5.

ABOVE: Desert 'Deux Milles'. These 'first-generation' Mirage 2000s are part of the significant UAE fleet and are seen carrying ATLIS targeting pods and Al Hakim guided missiles on their forward fuselage stores stations.

ABOVE: The Dash 5 cockpit is based around five displays, including three full-colour MFDs, a head-level display and a HUD.

with the RD series of air interception radars available for the air defence versions, and the Antilope series for the air-to-ground specialists.

'On the Mirage 2000D version, the radar is not good for air defence,' claims 'Guss'. For the Mirage 2000D application, the Antilope radar is primarily intended to provide a terrain-following function, in keeping with the aircraft's low-level penetration role.

'The radar itself is the same [as on the Mirage 2000N] but the software has been updated,' 'Guss' explains, and compared to the Mirage 2000N, the Mirage 2000D introduces an increased degree of digitalization and updated instrumentation in the cockpits, plus an embedded global positioning system (GPS) for navigational accuracy.

The Mirage 2000D's radar is designed to operate in high-threat environments.

'If the radar is jammed you can switch to the database and continue the terrain-following mode without using the radar without any problems,' 'Guss' reveals.

With a number of different front-line versions active in the Armée de l'Air inventory, and with different cockpits in the earlier and later versions, pilot conversion to type can prove challenging, as 'Guss' recalls of his own conversion to the Mirage 2000D:

'The problem is, at the OCU you learn to fly the aircraft, but when arriving in the front-line unit you still have a lot of work to learn the cockpit and the

[MISSION REPORT]
++++++++++++++++++++++++++++++

MIRAGE 2000N

France has long maintained an independent strategic nuclear deterrent, which, during the Cold War years, included land-based intermediate-range ballistic missiles, submarine-launched ballistic missiles and various forms of air-delivered weapon, both guided and free-fall. Strategic-level airborne nuclear weapons were originally entrusted to the Mirage IV fleet, but the arrival in service of the Mirage 2000N from 1988 allowed the earlier type to be re-roled for the reconnaissance mission.

The two-seat Mirage 2000N fleet falls under the command of the Armée de l'Air's Commandement des Forces Aériennes Stratégiques (CFAS – Air Strategic Force Command) and is divided between three squadrons within Escadre de Chasse 4. The first of these units to equip was Escadron de Chasse (EC) 1/4 'Dauphiné' at Luxeuil in 1988, followed by EC 2/4 'La Fayette' at the same base, and EC 3/4 'Limousin' at Istres.

Although the Mirage 2000N can deliver a limited range of conventional weapons, its primary undertaking involves the ASMP (Air-Sol Moyenne Portée – air-to-surface, medium range) ramjet-powered missile, armed with a nuclear warhead with a maximum yield of 300 kilotons. This is carried on the aircraft's centreline, and is normally complemented by one or two infra-red-guided Magic 2 AAMs for self-defence and a pair of 2,000 litre (440 Imp gal) long-range fuel tanks. The Mirage 2000N's range is further extended through the use of aerial refuelling,

ABOVE: This Mirage 2000N carries the ASMP on the centreline station,
Magic 2s and long-range fuel tanks. The aircraft belongs to EC 1/4, and wears the historic insignia of SPA 37 – a white vulture in

and CFAS maintains an organic tanking capacity in the form of the Boeing C-135FRs assigned to ERV 93 'Bretagne' at Istres.

The Mirage 2000N is designed to exploit its Antilope 5 terrain-following radar to penetrate enemy territory at low altitude. Protection from enemy air defences is entrusted to a combination of a low-level, high-speed mission profile flown under automated control, and a comprehensive onboard electronic warfare suite that provides both sophisticated jamming and decoys. Controlled by the navigator/WSO in the back seat, the EW suite includes missile launch detectors on the outer wing pylons and chaff and flare dispensers. Targets can be identified using the Antilope 5's air-to-ground mode, and the ASMP can be launched from low level at a range of around 100km (62 miles) from the target, increasing to a reported 300km (186 miles) when launched from high altitude. Flying at a speed of up to Mach 2 at low level, the ASMP stands every chance of defeating even the most sophisticated air defences.

switchology. Especially the lateral displays, because they give you a lot of information. What is tricky initially is not to get too focused inside the cockpit, because you still have to look out. You must learn how to use the system without looking too much inside the cockpit. The HOTAS concept is good for that.'

The latest *Armée de l'Air* air defence variant, the Mirage 2000-5F (or 'Dash 5') provides the pilot with an even more advanced cockpit interface.

'It's got five displays: two lateral, one head-down, one medium and one high,' 'Guss' explains. *'They can carry the Mica, and the radar is totally different. It's very difficult to defeat even with our jamming, because it changes the wavelength continuously to defeat the jamming. The Mirage 2000C is only semi-active, or Fox 1, capable, and the Dash 5 is Fox 3 (active missile) capable. The problem is that we have only two squadrons of those aircraft in France.'*

CREW COMMITMENTS

The pilot of the two-seat Mirage 2000D is provided with a full set of flight and mission controls at the front seat, including duplicated versions of the navigator's controls. According to 'Guss', *'if the navigator is unable to work, you can get the control and still deliver the weapon. So that gives you more workload – you have to learn that also.'*

Meanwhile, in the back seat, the navigator is provided with a basic stick controller, so he or she can take over flying the aircraft in an emergency. However, the duplicated controls serve only as a safety back-up, and the navigator is not generally supposed to fly the aircraft. *'Normally the navigator works the laser, the electronic warfare suite and the navigation system,'* 'Guss' explains, *'but you can do it in the front cockpit also. It's much the same concept in the Rafale.'*

Both the Mirage 2000N and Mirage 2000D routinely carry Magic 2 heat-seeking AAMs for self defence, and the Mirage 2000D will soon add the advanced infra-red version of the Mica to its inventory. However, in a combat environment, the aircrew rely primarily on their flight profile and all-out performance to reach the target and survive the mission.

'As a striker,' says 'Guss', *'our best defence, I would say, is speed at low level. At Red Flag, I've seen that the first shot they've got on the other side is on the slowest guys, the A-10s, the Tornados, because they can't really accelerate to what they want. With the Mirage you can really increase your speed a lot, and with the delta wing, the manoeuvrability of the aircraft is still very good, even at 600 knots [1,100km/h] or Mach 0.9. There are automatic limitations, so even if you pull really hard you will never over-stress the aircraft, which is very good. You don't really have to think – just pull hard and see what happens.'*

And if the Mirage 2000D runs into enemy fighters? *'We train a little bit for dogfights: one versus one and two versus one, and it's just a matter of keeping skills for the pilots and to hone initial reactions during combat, just to cause the damage and leave, to stay alive. But to be honest I would not continue a fight, because I'm not really trained for that. It's a very secondary mission.'*

While the air defence and nuclear strike variants of the Mirage 2000 are planned to be superseded in time by the Rafale, the future remains bright for the Mirage 2000D, and pilots and crew are confident of its potential as a Mirage F1 successor for the ground-attack and peacekeeping missions. 'Guss' expects that the Mirage 2000D will stay in the air force until 2032.

'It's going to be basically the aircraft of the French air force for the strike mission, together with the Rafale of course, but the Rafale will also do air defence... the Mirage F1 will finish in five to ten years and we will definitely need another aircraft... We've already got Mirage 2000Ds in Africa, in Djibouti; we've got a station there with a mixed squadron of Mirage 2000Cs and Mirage 2000Ds, as a pre-positioned element for the Gulf and Africa.' And, unlike the Mirage F1, the Mirage 2000D will be much more capable of countering any possible air-to-air threats.

ABOVE: Contrails streaming from wingtips and intake strakes, a Mirage 2000D takes on fuel from a USAF KC-135R Stratotanker during a mission over the Adriatic, flown in support of the NATO effort over the Balkans. Noteworthy are the Mirage's Magic 2 AAMs on the outer wing pylons, and the PDL thermal imaging and laser designation pod carried under the starboard wing root.

BELOW: This Dassault-operated two-seater was built as the Mirage 2000B prototype before becoming the demonstrator for the Dash 5 programme, making its first flight as such in 1990. It is seen here in Dash 5 Mk II configuration, with centreline Scalp EG.

Flying the Hornet

A track history of excellence in combat spanning more than 20 years, combined with its robust multi-role capabilities, has made the F/A-18 Hornet popular the world over. It is currently flown by the armed forces of eight nations, and with the recent retirement of the F-14 Tomcat, the Hornet has become the U.S. Navy's only fleet defender.

The Hornet is particularly renowned for its low-speed handling capabilities in a dogfight. Major Chris 'Elwood' Evans, a U.S. Air Force exchange pilot flying the F/A-18E/F Super Hornet with the Navy, and an experienced F-15E Strike Eagle pilot, characterized it as *'extremely agile'*. Lt. Ed 'Speed'

Whelan, a U.S. Navy F/A-18C/D pilot, agrees:

'One of the Hornet's most lethal strengths is its slow-speed manoeuvrability in a fight. I can get the jet down under 100 knots [185km/h], and still have full authority of the nose to point and employ weapons. The jet can be fully stalled, falling out of the

ABOVE: An unarmed
F/A-18C Hornet assigned to
the 'Golden Warriors' of
Strike Fighter Squadron 87
launches from one of the
waist catapults of the USS
Theodore Roosevelt (CVN
71) for a training sortie.

sky, and I can have the nose
parked up taking shots.'

Much of this agility comes from
the Hornet's aerodynamically
unstable design, but to get the
most from it requires a very good
fly-by-wire control system.
Whelan explains why:

'The Hornet's Flight Control
System, or FCS, is probably one of
the most amazing facets of the jet.
It allows you to take the jet to the
edge of its envelope – and beyond –
with complete confidence that
you'll still be able to maintain
control of the aircraft. This is
because the flight control
computers are doing all the
thinking. I give the computer an
input with the stick and rudders
telling it what I want the jet to do,
and it manipulates all the control
surfaces to make it happen.
Coming from conventional
mechanically-controlled aircraft, it
really is pretty amazing.'

Evans remarks that that bigger
Super Hornet is exactly the
same. 'The FCS allows the pilot
to manipulate the stick and
throttles just about any way
possible and still not worry about
whether or not he is going to put
the jet into a spin.'

The reason that this
manoeuvrability is so important

becomes clear when Whelan
goes into more detail. 'Regardless
of what you fly, you have to know
the strengths and weaknesses of
who you're fighting. With that
knowledge you know how to
exploit his weaknesses, and
prevent him from using his
strengths. Our manoeuvrability
allows us to "drive the fight", so to
speak. For example, an F-16 pilot
has a better power-to-weight ratio
and can out-turn a Hornet when
he's flying at optimum speed; so,
using our slow-speed ability and
nose authority, we can drive him
around, keep him running from
our nose, and in doing so prevent
him from building up to his
optimum speed. In theory,
anyway. Of course, 90 per cent

of any fight is down to how good
the guy in the seat is.'

Evans adds that there is another
very important advantage to low-
speed manoeuvrability – 'It allows
us to engage fourth-generation
fighters at slow speed, and to keep
them close so that they can't employ
their high-off-boresight weapons,
like the AA-11 Archer, against
us.' Such missiles have
incredible manoeuvrability
and can engage another
aircraft located as much
as 90 degrees away from
the missile's boresight.

The Hornet's versatility and ability to perform multiple missions makes it an ideal aircraft for operations on aircraft carriers, where space is limited, and also makes it attractive to international operators whose budget is tight.

'The Super Hornet and Hornet are multi-purpose, "do all" fighter/attack aircraft. The U.S. Navy employs the full range of capabilities that the jets have to offer in both air-to-air and-air-to-ground roles.'

MULTI ROLE FIGHTER

The Hornet, and the Super Hornet, have the ability to take on both 'attack' and 'fighter' missions. This is made possible by their excellent cockpits, which make use of Multi Function Displays to present the pilot (and Weapon Systems Operator [WSO] in two-seat variants) with a whole raft of information. *This allows us to process what's going on in the battlespace more quickly, and to use this data to target a greater number of enemies,'* Evans elaborates.

Whelan clarifies this:

[MISSION REPORT]
++++++++++++++++++++++++++++++++++
HARM SHOOTERS

ABOVE: Any aircraft capable of launching an AGM-88 is an invaluable asset for Suppression of Enemy Air Defence (SEAD). In recent years, the F/A-18 Hornet has adopted an important SEAD role for the U.S. Navy and Marine Corps.

The Hornet's versatility as a multi-role fighter is underscored by its ability to carry and employ the AGM-88 High Speed Anti Radiation Missile (HARM). This 226kg (500lb) device detects and seeks out the energy emitted by radars, and is used to destroy the antenna by homing in on it and detonating as it passes by. In 1986, when the U.S. used Navy and Air Force warplanes to attack terrorist facilities on the Libyan mainland, and again in 1991 against Iraq, the Hornet carried HARMs and supported the main strike packages by firing their AGM-88s at the radar sites that might threaten them. The Hornet's ability to do this, at the same time as defend itself from both Surface-to-Air Missiles and air threats, made it an invaluable tool for the war planners located deep underground in Riyadh, Saudi Arabia.

'The more situation awareness you can have... the better you can employ the systems on the jet, and operate the jet itself. Rather than have a swath of dozens of gauges and dials and displays, we can choose what we want to be looking at, or need to see. We can streamline the information we get, be it FLIR [Forward-Looking Infra-Red], *radar, TCS* [an optical television camera

MAIN PHOTOGRAPH: A U.S. Marine Corps Hornet approaches the 'basket' for refuelling somewhere over Iraq. Reflecting changing priorities in Iraq, the jet is loaded with AIM-9M Sidewinder missiles on the wing tips, a 226kg (500lb) GBU-12 laser guided bomb (left), and a 454kg (1,000lb) GBU-32 Joint Direct Attack Munition (JDAM).

FOREIGN OPERATORS

Operator	Variant	Quantity
Australia (*Royal Australian Air Force*)	F/A-18A/B	75
Canada (*Canadian Forces Air Command*)	CF-188A/B	138
Finland (*Suomen Ilmavoimat*)	F/A-18C/D	68
Kuwait (*Al Quwwat Aj Jawwaiya Al Kuwaitiya*)	KAF-18C/D	40
Malaysia (*Tentera Udara Diraja Malaysia*)	F/A-18D	8
Spain (*Ejército del Aire*)	C.15/CE.15	72 + 24
Switzerland (*Schweizer Luftwaffe/Forces Aériennes Suisses*)	SF/A-18C/D	34

system], *etc. to give us exactly what we need, and in doing so eliminate the "clutter" of information we don't need.'*

Each Hornet operator will place an emphasis on one mission over the other. For example, the Swiss Air Force uses its SF/A-18C/D Hornets exclusively for air-to-air operations and does not train for ground attack, whereas the U.S. Navy *'primarily employs its Super Hornets in the attack role, assigning us the secondary role of air-to-air fighter which we also practise. As such, we spend the majority of time practising our attack skills,'* remarks Evans.

The emphasis from one role to another can be changed or rebalanced at any time, but Whelan points out that since the Hornet is currently supporting troops on the ground in the Middle East, the current balance makes sense.

HORNET WEAPONS

The Hornet is cleared to carry a wide range of munitions to allow it to complete nearly every mission type that military planners require.

When it is being tasked to protect other aircraft in the escort and Combat Air Patrol (CAP) roles, it will make use of AIM-9M Sidewinder, AIM-7 Sparrow and AIM-120 AMRAAM (Advanced Medium Range Air to Air Missile) air-to-air missiles. Its nose-mounted M61A1 Gatling gun serves as a weapon of last resort in this arena, since in an ideal world it will use its powerful radar and far reaching AMRAAM to destroy opponents long before they come into the gun's relatively short 1,800-M (6,000-ft) envelope.

Should the F/A-18 be called upon to provide Suppression of Enemy Air Defence (SEAD) support, two AGM-88 High Speed Anti Radiation missiles

[MISSION REPORT]

MIG KILLS

On 17 January 1991, a U.S.-led Coalition attacked Iraqi forces that had illegally occupied Kuwait in late 1990. Part of the Coalition team assembled to push Iraqi forces out of Kuwait included the USS *Saratoga*'s (CVW-17) VFA-81 'Sunliners', piloting F/A-18C/D Hornets. On the opening night of the war, the Saratoga launched several waves of 'Sunliners' Hornets. One, flown by Lieutenant Commander Mark Fox, detected an Iraqi Air Force MiG-21 Fishbed fighter, and downed it with an AIM-9M Sidewinder missile from very close range.

Not long after, Lieutenant Nicholas Mongillo, flying a ground attack mission, was alerted by a Navy E-2C Hawkeye AWACS of the presence of two more MiG-21s. With his Hornet laden with bombs and too heavy for combat manoeuvring against the agile Fishbeds unless he jettisoned his stores, Mongillo used the Hornet's radar to detect the lead Iraqi from far away, and downed him with a single AIM-7 Sparrow missile. He then went on to successfully bomb his target when the second MiG fled the scene.

LEFT: A pair of AIM-9 Sidewinder-armed F/A-18C Hornets of Strike Fighter Squadron 136 (VFA-136), pictured over the Persian Gulf in 1994.

Mongillo's kill was the second, and the last, Navy kill of the war; it served to validate the Hornet's superb multirole capability.

LEFT: The Hornet's carefree handling makes it an ideal mount for the U.S. Navy's Blue Angels aerobatic display team. As seen here performing the Diamond Dirty Loop manoeuvre, such a refined control system is essential to prevent midair collisions!

PILOT'S VERDICT

"The engines in the Hornet are superb. We have confidence in knowing you can slam the throttles around, under all conditions, and you're not going to cough up a motor to a compressor stall. "

Lt. Ed 'Speed' Whelan, U.S. Navy F/A-18C pilot

can be carried in addition to the standard load of AIM-7/AIM-120 and AIM-9 missiles. The Hornet's onboard radar warning receiver supplements the sensitive seeker head of the HARM in detecting hostile radar emissions, although a 'pre-emptive' mode – where the known location of a threat radar is programmed into the missile before flight – is most often used. The missile is launched against the site based on the timings of the strike package; hopefully the threat radar will come on air just as the HARM is bearing down on its location, and while the strikers are still outside of the radar's missile envelope.

For ground attack and interdiction missions, the Hornet is compatible with many of the latest GPS (Global Positioning System) bombs, including the GBU-31, GBU-32 and GBU-38 JDAMs (Joint Direct Attack Munitions). Similarly, Cluster Bombs and unguided 'dumb' bombs are also carried when the mission and target type dictates. For better stand-off capability and precision, the Hornet boasts the ability to employ powered weapons ranging from the simple AGM-65 Maverick to the sophisticated Standoff Land Attack Missile – Extended Range (SLAM-ER) and the AGM-154 Joint Standoff Weapon (JSOW). Again, the

Gatling gun in the nose can also be used to strafe 'soft' targets when friendly forces are perilously close by.

Finally, the Hornet can carry a range of powered, unmanned drones for deceiving enemy radar operators. Hornets launched these drones at the start of the 1991 Gulf War, and again during the 2003 invasion of Iraq.

MAIN PHOTOGRAPH: The U.S. Navy's Air Test and Evaluation Squadron Two Three (VX-23) tests the Hornet's weapons systems. It is seen here releasing MK-83 454kg (1000lb) bombs during a series of Advanced Targeting Forward Looking Infrared (ATFLIR) adjacent stores release tests.

Flying the F-117

Often misunderstood by the media, the Lockheed F-117 Nighthawk was soon dubbed the 'Stealth Fighter' after its starring role spearheading the Coalition air forces' offensive during Operation Desert Storm in 1991.

Others applied the name 'Wobblin' Goblin' to the F-117, which some took as a reference to the fact that the aircraft was far from easy for the pilot to control – presumably on the basis of its highly unorthodox appearance. Pilots themselves, for whom the F-117 is normally known simply as the 'Black Jet', will confirm the value of the aircraft in operations against Iraqi forces in 1991 and subsequently, but they disagree that the Nighthawk's radical design makes for difficult flying.

'Bandit 329', who led the US Air Force's 416th TFS 'Ghostriders' during Desert Storm, graduated top of his class in pilot training and previously flew F-4s and F-15s before being assigned to the 'Black Jet' community in 1990:

'For me, operationally, the F-117 flies very similar to what I remember from the F-4.

MAIN PHOTOGRAPH:
Cornerstone of the F-117's 'stealth' characteristics is the unique 'faceted' exterior, made up of a series of radar-defeating flat panels and coated with radar absorbent material (RAM).

PILOT'S VERDICT

❝ The F-117 allowed the Air Force to go into places that they could never go before...❞

'Bandit 329'
Former F-117 Squadron Commander
416th TFS 'Ghostriders', USAF

It doesn't have the performance potential of the F-15 or F-16, but it is a very, very stable platform. Every mission we flew seemed more like an instrument ride. But if you looked at it – I've seen it from the inside of a tanker – the flight controls are always moving; because it's computer-controlled, the flight controls are moving about a hundred times a second, but from the cockpit it's not noticeable. It is dynamically unstable, but so is the F-16. So if it goes out of control or you lose your flight computer it is impossible to fly. However, from the pilot's perspective, it is a very "solid" aircraft.'

Far from being the 'Fighter' of its popular epithet, the F-117 has essentially a single

role, and in its day it performed this without equal. Clutching a pair of laser-guided bombs within its weapons bay, the F-117 is designed to penetrate enemy air defences and deliver a knock-out blow to high-value assets: typically the enemy's leadership structure, communications assets and weapons-production facilities.

BACK TO IRAQ

Most recently, the F-117 was used for 'decapitation' strikes on priority targets during Operation Iraqi Freedom in March 2003. The F-117 remained in the public eye on

LEFT: While initial test-flying was conducted at the remote Groom Lake and Tonopah facilities in Nevada, the deserts of New Mexico are the current home of the Nighthawk. This example is from the 9th Fighter Squadron based at Holloman AFB.

have primarily made their name in the air-to-air arena.

Another pilot with both F-15 and F-117 flight time, 'JB' is an experienced test pilot selected for the F-117 programme in 1994, and now flying the F-22 Raptor:

account of high-profile missions such as these, coupled with an enviable mission success rate. However, it is far removed from glamorous USAF 'hot ships' such as the F-15 and F-16, which

'My impression of the airplane was that it had the handling qualities – the feel – of the F-15, and the power and the energy capability of an A-7. Once you got the airplane up and moving – and I'm talking over about 400 knots [740km/h] – it did just about anything any other fighter would do, it just wouldn't do it very long. You had one really good turn and then you were cut and dead in the water.'

LEFT: Inflight refuelling provides the F-117A with a truly global reach. The receptacle – seen here in the open position – is located on the aircraft's spine, and is illuminated for night sorties.

BELOW: F-117As of the 37th TFW are prepared on the Langley flight line prior to deployment to Saudi Arabia, during Operation Desert Shield. The first aircraft arrived in theatre in August 1990.

[MISSION REPORT]
+++++++++++++++++++++++++++++++

DESERT STORM: 1991

The F-117 first went to war during Operation Just Cause, the U.S. invasion of Panama in December 1989. Then, six F-117s flew non-stop from Tonopah, Nevada, with five aerial refuellings, as part of the campaign to topple Manuel Noriega. However, it was to be the 1991 Gulf War that cemented the F-117's reputation as a media star.

Soon after Saddam Hussein's invasion of Kuwait, the 37th Tactical Fighter Wing deployed the first F-117s to King Khalid air base in Saudi Arabia, and by end of 1990 the wing had its two combat units in theatre: the 415th and 416th Tactical Fighter Squadrons. In addition, the wing's strength was boosted by pilots and crew from the 37th TFW's 417th Tactical Fighter Training Squadron, who were rotated between the two combat units. The 'Black Jets' were involved from the start, taking out key Iraqi installations on the first night of the Desert Storm offensive on 17 January 1991. Targets included hardened command bunkers, communications facilities and fixed air defence assets. By tearing a hole in the Iraqi air defence and C2 network, the F-117s opened up the skies for forthcoming waves of Coalition aircraft.

'BLACK JET' OVER BAGHDAD
Among those flying on the first night of the war was 'Bandit 329', who led his F-117 squadron, the 416th TFS, during the second wave of strikes that hit the capital, Baghdad:

'We flew in two waves. I led the second wave, about an hour and a half or two hours after the first wave. Our time over the target was roughly 03.00 in the morning. I remember I was heading north from our base in Saudi Arabia. I looked up, the sky was dark, and you could see explosions going around the desert. Iraq is a country with a lot of nothing – and cities. I looked up to my 11 o'clock and I saw this boiling cauldron of tracers and AAA. A witch's cauldron, just bubbling and boiling. I

thought it was an airfield probably just getting hammered by F-111s... I unfolded my map, to realise that that boiling cauldron was Baghdad, which is where our target was. I just kept thinking to myself: there's no way an airplane can fly through that and survive. There's no way. And I realised that that's where my entire squadron, my entire wave, was going...it was just unbelievable. The F-117 in the cockpit is a pretty noisy airplane – I wore earplugs. But you start hearing all the clanks and all the noises...it was pretty terrifying. But I'm the commander of the squadron and I can't very well just turn around. Even if something went wrong I felt that I would have to go...And then coming into Baghdad... I looked through the HUD and all I could see was tracer. Just amazing. All I could see was tracer, and the only thing I could do was lower my feet so I couldn't see the tracer any more. It was the most terrifying moment of my life...but nobody took any hits. I don't know how they missed...'

But the F-117s continued to elude the Iraqi defences, and by the time Desert Storm had ended, the 'Black Jets' had delivered over 2,000 tons of bombs during 43 nights of operations. They were the only Coalition aircraft to venture into heavily defended 'downtown' Baghdad. Most of the ordnance expended comprised 907-kg (2,000-lb) GBU-10 Paveway II and GBU-27 Paveway III LGBs. 'Bandit 329' explains:

'We carried two different LGBs, the GBU-10 and GBU-27. The first used what we called a "slam-bam" type of guidance system with a gimbal-to-gimbal action, and the other used proportional guidance. The GBU-10 had different launch parameters, the GBU-27 was a more accurate weapon, but it also put us in a different threat regime, making it more dangerous to carry. But we could put the GBU-27 basically inside of a three- to four-foot [0.9–1.2m] section of carriageway... We dropped both on the same type of target, but the GBU-27 had a harder body so that it could penetrate deeper. The GBU-10 was a soft-target type of weapon, for a building for example.'

BELOW: During Operations Desert Shield and Desert Storm, the 37th TFW's F-117 contingent operated from a Royal Saudi Air Force base, King Khalid. Soon dubbed 'Tonopah East', the base offered modern facilities within mountainous southwestern Saudi Arabia.

RIGHT: One of two operational Nighthawk units, the Holloman-based 9th Fighter Squadron, changed identity from the 'Iron Knights' to the 'Flying Knights' in the mid-1990s. Established as a successor to the 415th FS in 1993, the squadron took part in Operation Allied Force.

'Bandit 329' continues:
'One of the things about the F-117 is that it does not accelerate well, it does not decelerate well... It has the F/A-18's engines, but they don't have afterburners, because of the "platypus" tail...We don't have nozzles, like you have on an F-15 or F-16, to concentrate the thrust. Because the thrust is spread out over the tail, *our actual acceleration capabilities are somewhat limited.'*

Resulting in a very low heat signature, the 'platypus' tail is just one of a number of design features tailored to reduce the F-117's radar and infra-red profiles. The F404 engines are thrust-limited and propel the Nighthawk to a normal cruising speed of Mach 0.81. With the exhaust 'slots' located above the fuselage and ahead of the tail surfaces, heat emissions are screened from detection.

'STEALTH' PIONEER

Today, low observable (LO) or 'stealth' characteristics are recognized features of the latest-generation warplanes, but the F-117, designed in secrecy from the mid-1970s, was the first true, in-service 'stealth' warplane. The Nighthawk's remarkable wedge-shaped appearance contributes to its low-observable characteristics, dramatically reducing its radar cross section (RCS) to avoid detection by enemy air defences. For the pilot, however, the use of fly-by-wire flight controls makes the F-117 feel much like any other single-seat fighter. Aside from its unusual angular, heavily framed canopy, the Nighthawk's cockpit provides the pilot with controls similar to those of any other single-seat fighter of its generation. These include a head-up display, multifunction displays and, most importantly, a large monochrome CRT screen serving the forward-looking infrared system used to locate and identify the target.

'It is a very large cockpit,' explains 'Bandit 329'. *'It isn't cramped at all and it is laid out*

[MISSION REPORT] +++++++++++++++++++++++++++++++++

ALLIED FORCE: 1999

As it had done previously over Iraq in 1991, the F-117 led the Coalition air strikes on Yugoslavian targets during Operation Allied Force in 1999. Conducting a series of attacks against the Serbian armed forces and government, the aim of the 78-day, NATO-led air campaign was to put an end to the deportation of the ethnic Albanian population from the province of Kosovo. In the war over Yugoslavia, the F-117 was once again assigned the toughest targets: heavily defended installations, including objectives in Belgrade. A maximum of 24 'Black Jets' was eventually deployed in two batches from Holloman, New Mexico, to two USAF bases in Europe: Aviano in Italy and Spangdahlem in Germany.

Allied Force marked the only combat loss of the F-117 to date, 'Vega 31' falling outside Belgrade on 27 March 1999, during the fourth night of the Coalition air campaign. Serbian air defence units had carefully planned the operation to down a low-observable target like an F-117, modifying their radar and fire control equipment and tracking the aircraft's flight

ABOVE: A Serbian trophy hunter with the ejection seat of F-117 'Vega 31', which was downed outside Belgrade on 27 March 1999.

path from Aviano. In addition, a veteran U.S.-made radar was used to detect the aircraft, with missiles being guided electro-optically to avoid electromagnetic jamming. Two SA-3 'Goa' surface-to-air missiles were fired at the F-117, with one scoring a lucky hit – and a major propaganda coup for Slobodan Milosevic's Yugoslavia. Lt Col Dale Zelko, the Nighthawk pilot, ejected safely and was picked up by a Combat SAR team in a mission that involed three special operations helicopters covered by A-10 close support aircraft. 'Vega 31' was one of only two NATO aircraft lost to Serbian defences during Allied Force.

very well for its time and for the type of mission. Remember, it is late '70s technology and not modern technology... Everything they put in was "off the shelf", so in that respect the cockpit was not state-of-the-art. But it is very simple and straightforward... Our primary mission instrument is the infrared screen to try and find the target...it is in the centre of the cockpit, so you were looking down – you weren't looking outside.'

UPGRADES

The F-117 was the subject of continued upgrade, especially in regard to its all-weather capability, something that was found lacking in Operation Allied Force, as F-117 test pilot 'Cools' outlines:

'[One of] *the newest weapons we put on the F-117 is the EGBU-27, which is an enhanced version of the GBU-27 that adds GPS capability... With that weapon, the has the*

capability to go out and strike the target no matter what the weather, night or day.'

ELITE PILOTS

The pilots selected for the small fleet of 'Black Jets' were truly an elite within an elite. However, the training programme ended in 2006, and in April 2008 the aircraft was retired from service.

In every sense a revolutionary aircraft, the Nighthawk's legacy is neatly summarized by Desert Storm veteran 'Bandit 329':

'The F-117 was a great weapon... It was there at the right time in history, but it was a stepping-stone and I think the Air Force is retiring it because it has something better.'

Flying the Rafale

Developed to replace six different aircraft in use with the French Armée de l'Air (air force) and Aéronavale (navy), the Rafale is one of the most sophisticated warplanes of its generation, with a superb balance of agility, performance and weapons system capability.

MAIN PHOTOGRAPH: The Rafale continues Dassault's tradition of delta-winged multi-role fighters. EC 1/7 was the initial air force unit to equip, flying a first QRA sortie on 26 June 2006.

The Dassault Rafale has outflown the F-15, F-16 and F/A-18 in mock dogfights and, according to pilot Colonel François Moussez, the French fighter has also *'systematically won against the F-15 and the Eurofighter Typhoon'* during simulated air combats. However, it is not just in the air-to-air arena that the Rafale shows its class, as Colonel Moussez explains:
'With the Rafale we can do simultaneous multi-mission management: air-to-air, air-to-ground [and] reconnaissance at the same time.'

Furthermore, unlike its direct European rivals, the Rafale was designed from the outset to operate from aircraft carriers, with Flottille 12F of the Aéronavale becoming the first operational unit – with the navalized Rafale M variant – in June 2004.

The naval specification means that the Rafale incorporates a significant degree of automation, reducing the pilot's workload and allowing him to focus on his mission. During a catapult launch, for example, the aircraft flies itself for the first 10 to 15 seconds after departing the catapult, facilitating safe carrier operations at night or in poor weather. The 'carefree' flight control system also translates into an aircraft of exceptional agility, exploited by the pilot via a sidestick controller, as also found on the F-16 and certain modern airliners.
'The Rafale is fantastic to fly,' comments one pilot.

'You can control it with two fingers on the sidestick. The thrust is enormous. As soon as one has understood the systems, one can concentrate fully on the mission and weapon deployment. Flying the plane then becomes a trivial matter.'

VOICE-ACTIVATED CONTROLS

A further reduction in aircrew workload is provided by the introduction of a combined Voice, Throttle and Stick (VTAS) system, which allows the pilot to call up information on the various displays and to execute certain non-essential cockpit functions using voice commands alone.

'As an alternative to using manual methods, the direct voice input technology allows the pilot to activate data entry functions, and select non-safety-critical modes,' explains Philippe Rebourg, Dassault's Chief Test Pilot for Military Aircraft. *'In some demanding combat scenarios, manual actions can prove painfully slow, and the voice command system increases overall effectiveness: the pilot does not have to look into the cockpit any more. That enables him to focus on the mission and on systems operation. Numerous foreign test pilots have evaluated the system, and they all praise its efficiency... The response time is extremely short, and critical voice command selections are confirmed by visual feedback.'*

Chris Yeo, a former EF2000 test pilot, also has some experience on the Rafale, having flown prototype B02:

PILOT'S VERDICT

"The most noticeable difference compared to other aircraft is that the Rafale is a flying computer. It manages its own flight parameters, leaving its pilot free to concentrate on the tactical mission."

Capt. Nicolas Lyautey,
Escadre de Chasse EC 1/7 'Provence'

'First impressions are important to a test pilot – the human body adapts to a new environment quickly, so I used this period to start to become acquainted with the Rafale. Despite not having flown a fighter for several months, I quickly felt at home with the flight control system and the cockpit. The aircraft responded quickly and positively to control inputs and could be placed accurately. The control forces were pleasant and well balanced.' While the advanced man-machine interface means that the pilot is provided with the mission information he requires, the Rafale's manoeuvrability is ensured through a combination of the sophisticated fly-by-wire flight control system and two powerful M88-2 turbofans. These latter provide a thrust-to-weight ratio of 8.5 and allow the pilot to accelerate rapidly – and

safely – around all corners of the flight envelope. From the engines running at idle, the pilot can switch to full throttle and afterburning within just three seconds. Engine reliability is a key factor when it comes to performing a carrier landing. This is achieved with the aid of a laser-based landing aid, resulting in a landing run of just 200m (650 ft), with only a 3m (10 ft) margin of error to the edge of the deck: *'an impressive manoeuvre'*, in the words of one navy pilot.

The Rafale has also demonstrated its agility in the low-speed flight regime and at extreme angles of attack, and during test flights has flown at an incidence of in excess of 100° and at negative speeds of 75 km/h (40 knots) while remaining under control. While such extreme manoeuvres can be exploited by the pilot to gain an off-boresight missile lock during a dogfight, or to cause a hostile fighter to 'overshoot', the Rafale's

'fire and forget' Mica missiles allow targets to be engaged at safer stand-off ranges. Jean Camus, a test pilot with extensive Rafale and Mirage 2000 experience, explains:
'We consider that firing after a brutal nose-up like a Cobra is a risk during combat because weapon separation problems can arise and the pilot can be in a very dangerous situation if he fails to destroy his opponent. We prefer to use a very agile weapon, like the Mica, and a helmet-mounted sight.'

DATA FUSION

In addition to the helmet-mounted sight, the Rafale pilot is provided with an RBE2 electronically scanned multi-function radar, a Spectra electronic warfare self-protection suite, and an OSF (*Optronique*

[MISSION REPORT]
+++++++++++++++++++++++++++++++++
FLYING WITH THE AÉRONAVALE

Following his final pre-flight briefing in the ready room of the aircraft carrier *Charles de Gaulle*, the Aéronavale Rafale pilot dons his flight suit and life-support equipment and heads out onto the carrier deck. Here, he will perform a last walk-around with his air boss to ensure that the assigned aircraft is in full working order. Entering the air-conditioned cockpit via the Rafale M's integral ladder, the pilot is strapped into his Mk 16F ejection seat and can now begin the start-up procedure. The inertial navigation system is switched on first, while the signal officers on the flight deck initiate the launch sequence of the various aircraft earmarked for the upcoming sortie.

After starting the engines, the pilot tests the catapult launch bar, then releases the aircraft's brakes and opens the throttle to begin the roll towards the catapult. The Rafale's heavy-duty undercarriage features 360° steering on the nose gear, allowing the pilot to manoeuvre accurately into position. On selecting 'launch' mode, the fighter's leading-edge slats are deployed to maximize lift, the canards are deflected and the elevons selected in the nose-up configuration. The Rafale M is now ready to go.

AUTOMATED LAUNCH
While the pilot forces himself back into his seat to help take the force of the catapult, the launch itself is controlled from below-decks. The catapult officer on the deck signals with his flag and the launch officer initiates catapult release with the touch of a button. Within a distance of only 75m (250 ft) the Rafale is propelled to a speed of 270 km/h (145 knots) and on leaving the deck the pilot selects full afterburner to begin a high angle of attack climb-out. 'It is quite violent,' describes one pilot of the launch, 'the plane makes rather abrupt movements, but it all goes very smoothly.'

At this time the aircraft remains under automated control, which ensures that any pilot error will be corrected, with an override function acting on the pilot's stick and the throttle. Such is the power provided by the twin M88-2 engines that, should one turbofan malfunction, the pilot can abort the mission

safely and return for a single-engine landing. On reaching an altitude of around 120m (400 ft), the pilot resumes control of the Rafale and begins the transit to medium altitude.

RENDEZVOUS
For a typical combat air patrol (CAP) mission, the E-2C Hawkeye airborne early warning aircraft will have been launched from the *Charles de Gaulle* prior to the Rafales, in order to take up its racetrack pattern. From here it will use its powerful radar to scan the airspace around the carrier for any hostile contacts. The Rafale M pilot then takes up his racetrack pattern at a pre-planned altitude, aiming to minimize fuel consumption while awaiting the call to action from the Hawkeye. Should any unidentified aircraft be detected, the Hawkeye will guide the Rafale M onto the contact, the pilot now selecting afterburner for a supersonic 'dash' to his reference point.

TARGET INTERCEPTION
Once the pilot has the target within the range of his onboard RBE2 radar, he assumes responsibility for the interception. At this stage he will most likely be operating as a pair, or as part of a four-ship formation. The fighters' radars will be used sparingly, to avoid detection, with the pilots taking it in turns to track the target aircraft. The pilot will then close to within visual range for a positive identification. If the target is confirmed as hostile, the Rafale M pilot can now move in for the kill, selecting a Mica RF missile. With the target now designated by the Rafale's radar, the radar-guided missile is launched under inertial guidance mode, before locking on to the target using its own seeker head. The Rafale's radar can detect and track up to 40 air targets and, if required, up to eight high-priority targets can be engaged, with the possibility of launching four missiles simultaneously.

[MISSION REPORT]

+++

MICA AIR-TO-AIR MISSILE

The Mica fully autonomous ('fire and forget') air-to-air missile entered service – initially only in radar-guided form – on French air force Mirage 2000-5F interceptors. From Standard F2, however, the Rafale pilot will have a choice of two different Mica missiles: the active radar guided RF variant or the passive homing IR model.

While the Rafale pilot will normally select the Mica RF for engaging targets at long range – in excess of 60km (37 miles) – the Mica IR version can be employed for close-range combat, without the need to generate tell-tale radar emissions. In this case, the pilot receives target information from the passive OSF sensor array, or even from threat data generated by the Spectra elecronic warfare self-protection suite. Another advantage of the Mica's 'dual role' design ethos is its high degree of agility, unusual for a medium-range AAM. The Mica uses long-chord wings and tail control surfaces together with thrust vectoring to manoeuvre at up to 50 Gs.

Once in the vicinity of the target, the Mica relies upon a blast-fragmentation warhead that is triggered by an impact or a radar-proximity fuse.

LEFT: In typical long-range air defence configuration, the Rafale is armed with four Mica missiles and three fuel tanks. For shorter-ranged taskings, up to eight air-to-air missiles an be loaded, with one tank.

BELOW: A Rafale M departs the deck of the *Charles de Gaulle* with a centreline Thales Reco NG pod. This provides the Rafale with its reconnaissance capability and is equipped with two infrared sensors: bi-spectral for medium/high altitude and mono-spectral for high speed and low altitude.

Secteur Frontal) passive sensor suite. The OSF incorporates an infrared search and track system, forward looking infrared (FLIR) sensor and a laser rangefinder. Information gathered from all these sources is managed via data fusion to form a single tactical picture. This is then presented to the pilot on a head-up display and three full-colour liquid-crystal multi-function displays (MFDs).

'*This data fusion capacity between the different sensors is certainly the most significant point of the Rafale weapon system,*' according to Philippe Rebourg.

'*It is a revolution by comparison with planes of the generation of the Mirage 2000 or F-16 whose pilots have to build an image of the tactical situation by analyzing information provided by radar or threat warning systems. With the Rafale the crews can obtain a clear view of the whole air battle with one look and take the advantage.*'

PRIMARY FLIGHT CONTROLS

Yves 'Bill' Kerhervé, Dassault Aviation Chief Test Pilot, describes the primary flight controls with which the Rafale pilot carries out his mission: '*The joystick and the throttle lever are of course the classic controls for flight: the joystick is lateral* [i.e. a sidestick], *so as to free up space in the cockpit. Most of the main controls have been placed on these two levers so that the pilot can control his entire weapons system, adjust his sensors and give orders to his automatic pilot without taking his hands off them. There are 13 such "real time" controls on the joystick and 24 on the throttle lever. It is easy to understand that the pilot requires some training to use them instinctively.*'

The pilot is also provided with specially tailored gloves that

RIGHT: First flown in April 1993, Rafale B01, the first two-seat prototype, has been used for a variety of avionics and weapons trials. Here, B01 is seen carrying the Apache stand-off submunitions dispenser, which is already in service on Armée de l'Air Mirage 2000D interdictor aircraft.

ensure effective operation of the two touch-sensitive MFDs on the left and right of the primary wide-field MFD screen.

'OMNI-ROLE FIGHTER'

While previous generation warplanes may be described as multi-role, they can rarely exploit the full range of combat functions during the course of a single mission. With the 'omni-role' Rafale, however, the pilot can adapt to the changing combat scenario, selecting appropriate sensors and weapons as required.

'The air-to-air and air-to-ground functions can be activated simultaneously,' explains Philippe Rebourg. 'It's the real innovation that gives the Rafale her superiority over her competitors. During the Scalp [conventionally armed cruise missile] attack, the air-to-air mode was active with the radar and OSF dedicated to this function. Naturally the radar tracked some targets and the OSF has locked the target classified as the most dangerous by the system. Only one push would have

been sufficient to engage this target. The complete firing sequence can be realized through the autopilot by simple inputs...On the Rafale, the autopilot is completely integrated to the flight control system.'

For its pilots, the Rafale represents a significant advance over previous equipment, and its performance and capabilities will continue to evolve in the coming years as further improvements are incorporated into the basic design.

PILOT'S VERDICT

"The Rafale is easy to fly. The responsiveness of the flight controls is a tremendous advantage for the pilot in the most hazardous stages of flight, including the catapult launch and during air combat..."

French navy Rafale pilot, Flottille 12F, Landivisiau air base

LEFT: The Rafale is currently maturing to become a very capable all-weather attack aircraft, as new weapons and mission system avionics are introduced and refined. This example carries a 'six-pack' of 500-lb (227-kg) GBU-12 Paveway II LGBs, which the Rafale can self-designate using the Damocles targeting pod.

Flying the Gripen

Sweden is justifiably proud of Saab's long tradition of producing innovative indigenous warplanes. The latest of these is the JAS 39 Gripen, the first fighter of its generation to enter front-line service and a superbly agile 'swing-role' combat aircraft.

MAIN PHOTOGRAPH: This JAS 39B demonstrates a precision-attack payload of laser-guided bombs. The Swedish air force is putting increasing emphasis on the Gripen's battlefield support mission, and the aircraft introduced the Litening laser designation pod in 2004.

After being kitted out in an anti-g suit and survival pack, the Gripen pilot enters the cockpit. He or she is then strapped into the inclined Mk 10L 'zero-zero' ejection seat with the aid of a five-point harness and leg restraints, and mission data is uploaded into the aircraft's central computer using a portable Data Transfer Unit 'black box'.

In contrast to previous-generation warplanes, the JAS 39C Gripen's cockpit is entirely digital, with no analogue back-up instruments. The result is a notably 'uncluttered' workplace, and one in which information is prioritized according to the situation, in order that the pilot is not overwhelmed by non-vital data. As such, a wide-angle head-up display and three multi-function colour display screens dominate the cockpit.

The head-up display presents essential flight data and weapons aiming parameters. The three MFDs are arranged below the HUD. The screen on the left provides the pilot with flight data and system status, including reports on the condition of the engine, fuel load and weapons, and also presents the electronic warfare scenario. On the right, the multi-sensor display provides the radar and fire control picture, including information from

PILOT'S VERDICT

"*From the pilot's perspective, Gripen is a delight to fly. As a pilot myself I can say that Gripen itself is easy to operate on the ground and in the air. So flying is real fun...*"

**Major General Sági János,
Hungarian Air Force**

ABOVE: Although not part of the Swedish air force's traditional repertoire, aerial refuelling is a capability demanded by foreign Gripen customers. In this case, the tanker is a South African Air Force (SAAF) Boeing 707.

in danger... If you pull past 2g you don't even notice [that the HMD is] there and up to 5g it still feels good. Beyond 6g weight becomes an issue but, HMD or not, a pilot always wants to avoid moving their head under g. I was very impressed with how stable the helmet was. It didn't move under manoeuvres at all and that was an important test point for us.'

HOTAS CONTROLS

The pilot flies the aircraft using the HOTAS principle, introduced on the F-16, with a conventional central control column that incorporates switches for operating the weapons systems and allows different information to be called up on the displays via a throttle-controlled cursor. The throttle itself operates as an additional joystick, providing the pilot with 14 different functions. According to the 'swing-role' principle, the pilot has the flexibility to literally switch from one mission type to another with a simple input. The central computer then adapts the Gripen's onboard systems accordingly and modifies the pilot's displays based on the new mission profile, whether it is counter-air, air-to-ground, maritime attack or reconnaissance. Major General Jan Andersson, Chief of Staff of the Swedish Air Force, highlights the value of the Gripen's multi-mission capability:

'Gripen is essential for the modern Swedish air force because it gives us that multi-role flexibility.

The traditional Swedish emphasis was on air defence and the anti-ship mission, but now we need more than that – and Gripen does it. For example, we have put a lot of effort into developing a precision-attack capability on the battlefield.'*

The Gripen's air-to-ground prowess has also been demonstrated in multinational exercises, including the Red Flag war games in Alaska in 2006, as Lieutenant Colonel Ken Lindberg of the Swedish air force reveals:

'Every day we flew two missions, each with four aircraft. We did offensive counter air missions as strike package escorts, "swing role" interdiction missions with a secondary offensive counter air tasking and close air support/offensive counter air missions – another swing role. We dropped 16 inert GBU-12 500-lb [227kg] laser-guided bombs which were either self-designated by the launch aircraft, "buddy-lased" by a second aircraft or targeted by forward air control teams on the ground. We also did strafing runs with our 27-mm cannon on close air support missions.'

Designed according to Swedish military doctrine, the Gripen is designed to get into the combat zone quickly, whether the pilot is tasked with interception of a hostile aircraft, or an attack on a fast-approaching naval target. Even when operating from improvised forward operating bases or battle-damaged airstrips, the Gripen is ready to roll within three minutes, with a simple start-up procedure. Under the power of its afterburning Volvo RM12 turbofan, the Gripen can take off in under 500m (1,640ft). Within two minutes of brake release, the Gripen can be at an altitude of 10,000m (32,800ft). Once in the air, the fighter relies on its

other onboard sensors. The central screen serves the navigation and mission components, and is dominated by an electronic map display upon which target information can be overlaid.

An optional further source of data is the pilot's Cobra helmet-mounted display (HMD), which presents real-time information in the line of sight. The Cobra is particularly valuable for weapons cueing, allowing air and ground targets to be engaged at off-boresight angles, while at the same time providing an indication of weapons status and flight data on the visor.

Charl Coetzee, a South African Gripen test pilot, notes that the Cobra HMD '*...gives you the unexpected position to shoot from. If your target is within 90° of a Gripen then he's*

RIGHT: This view of a single-seat Flygvapnet Gripen reveals the onboard cannon installation, the single Mauser BK 27 being built in to the left-hand side of the nose. The same weapon is used on the Tornado and Typhoon.

GRIPENS FOR NATO

The introduction of the Gripen to Czech air force service was completed smoothly and at astonishing speed for such an advanced piece of equipment, as Colonel Petr Mikulenka, Wing Commander of Cáslav air base makes clear:

'I'll be honest with you, we looked at this transition plan and we wondered "is it possible?" but we believed. Moving to the Gripen is not just about the aircraft – it's a whole new system. Everything changes; our rules, our whole approach. But in the end it was just another normal working day. We finished with the MiG-21s and minutes later we were working with the Gripens. There was no buffer zone. Yes it took a lot of preparation, but we did it for real. No cheating. We are fully integrated into NATO.'

The Czech military set a demanding schedule, with the new aircraft to be in service within 11 months of signing the contract in June 2004. Two months later, Czech pilots began training on the Gripen and over a 24-hour period from 30 June 2005, the Czechs stood down their ageing MiG-21 fighters and introduced their new Gripens to front-line service. At that point, the aircraft were declared operational within NATO and took on responsibility for the 24-hour quick reaction alert (QRA) mission over Czech airspace.

NATO MODIFICATIONS

The NATO-standard JAS 39C/D Gripen provides a number of new features that aid integration with other air arms and improve overall capabilities. Among these changes are new colour MFDs that provide the pilot with a 70 per cent increase in display surfaces and which are compatible with night-vision goggles. While aerial refuelling was never a Swedish requirement, the JAS 39C/D mounts a retractable refuelling probe above the port air intake. The aircraft also boasts strengthened wings and landing gear, the former supporting NATO-standard weapons hardpoints.

As the third Gripen operator, Hungary took delivery of its first five aircraft in March 2006, in the form of three single-seat JAS 39Cs and a pair of two-seat JAS 39D models. These were flown from Sweden by the initial cadre of Hungarian instructor pilots who had by now been trained by the Swedish air force. In Hungarian service the Gripen equips the 1st Tactical Squadron, the famous 'Puma' squadron under the command of the 59th air base wing at Kecskemét. The first group of instructor pilots was followed by another five who left for Sweden in summer 2006. In total 15 pilots will convert in Sweden, before training begins in Hungary.

ABOVE: The Gripen pilot is provided with some of the most advanced personal equipment of any combat aircrew.

'At the moment we plan to fly our MiG-29s until the end of 2009, and our Gripen schedule is tracking that date,' explains Colonel Nándor Kilián, Deputy Base Commander at Kecskemét. 'By the end of 2008 the Gripens will be ready to take on QRA mission and they will share that tasking with the MiG-29s. At the moment the plan is to wait until the MiGs are retired before the Gripens are declared fully air-to-air and air-to-ground capable – but they will be ready for the air-to-air mission a lot sooner.'

While Czech and Hungarian pilots develop their skills and tactics on their new mount, the capabilities of the Gripen itself are being gradually improved via software updates. Initially only cleared to fire the Sidewinder and onboard cannon, they will add the AMRAAM and a range of air-to-ground stores to their inventory. The aircraft are also receiving the EWS 39 electronic warfare suite. Eventually, the Czech and Hungarian missions will be able to take on a range of out-of-area NATO missions, exploiting their inflight refuelling capability in order to conduct overseas deployments.

BELOW: Securing export orders from the Czech Republic and Hungary was a major coup for Saab. Here, Czech (nearest camera) and Hungarian (centre) single-seaters are accompanied by a Swedish JAS 39D two-seater.

[MISSION REPORT]

+++

ANTI-SHIPPING STRIKE

Long a Swedish priority, the anti-shipping strike mission has been taken on by the Gripen, which can be armed with two examples of the turbojet-powered RBS 15F missile. The sea-skimming RBS 15F can be launched in 'fire and forget' mode, with the pilot uploading target data into the missile before turning away to avoid detection and hostile fire. The missile then flies under inertial guidance, switching over to its onboard active radar seeker for the terminal phase. The weapon's approach to the target is conducted at low level, with a series of evasive manoeuvres and dummy attacks to evade countermeasures.

MULTI-MISSION SORTIE

While its predecessor the Viggen required a dedicated anti-shipping derivative to prosecute this demanding mission over the Baltic Sea, the Gripen can switch from one role to another during the course of a mission. In one tactical training exercise, a Gripen four-ship made a low-level airfield attack before one aircraft broke off to conduct a reconnaissance mission over the Baltic. At this point, enemy vessels were detected, and the recce Gripen relayed target information by datalink to the remaining aircraft. These then launched RBS 15F missiles from stand-off range, without even turning on their radars. The sortie ended with an air-to-air component, with the Gripens deploying AMRAAM and Sidewinder missiles to suppress hostile aircraft.

ABOVE: A typical anti-shipping load-out for the Gripen includes a pair of RBS 15F missiles complemented by a pair of AGM-65 Mavericks. The latter, known as the Rb 75 in Sweden, employs TV or imaging IR guidance.

MAIN PHOTOGRAPH: On completing his or her mission, the Gripen pilot can land the aircraft in just 450m (1500ft) without the need for a braking parachute or arrestor gear. Once on the ground, ease of maintenance is such that the groundcrew will have the aircraft ready for the next sortie after a ten-minute turnaround.

impressive thrust-to-weight ratio, unstable aerodynamic configuration and fly-by-wire control system to maximize agility, as Gripen test and display pilot Fredrik Müchler explains:

'Flying the Gripen is an amazing experience. Not only does its low weight, high power and aerodynamic efficiency offer optimal acceleration, turn and cruise performance. It's also extremely manoeuvrable, thanks to its fully digital flight control.

Incredible performance and exceptional situational awareness makes flying Gripen the ultimate fighter pilot's dream.'

The Gripen's flight characteristics have also impressed the pilots of export operators, including Major General Sági János of the Hungarian air force, in which the Gripen has replaced the MiG-29 as that nation's premier fighter:

'...From the pilot's perspective, Gripen is a delight to fly. As a pilot myself I can say that Gripen itself is easy to operate on the ground and in the air. So flying is real fun...Gripen's new ergonomic concept means dynamic manoeuvres are rapid and precise and the aircraft reacts faster to control inputs, yet you know that you're protected by the safety systems at all times.'

In order to withstand the rigours of high-g flight, the

Gripen pilot is provided with a made-to-measure full-body anti-g suit with an assisted breathing facility that forces extra air into the oxygen mask during extreme manoeuvres. But it is not only the Gripen's agility that can give the pilot the edge in air combat. The aircraft is arguably the first 'netcentric' fighter, meaning that the pilot's situational awareness is expanded using information passed by datalink between the Gripen and other air and ground assets. The datalink can even transmit target imagery from one aircraft to another. A major advantage is that the pilot can receive target data from other sources while keeping his or her own radar and sensors 'silent', avoiding detection.

Lieutenant Colonel Ken Lindberg describes the datalink at work during a Red Flag training mission:

'During offensive counter air missions we used our datalink between four-ships which gave us fantastic situational awareness – better than we were getting from the E-3 AWACS. We were always on top of the air battle. We also found that our warning and electronic warfare systems are really, really good. It was almost impossible for the [enemy] *Red air forces to get through our EW systems. And we always had a good picture of where the air defences were, could avoid them and still do our work – even in very dynamic situations, with the threat getting more complex each day.'*

As well as this data exchange, the pilot uses the onboard Ericsson PS-05/A multi-mode pulse-Doppler radar, which can handle long-range engagements with the AIM-120 AMRAAM that forms the aircraft's primary air-to-air armament. For close-range aerial combat, the Gripen pilot can exploit the aircraft's agility, optional Cobra HMD, a wide range of short-range AAMs and the onboard cannon.

GRIPEN ON PATROL

Since 2005 the Gripen has taken on the vital Quick Reaction Alert (QRA) tasking in the Czech Republic as well as in Sweden. On several occasions Czech air force Gripen pilots have flown 'live' QRA scrambles to intercept intruders – normally civilian aircraft that have either broken contact with air traffic control or departed unintentionally from their planned course. Colonel Petr Mikulenka, Wing Commander of Cáslav air base,

flew the first such sortie on the Czech air force Gripen in 2005:

'We launched to intercept a Turkish Airbus A320 that had lost communications over Slovakia. We escorted it through Czech airspace and 85 nautical miles [160km] *into Germany, just to make sure everything was OK. This was just a few weeks after the Helios Airways 737 crash in Greece, so we were obviously concerned, but it all had a happy ending.'*

JAS	39A	39B	39C	39D
TABLE OF DELIVERIES				
Sweden	106	14	70	14
Czech Republic	0	0	12	2
Hungary	0	0	12	2
South Africa	0	0	19	9

BELOW: This JAS 39C is seen on trials with the FMV, the Swedish Defence Material Administration. The FMV is responsible for testing flight systems from Linköping air base and uses the test range at Vidsel to prove new weapons for the Gripen, including the Meteor AAM, beginning in 2006.

Flying the B-2

When Northrop built the YB-35 'flying-wing' prototype bomber in 1942, they did so because the design reduced aerodynamic drag, thereby increasing range. Although ultimately unsuccessful, little could they have known that 40 years later their successors would use the same concept, blended with low-observable technology, to build the world's most stealthy – and expensive – manned operational aircraft: the B-2 Spirit.

MAIN PHOTOGRAPH: Air refuelling is a vital link in the jet's ability to strike almost any target in the world, and is a skill that must be practised regularly by the B-2 pilot.

The B-2's flying-wing design makes it the most recognizable aircraft in the world today. In much the same way that people watched Concorde in awestruck silence, so too the Spirit captivates the imaginations of those lucky enough to see it in flight.

Whiteman Air Force Base, Missouri, is home to the 509th Bomb Wing, the parent unit of the only two operational B-2 squadrons in the world, the 13th Bomb Squadron and the 393rd Bomb Squadron.

So what does the B-2 actually do? Major Geoffrey 'Roman' Romanowicz, a Spirit pilot with the 393rd Bomb Squadron, explains: *'It's a long-range, intercontinental bomber. We have four key attributes that we bring to the fight: stealth, long range, lots of weapons and precision capability.'*

These four attributes combine to allow the US Air Force to enforce America's powerful global strike capability. This, says Romanowicz, *'means that from Whiteman here in the middle of the United States we can hold pretty much any target, anywhere on the face of the earth, at risk. Our enemies know that and have to account for it.'*

Commander of the 13th Bomb Squadron, Lt. Col. Bill 'Rudy' Eldridge flew B-1B Lancers for eight years before being assigned to the B-2, at a time when it was still shrouded in mystery. He joined the programme keen to know how it could accomplish with two crew the same tasks that it took four crew to complete in the B-1. What he found was that *'the B-1 is a stick and rudder aircraft hat uses WSOs to operate the weapons systems, whereas the B-2*

ABOVE: The B-2's flying wing design generates a tremendous amount of lift: here a B-2 retracts its undercarriage long before it crosses the runway threshold at Nellis Air Force Base, Nevada.

BELOW: Landing is perhaps the most challenging part of flying the B-2. Whereas traditionally care is taken to ensure that aircraft do not stall on landing, the B-2 pilot has the opposite problem – too much lift!

is less intensive to fly, but is much more mission-intensive. The B-2's strength lies with its stealth, and that allows us to fly at high altitude. When you're up at very high altitude you spend more time looking at your timings and concentrating on the threat. Also, we're the guys who'll knock the door down – clean out the radars and threat systems that the bad guys have – so that others like the B-1 can follow. In that sense I

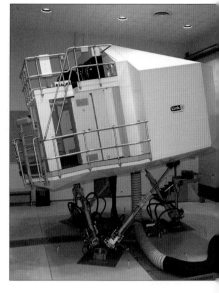

RIGHT: The full-motion B-2 aircrew training simulator allows pilots to simulate full-profile missions and practise flying those missions. Pilots also use the simulator to maintain currency and practice endurance flights.

found that there was a different mindset: the B-2 is more of a lone wolf, operating separately and with minimal mutual support.'

PILOT TRAINING

Being able to execute such a mission at a moment's notice means that the B-2 pilot must be well informed about hostile nations and the armed forces they could be called upon to strike. 'All Air Force pilots are kept busy reading up about the enemy because we are in so many places around the world at the moment, but we could go anywhere at the drop of a hat, and so the B-2 pilot spends a lot of time studying about different areas of the world,' Romanowicz observed.

Having flown two operational tours in the Lockheed Martin F-16 fighter before moving to the B-2 in 2004, Romanowicz explains that the mission of the B-2 is, of course, exclusively air-to-ground. 'We employ a mix of unguided weapons, nuclear weapons and precision weapons. All of those missions involve air-to-ground employment, but they

are very different missions that can arise in very different circumstances. Every B-2 pilot has to keep up and train to all three of those missions.'

To aid this ongoing learning process, the simulator at Whiteman is used extensively. 'We use the simulator a lot more than you would in other communities, and we use it more effectively, too. This is a fact of life that comes simply because the B-2 is a limited asset. Our simulator is very good and helps us remain combat ready,' Romanowicz expounded. With only 21 B-2s ever built and flight time at a premium, this reliance on the simulator is to be expected.

[MISSION REPORT]
++++++++++++++++++++++++++++++
THE STEALTH BOMBER

The key to the B-2's success is its stealthy characteristics. Unsurprisingly, the Air Force says little on the subject, but Romanowicz did say this: 'The B-2 is not invisible; stealth just makes this aircraft have a smaller radar return than other aircraft of comparable size. This allows the B-2 to penetrate deeper into the enemy's defences than other aircraft to complete its mission.'

The Spirit's stealthy features include the actual flying-wing design itself, reduced aural and infrared signature from the exhausts, composite materials and coatings, a radar-absorbent structure, triangular-shaped leading edges on undercarriage and bomb bay doors that do not reflect radar energy back to the transmitter, the jet's overall reduced emissions output, and the low probability of intercept emissions from its APQ-181 radar.

ABOVE: Northrop's B-2 Spirit employs many measures to ensure it remains 'low observable', but in the visual spectrum its best form of defence currently is to fly at night.

Learning to fly the B-2 'takes about nine months to a year,' Romanowicz explained. 'The initial training qualification course [ITQC] takes you through everything from basic take-off and landing through to air-refuelling and actually employing the jet. With the B-2 you are managing a lot more weapons and those systems responsible for managing the bombs are much more complicated than the F-16. So, a lot of the time in your initial spin-up is spent learning about all of the weapons, and how to manage and employ them.'

NO CO-PILOT
When a new B-2 pilot completes the ITQC he is qualified to conduct all missions in the B-2.

'We don't really have co-pilots in the B-2,' Romanowicz clarifies, 'but the way we break things up in a mission environment is to have a Mission Commander and a pilot. The pilot is concerned primarily with the flying and navigation of the aircraft, and the Mission Commander plans the bomb runs, manages the weapons and gets ready for the attacks. Each pilot in the B-2 can perform both of those functions, so it doesn't matter which

seat you sit in, but during the brief before the flight we are very specific about who is going to be taking care of specific duties.'

FLYING THE B-2
As a 'flying-wing,' the B-2 has no vertical stabilizers – tail fins – to keep it stable in yaw and allow the pilot to yaw the aircraft left and right. 'The B-2 is flown by computer, by fly-by-wire [FBW], which makes the jet very stable and very safe, and enables us to fly without a tail,' says Romanowicz. 'To control yaw in the B-2 we have devices that are like speed brakes at the end of each wing. The computer opens these to create drag – and therefore yaw.'

The B-2 might be easy to fly, but it does have some aerodynamic idiosyncrasies, revealed Romanowicz. 'The flying-wing design continues to want to fly. With most jets you pull back gently on the stick flare to stop the sink rate on landing, but in the B-2 you almost need to apply a little forward stick pressure to push the nose down to get it to land.'

AVIONICS AND WEAPON SYSTEMS
To make managing the capabilities of the B-2 as uncomplicated as possible, its

spacious cockpit is equipped with nine multi-purpose display screens, providing both pilots with a plethora of weapon, flight, navigation and battlespace information. But despite the incredible array of data available to both pilots at any given time, 'the odd thing is that you can never have too many

BELOW: Pilots from the 509th Bomb Wing climb into the Spirit's spacious cockpit ahead of a Global Guardian sortie. Global Guardian is designed to exercise the ability of USAF forces to effectively deter a military attack against the United States.

ABOVE: Noteworthy in this shot is the lack of protruding bumps and antennae normally found on aircraft to enable them to transmit and receive signals, and to measure altitude, angle of attack and air speed. The B-2 can certainly do all of this, but the associated sensors and antennae are flush-mounted with the skin.

MAIN PHOTOGRAPH: The B-2 is painted in a non-reflective blue-grey paint that helps reduce its visual signature by day. Although the planform view provides a huge visual target, when viewed head-on and from the side, it is more challenging to detect visually.

screens to manage the information that we need to process,' says Romanowicz.

The recent arrival of the Link-16 Data Link to the B-2 will mean that even more data is available to the Spirit's two-person crew. In particular, real-time data on the location of targets, threats and friendly forces is encrypted and transmitted to the Spirit by other aircraft occupying the battlespace.

GPS-GUIDED

Finding targets and refining coordinates on the run-in to the target is accomplished via the B-2's GPS Aided Targeting System (GATS), which combines a global positioning system with the APQ-181 radar mounted

flush in the port fuselage, below the leading edge of the aircraft's wing.

'The specifics are mostly classified,' says Eldridge, stating only that in addition to some surface targeting and mapping modes, 'it also has rendezvous and

RIGHT: The B-2's most obvious Achilles' heel lies with the need to keep its radar-absorbing skin in top condition to preserve its small radar signature. Unsurprisingly, there is a fine line to be trodden between flying the Spirits to keep pilots current, and keeping them on the ground to keep their skin in war-fighting condition.

air-to-air range while search modes more often found in fighter radars help us find the tanker for air refuelling.'

Tied to GATS and the APQ-181, or programmed independently, are an array of precision guided weapons: the B-2 can bomb 16 targets in a single pass when equipped with 454kg (1,000lb) or 907kg (2,000lb) JDAMs, or as many as 80 when carrying 227kg (500lb) JDAMs.

Eldridge confirmed the imminent arrival of the AGM-158 Joint Air-to-Surface Stand-Off Missile (JASSM), *'which will give us an even better stand-off capability,'* and went on to summarize: *'So, we will have stand-off precision with JASSM, gravity precision with JDAM, and a heavy-weight precision weapon with the 2,268kg (5,000lb) EGBU-28 Bunker Buster that we can also carry. The EGBU-28 can hit a set of GPS coordinates or be lased to the target by someone else.'*

RECORD-BREAKING MISSIONS

The B-2's unconventional look is matched only by the unconventionally long missions that it performs – a by-product of its ability to execute the 'Global Reach, Global Strike' doctrine.

The longest B-2 combat mission so far stands at a staggering 44-hour continuous, non-stop flight, punctuated by a precision attack against a Taliban stronghold in Afghanistan in October 2001. These missions were flown from Whiteman, with a brief stop at the the British Indian Ocean Territory of Diego Garcia on the return leg. When the US-led coalition invaded Iraq in March 2003, the B-2 flew direct to and from Iraq from Whiteman.

Romanowicz says that there is space behind the B-2's ejection seats for a pilot of average height to lay down in a sleeping bag or cot. *'It's important to manage your sleep cycles in these missions to ensure that once you get to where you're going and are over the target, you're both awake and alert. Having another person to talk to in the cockpit makes a huge difference – so does being able to get up and stretch your legs.'*

The B-2 could conceivably fly for as many as 70 hours at a time – at least, that's how long tests have shown its four engines can run continuously before needing to be topped-up with lubricating oil – but for now the practical limit is set at 50 hours. This is one upgrade that is being considered for the jet in the future, according to Romanowicz.

RIGHT: The B-2's trailing-edge control surfaces can be deflected as a single control surface like an aileron to control roll, but can also be split open like a clamshell to create yaw.

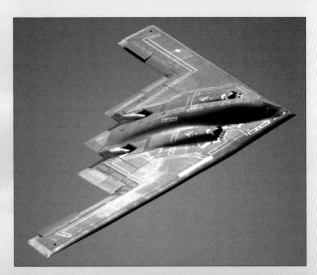

[MISSION REPORT]

FLYING THE B-2 INTO COMBAT

The B-2 made its operational debut on 24 March 1999, when two Spirits dropped 32 907kg (2,000lb) JDAMs during a 31-hour, non-stop Operation Allied Force mission from Whiteman to the Federal Republic of Yugoslavia. Over the course of OAF, 45 B-2 sorties delivered 656 JDAMs.

But it was three days of Operation Enduring Freedom missions against Afghanistan in October 2001 that put the B-2 into the record books for the longest non-stop combat missions ever. Eldridge, now the 13th Bomb Squadron commander but at that time the chief of weapons and tactics in the B-2's training squadron, flew a 40.2 hour mission on the 10th–11th October 2001.

'I flew into Afghanistan on the third day of the conflict, and we carried a mixed load of 14 GBU-31 2,000-pound [907kg] JDAMs, and two GBU-27s, the precursor to the EGBU-28. Because the mission was so long, we took off without having a target assigned to us. As we approached Afghanistan, our target were passed to us by AWACS [Airborne Warning and Control System]. Our target was a terrorist training facility near Kandahar. In the two days prior, we'd been hitting the targets that stealth was designed for – the few radars operating there and a few of the airfields with capability – but now we had moved on to strike terrorist command and control targets.

'Almost two days in the cockpit was tough, but we have a whole team of physiologists and aerospace medicine guys here at Whiteman who prepare us for it and give us a product before the mission that tells us when the sun will be up, when it'll be dark, who should sleep first and when they should

ABOVE: While the B-2 has excelled in combat over Afghanistan and Iraq, it was built to take on a far more sophisticated threat: that posed by the former Soviet Union. Today, China, North Korea and Iran represent the most obvious threats to the United States.

sleep, and lots of very good information. We also have a nutritional plan and in-flight meals that are designed to help make the missions successful.'

These missions saw the B-2s fly the 40 or so hours from Whiteman to Afghanistan non-stop, but the return leg of the trip involved a brief stop at Diego Garcia before a replacement crew flew the jet back to Whiteman.

Eldridge continued: *'My wife knew that I was working late planning missions, but I couldn't tell her that I was about to actually go on a mission. I just packed my bag and said, "I have to go away for a few days." When we had hit the target and had landed [at Diego Garcia], my commander called her to say, "Rudy is feet dry" [a term that describes overland flight. 'feet wet' is used when flying over the ocean], which was supposed to let her know I was safe. It was only a few weeks later that she turned around to me and said, "What does feet dry mean?" She'd had no idea what he'd been talking about, she'd just known it was good news!'*

Flying the Typhoon

The result of a collaborative venture involving the UK, Germany, Italy and Spain, the Eurofighter Typhoon is set to spearhead the air arms of these nations for many years to come. Providing a counter-air capability that is arguably rivalled only by the US Air Force's F-22 Raptor, the highly agile Typhoon is equally adept at long-range penetration missions.

MAIN PHOTOGRAPH: The RAF's next generation of fighter pilots are training on the Typhoon with No. 29 (R) Squadron, the Operational Conversion Unit. The first front-line unit was No. 3 Squadron, joined by No. 11 Squadron, which began to receive aircraft in 2006.

Although its early development may have been tortuous, the Eurofighter Typhoon – known in some countries as the EF2000 – has survived political intrigue to emerge as one of the most promising 'next-generation' combat aircraft. According to the manufacturers, orders for the Typhoon exceed those of any direct competitor, while a series of planned improvements will see the aircraft's capabilities gradually expanded by production block, as deliveries continue to the four partner nations and to export customers.

The Typhoon was originally intended to outfight projected advanced developments of the Soviet MiG-29 and Su-27, and the aircraft's design therefore stresses a very high level of manoeuvrability. This is primarily achieved through a combination of a sophisticated fly-by-wire flight control system with an unstable canard/delta aerodynamic configuration.

Flying Officer Andy Hawkes of No. 3 (Fighter) Squadron, RAF, outlines some of the key characteristics that contribute to the Typhoon's air combat credentials:

PILOT'S VERDICT

❝Flying the Eurofighter is the highlight of my career as a test pilot. Even for an F-16 pilot the maximum power of the aircraft is absolutely impressive.❞

Major Frode Andre Evensen
Norwegian F-16 pilot
and USAF Test Pilot School graduate

MAIN PHOTOGRAPH: The first Typhoons to take on an operational tasking were those of Italy, which provided aerial protection of the 2006 Winter Olympics in Turin. The early single-seat aircraft are the first to offer a weapons capability – based around the AMRAAM and AIM-9L – and have the initial version of the DASS self-protection suite.

RIGHT: In July 2006 the Luftwaffe began to re-equip JG 74 with the Typhoon. This is Germany's first operational Typhoon air defence wing, following JG 73 'Steinhoff', which is responsible for tactical training and evaluation. Eventually, Germany will also replace the majority of its Tornado IDS fleet with ground-attack configured Typhoons.

'The seat's a little bit higher to give the pilot the view around in air combat, so you can see everything without any kind of blockage. The wing area that we have allows us to turn the aircraft extremely tightly, which adds again to the performance...and we've got two great big engines which really do give a good kick to the aircraft.'

The Typhoon's power and agility alone do not ensure its lethality. The pilot is provided with the purpose-designed Captor pulse-Doppler radar. A true multi-mode unit, the Captor allows the pilot to switch between air-to-air and air-to-ground modes, and automatically selects the required frequency as it tracks, identifies and prioritizes threats. In addition to the radar, the Typhoon pilot will ultimately be provided with a passive sensor suite, known as PIRATE, which incorporates a scanning infra-red search and track (IRST) system and an imaging forward-looking infra-red (FLIR) component.

Craig Penrice, the BAE Systems Typhoon project pilot, has flown the F-14, F-15, F-16, F/A-18 and MiG-29, and is well placed to compare these fighters.

'Everybody holds up the F-15 Eagle as the example of what a fighter should be... Pilots of the "teen series" will tell you how good their particular jet is, but when you have flown them all it is difficult to notice any particular performance differences between them. When you experience the Eurofighter you do not need a force gauge and a stop-watch to work out the performance differences – you can feel them. As can be seen from the air display performance of the Eurofighter, it is a highly agile aircraft. It has the ability to change its energy state very quickly. When this is combined with high turn rates and small turn radii, you have an excellent fighting machine.'

MULTI-MISSION FLEXIBILITY

The air defence mission reflects only one facet of the Typhoon's capabilities, however, and the aircraft is systematically receiving avionics refinements and new hardware for the air-to-ground mission. This will ultimately allow the aircraft to conduct 'swing-role' missions: switching between offensive

[MISSION REPORT]
++++++++++++++++++++++++++++++++

'SWING-ROLE' OPERATIONS

Block 5 Typhoons will be the first to have an 'austere' ground-attack capability, although this will initially only be exploited by the RAF. The RAF will ultimately clear its entire Tranche 1 fleet to carry Paveway and Enhanced Paveway LGBs and Litening III laser designation pods. The result – which will effectively replace the Jaguar in RAF service – is a long-range precision strike aircraft capable of fighting its way to the target through hostile airspace and returning to base unscathed. Using Litening III, the Typhoon pilot can self-designate his or her own targets for Paveway LGBs, or groups of aircraft can pinpoint targets for one another.

PAVEWAY ATTACK

When using the Enhanced Paveway (EPW), the pilot can choose from two guidance modes, either laser designation or GPS, the latter providing a true all-weather capability. The pilot would normally select the laser guidance option to destroy a moving target or in order to employ remote designation. Meanwhile, GPS would be used for attacking targets with known coordinates to increase accuracy.

By the time Tranche 2/Block 10 deliveries get underway from 2010, the Typhoon's air-to-ground credentials will have been further improved, with a full day/night and adverse-weather precision attack capability that will extend to the German, Italian and Spanish fleets. Employing the 'swing-role' concept, a ground-attack configured Typhoon can be loaded with up to six LGBs in addition to four medium-range AAMs, two short-range AAMs and external fuel tanks.

After test-flying the Typhoon with a load of six Paveway II LGBs, two AIM-9L Sidewinders and a centreline fuel tank, Typhoon Project Pilot Mark Bowman commented:

'The advanced flight control system of Typhoon means that even with this heavy warload, the pilot is still able to manoeuvre the aircraft as a 'carefree' fighter, safe in the knowledge that the computers will be wringing out every ounce of turning and rolling performance.'

NEW WEAPONRY

Most significantly, the Block 10 aircraft will add stand-off precision weaponry to their arsenal – in the form of the British Storm Shadow and German Taurus cruise missiles – in addition to the Brimstone anti-armour weapon for the RAF. Other weapons options from Block 10-15 may well include the GPS-guided JDAM 'smart' weapon, one or more anti-radar missiles and anti-ship weapons such as the American

ABOVE: The Typhoon is gradually expanding its air-to-ground options to offer a true multi-role capability. This line-up includes both Taurus and Storm Shadow long-range weapons, visible left and right directly under the canard foreplanes.

Harpoon or Norwegian Kongsberg NSM. Software revisions for the Block 10 aircraft will also allow the pilot to attack multiple targets on a single pass, whereas the RAF's Block 5 is limited to a strike on a single target.

This will not be the end of the Typhoon's 'swing-role' evolution, however, since the Tranche 3 version is being planned and will almost certainly feature enhancements for the precision strike role. Tranche 3 may also feature some degree of 'stealth' technology in order to evade detection by hostile radar, while an increased payload and extended range will allow the pilot to attack more targets during a single mission deep into hostile airspace. The aircraft may also use conformal fuel tanks.

ADDITIONAL ROLES

Radar improvements from Tranche 3 will introduce a new reconnaissance capability, such that the pilot can alternate between air defence, ground-attack and surveillance modes during a single sortie. The Typhoon also offers the potential to develop a SEAD (suppression of enemy air defences) version, which would be used to detect, locate and then neutralize enemy air defences.

MAIN PHOTOGRAPH: Initially provided to customers with a single-role air defence function, as demonstrated by this AMRAAM/Sidewinder-equipped machine, the Typhoon was always intended to operate equally effectively in the air-to-ground environment and even to switch between missions in flight when required.

THE TYPHOON AIR DEFENCE MISSION

The baseline Block 1/Tranche 1 Typhoon standard – covering 31 two-seat aircraft for the four partner nations – is primarily intended for training and developmental flying, but is also capable of taking on a limited air-to-air role. With the arrival of the Block 5 aircraft at the end of Tranche 1 deliveries, the Typhoon's air defence capability will be enhanced through the addition of the improved AIM-120C-5 AMRAAM model and a voice-input system for the pilot. In addition, all Block 5 Typhoons except the German aircraft will be provided with the full DASS (Defensive Aids Sub-System) including a towed radar decoy, and will be equipped with the initial version of the PIRATE sensor suite, based on a FLIR system and IRST.

The Tranche 2 variant of the Typhoon will ultimately add the Meteor beyond visual range air-to-air missile (BVRAAM), a further refined DASS and the definitive pilot's helmet. Meteor will dramatically extend the fighter's lethality, allowing the pilot to engage hostile aircraft at extended range by virtue of the missile's air-breathing motor.

Looking further to the future, the Typhoon may add thrust-vectoring engines under Tranche 3, which would bring a new level of agility, permitting, for example, off-boresight missile shots at extreme attitudes.

BELOW: Pictured wearing the markings of Ala 11, this two-seat Typhoon bears the Spanish designation CE.16. 113 Escuadrón of Ala 11 operates the Spanish Typhoon OCU.

and defensive modes during the course of a single sortie.

POWERFUL ENGINES

Using full afterburner, the Typhoon's twin Eurojet EJ200 turbofans can propel the fighter off the tarmac and into a vertical climb within five to six seconds, and provide the pilot with more than enough power for air combat, as Maurizio Cheli, Chief Test Pilot with Alenia Aeronautica, describes:

'*I have flown the aircraft throughout the whole flight envelope, from minimum speed up to Mach 2 and from 0 to 55,000 ft [16,750 m]. This is the most exceptional engine I have ever flown, with a lot of thrust.*'

TYPHOON INITIAL OPERATORS BY COUNTRY

Country	Unit	Base	Service entry
UK	No. 17 (R) Squadron	Coningsby	18 December 2003
Germany	JG 73 'Steinhoff'	Rostock-Laage	30 April 2004
Italy	IX Gruppo, 4° Stormo	Grossetto	29 March 2004
Spain	113 Escuadrón, Ala 11	Morón	27 May 2004
Austria	Air Surveillance Wing	Zeltweg	12 July 2007

In addition, the engines allow the pilot to 'supercruise' in certain regimes – flying at a speed of around Mach 1.2 without the need to engage the fuel-thirsty afterburners.

Wolfgang Schirdewahn, Chief Test Pilot with EADS, continues:

'The Eurofighter has a lot of thrust and little drag. Acceleration from 800 km/h [497 mph] to Mach 1.2 is therefore markedly faster than with all known models. We build up a lot of speed, which we then pass on to medium-range guided weapons. And once were are travelling at supersonic speed, we can sustain it without using afterburners.

'The aircraft has been designed to be aerodynamically unstable at any speed, which means that it is only controllable with the aid of the fly-by-wire system. This is why during manoeuvres very high acceleration forces are built up. Because of the abrupt increase of g-forces, care must be taken that the pilot does not black out. This is why we have a comprehensive anti-g system to protect the pilot.

'As far as turning circles and rates are concerned, we are definitely better than the F-16. What is more, the pilot can make full use of the aircraft's agility without a second thought, since the fly-by-wire system will keep the aircraft within its aerodynamic limits in any situation. We won't lose energy quickly, or are able to build it up again thanks to powerful engines. It takes the EJ200 engines less than five seconds to accelerate from idle to full dry output.'

SELF-PROTECTION

Once in the battlespace, the Typhoon pilot can call upon a sophisticated electronic warfare self-protection suite, known as DASS (Defensive Aids Sub-System). The pilot's overall awareness is further enhanced by MIDS (Multifunction Information Distribution System), a secure datalink that allows up to eight Typhoons to share tactical information, and which also exchanges data with ground-based

command posts and airborne early warning and control (AEW&C) aircraft.

After a Typhoon test flight, Major Evensen, a Norwegian F-16 pilot and USAF Test Pilot School graduate, said:

'Flying the Eurofighter is the highlight of my career as a test pilot. Even for an F-16 pilot the maximum power of the aircraft is absolutely impressive. The Eurofighter is the easiest aircraft to land that I have ever flown.'

In terms of overall capability, the Typhoon may not be on a par with the far more costly F-22 Raptor, but it represents a significant advance over the fourth-generation combat aircraft that currently form the mainstay of most Western air arms, and offers unrivalled growth potential.

ABOVE: Current RAF Typhoon operations are centred at Coningsby, where the Eurofighter Cockpit Demonstrator serves as a vital training aid, offering a variety of realistic simulated mission scenarios.

MAIN PHOTOGRAPH: The RAF plans to equip four air defence squadrons with the Typhoon. The aircraft is seen here in two-seat T.Mk 1 form (the first version to be delivered to the UK) and in the colours of No. 29 (Reserve) Squadron.

PILOT'S VERDICT

❝ *Particularly impressive is the engine performance and handling at high altitude and high speed, where modern beyond-visual-range combat takes place.* **❞**

Chris Worning
Eurofighter Project Pilot
EADS Military Air Systems,
Germany

Flying the Super Hornet

The F/A-18E/F Super Hornet is a much-improved version of the original F/A-18A/B/C/D Hornet. The single-seat F/A-18E and two-seat F/A-18F are known to pilots and Weapons System Operators (WSOs) as the 'Rhino', because the Super Hornet is large, grey, and very dangerous.

MAIN PHOTOGRAPH: An F/A-18F from VFA-41 'Black Aces' during a mission over the Persian Gulf. The aircraft carries a warload typical of the 'Global War on Terror', comprising a wingtip AIM-9X Sidewinder, an AGM-65 Maverick air-to-surface missile underwing, an AAQ-14 LANTIRN (Low-Altitude Navigation and Targeting Infra-Red for Night) pod under the intake, and a 1,400 litre (370 gallon) centreline drop tank.

Lt Ed 'Speed' Whelan summarized the main differences between the Super Hornet and the Hornet as, *'More power; more capability; better radar; lower radar cross-section; more fuel; more efficient engines; more manoeuvrability; dozens of cubic feet of empty space for future upgrades and magic boxes; made from fewer parts; and able to carry more weaponry.'*

Major Chris 'Elwood' Evans, a US Air Force exchange pilot flying the F/A-18E/F Super Hornet with the US Navy, and an experienced F-15E Strike Eagle pilot, elaborates on some of the finer points: *'The Super Hornet has improved avionics, and also has the advanced ASQ-228 ATFLIR [Advanced Targeting FLIR] as well as the AESA radar [Active Electronic Scanned Array]. However, the biggest improvement for carrier ops is the ability to land on the boat with 10,000 pounds [4535kg] of gas or ordnance.'*

Another Super Hornet pilot, Lt Pete Morgan, says that the main difference between single- and two-seat models is *'the way they are mechanized: the "E" and "F" can do the same missions, but the two big missions that "F" squadrons take on are FAC(A) and RMC. FAC(A) is the forward air controller (airborne) role, and requires a two-person crew. RMC is rescue mission commander, the overall airborne coordinator of a search and rescue mission.'*

This, he says, is because *'the two-man crew is better suited to the high task-loading associated with those two missions. We have also seen better effectiveness in air-to-ground missions, because the pilot can dedicate more time to looking out for surface-to-air threats while the WSO concentrates on sensors such as the ATFLIR or*

inputting coordinates into the JDAM, JSOW, or HARM.'

The Joint Direct Attack Munition (JDAM), AGM-154 Joint Stand-Off Weapon (JSOW), laser-guided bombs (LGBs), and the 'radar-sniffing' AGM-88 High-Speed Anti-Radiation Missile (HARM) are the main weapons employed by the Super Hornet.

'JDAM and laser-guided bombs are used to destroy surface targets, with JDAM having a "through the weather" capability, while LGBs require you to be able to see the target with a sensor such as a FLIR or have a ground designation (such as a SEAL [Sea, Air and Land] team with a laser). JSOW is used for long-range surface attacks – JSOW has a much longer range than other weapons such as JDAM, LGBs and

unguided munitions. It also has a low radar cross-section and is GPS-guided, which results in much greater accuracy and less collateral damage, as well as fewer weapons required to destroy a given target. Finally, HARM is used to suppress and destroy surface-to-air emitters in order to allow strikers to ingress and destroy targets.'

MULTI-ROLE FIGHTER

The Super Hornet's versatility and ability to perform multiple missions makes it an ideal aircraft for operations on aircraft carriers, where space is at a premium, and also makes it

attractive to international customers, the first of which is the Royal Australian Air Force.

Whelan agrees, commenting that, *'The Super Hornet is a multi purpose, "do-all" fighter/attack aircraft. The USN employs the full range of capabilities that the jets have to offer, in both air-to-air and-air-to ground roles, and the Super Hornet also takes on air-refuelling tanker duties for the Carrier Air Wings.'*

This ability to assume both attack, fighter and refuelling

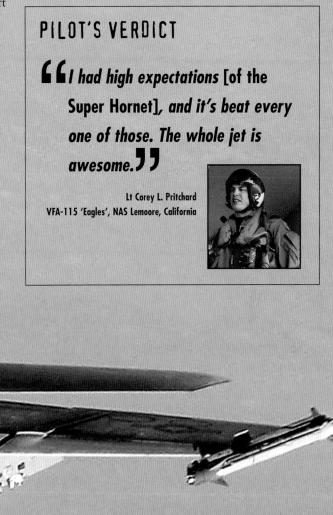

PILOT'S VERDICT

❝I had high expectations [of the Super Hornet], and it's beat every one of those. The whole jet is awesome.❞

Lt Corey L. Pritchard
VFA-115 'Eagles', NAS Lemoore, California

and F-15C Eagles for air-to-air; the Super Hornet must accomplish all these missions.

When asked how the Super Hornet community avoids being a jack of all trades, but master of none, Morgan responded:

'Unfortunately, there is a tendency to get proficient in one mission area, then not practise it for a long time while you practise another. The F/A-18 is a very forgiving airplane, easy to fly and easy to operate the systems. It does require more work to be prepared for all of our missions, but it is also very rewarding to know that you can be called on for any mission. There is a training matrix that ensures you keep a certain level of currency in all mission areas. It does serve to keep you current; however, most of us would prefer to spend more time doing BFM [basic fighter manoeuvres] than tanking.'

Morgan's personal favourite mission is the *'self-escort strike mission. It involves fighting your way through an air-to-air threat, possibly a surface-to-air threat,*

missions, allowing an impressive level of expertise to be accrued in a particular role as a result. For example, the US Air Force has the luxury of being able to dedicate F-15Es and F-16CGs for precision strike, F-16CJs for SEAD/DEAD (suppression/destruction of enemy air defences), and F-22A Raptors

missions is both a strength and a weakness for the Super Hornet community. Land-based air arms can dedicate individual aircraft types and squadrons to specific

dropping a bomb on something, and then fighting your way back out. It allows you to execute all of the missions that you have practised – air-to-air, air-to-ground and BFM.'

COCKPIT DISPLAYS

The Super Hornet's multi-role capability is facilitated by its excellent cockpit, which makes use of multiple displays to present the pilot and the WSO with a plethora of information. *'This allows us to process what's going on in the battlespace more quickly, and to use this data to target a greater number of enemies,'* Evans explains.

Morgan reflects that the touch-screen Up Front Controller Display (UFCD)

ABOVE: Bearing the famous tailfin markings of the 'Jolly Rogers', an F/A-18F catches the wire aboard USS *Dwight D. Eisenhower*.

almost directly in line with the Super Hornet pilot's face is an excellent improvement over the push-button controller found on the 'legacy' Hornet. *'The touch-screen display is nice because you can use it as either another display or as a touchpad. The F/A-18C keypad occupied a prime spot of real estate in the jet. Having a display right in front of you makes it very easy to see whatever is there. While scanning displays, taking a second to move your head is a big deal. Not having to look around is very nice. The touchpad also controls almost all of the avionics in the*

jet, which eliminates a lot of switches and dials in the cockpit. I have found the touchpad very reliable. You do not have to use anything on the touchpad while manoeuvring, since the Hornet has hands on throttle and stick [HOTAS] capability. It allows you to operate the jet tactically

ABOVE: Final pre-flight checks for an F/A-18E on the flight deck of the carrier USS *Ronald Reagan*. The revised engine air intakes introduced on the 'Super Bug' are clearly evident. These are tailored to reduce radar cross-section.

[MISSION REPORT]
AIRBORNE TANKERS

ABOVE: An EA-6B Prowler electronic attack aircraft tops up from an F/A-18E 'buddy tanker' of VFA-137 over the Pacific.

When the US Navy retired its ageing fleet of KA-6D Intruder carrierborne tankers, the S-3 Viking was employed as a temporary measure to fill the resulting void. However, a more permanent solution was required since the Navy knew that the old Viking was soon to reach its retirement date and would also be put out to pasture.

The solution lay in the F/A-18E/F. In its role as 'buddy tanker' it uses external fuel tanks and a removable pod containing the drogue that all Navy warplanes can plug their probe into to receive fuel. *'You have to have gas available airborne over the ship during ops,'* confirms Whelan, *'it's just a way of life, and we can't constantly depend on the US Air Force to do it... it would be too overwhelming.'* Providing this service is crucial because aircraft struggling to land on the carrier often require their fuel tanks to be topped-up lest

their engines starve of fuel and flame out, making ejection the only option.

Evans adds that the Super Hornet's buddy tanking role can also be utilized more aggressively; in dangerous combat environments, for example. *'The F/A-18 can extend the normal range of a Navy strike force, too.'* And, since the Super Hornet would become a very dangerous foe once it has jettisoned the bulky external fuel tanks associated with the role, it is more likely to fly closer to the edge of the combat zone than the more vulnerable Intruders and Vikings that preceded it.

[MISSION REPORT]
++++++++++++++++++++++++++++

SUPER HORNET
AESA RADAR

The Super Hornet is only the third jet fighter in US service to operate an AESA (Active Electronically Scanned Array) radar, the others being the F-15C Eagle and F-22A Raptor.

The APG-79 AESA radar, which is currently being rolled-out to the fleet, does not use the typical hydraulically driven planar array to steer a single radar beam, but instead uses a myriad fixed modules that transmit and receive pencil-thin beams. Multiple beams can be transmitted simultaneously and with great speed.

To the Super Hornet pilot and WSO, all of this means: 'no moving parts, a high power output, and the ability to track numerous targets with great precision,' according to Major Chris Evans. In air-to-air engagements, the radar allows targets to be engaged at very long ranges. For air-to-ground, the radar system offers high-resolution ground mapping at long stand-off ranges, and can also track ground targets at long ranges. There are other, less obvious, benefits to the Super Hornet's new radar. Because

it operates such a fast and precise scan, it is less likely to be detected by the enemy. Similarly, its fast, pencil-thin scans make enemy radar receivers less likely to gauge the Super Hornet's exact location if they do become aware of its transmissions, making it harder for them to use disruptive electronic jamming to confuse the AESA radar. And when jamming is encountered, the APG-79 should be able to use its sheer power to blast through it.

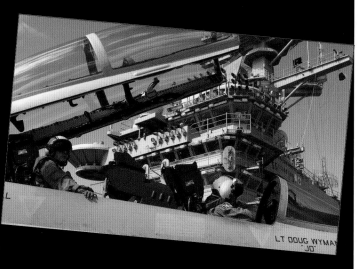

ABOVE: The ongoing introduction of the APG-79 radar on the Super Hornet provides pilots and WSOs with a warplane of dramatically increased lethality and survivability. This F/A-18F belongs to VFA-41 'Black Aces'.

BELOW: One of the most important advantages of the F/A-18E/F over its forebear is increased internal fuel capacity – around 33 per cent more than the 'legacy' Hornet. Nevertheless, this F/A-18E tanker is loaded with the maximum permissible external fuel load, plus 'buddy' pod.

without ever taking your hands off the controls.'

The F/A-18F's cockpits have two multi-purpose Digital Display Indicators (DDIs), a Multi-Purpose Colour Display (MPCD), and an UFCD. With all this surface area available to display information, how is it configured so that it doesn't all become too much for the pilot and WSO to digest?

'In the back seat, you will typically have the HUD on the UFCD, a moving map with the overall tactical picture on the MPCD, and two radar displays on the side DDIs. The front display layout is very similar, except that since there is a dedicated HUD, the UFCD can be used for another display, such as the electronic warfare or ATFLIR display. There is

definitely a lot of information available, and it takes a few years of flying before you become accustomed to when and where to look to find the particular bit of information that you are looking for. Personally, I would rather have too much information available than not enough'.

By way of comparison, Morgan said that he had recently flown an F-15C Eagle

pilot in the back seat of a Super Hornet: *'He was amazed at the amount of information – we call in situational awareness, or SA – available in the cockpit'.*

JHMCS

Another addition to the Super Hornet is the Joint Helmet-Mounted Cueing System (JHMCS), which projects weapons data and symbology onto the inside of the visors of both pilot and WSO. This device *'will revolutionize our capabilities when it fully matures,'* Whelan claims. Evans agrees: *'With JHMCS, you can see a target on the ground and slew the ATFLIR directly to what you see. Everyone talks about the greatness of JHMCS in the air-to-air environment during dogfights, but right now it's in the close air support world that its true lethality is being demonstrated.'*

Morgan further explained, *'The biggest advantage that the JHMCS brings is that you are able to see designations that are not in your HUD. In the air-to-*

air environment, you typically have to pull an enemy to your nose in order to cue a missile onto his jet. With the JHMCS, if you can see someone, you can cue a missile onto him and kill him. In the air-to-ground environment, in order to find a target, you must again put your nose on it. Since the HUD only has about a ten-degree field of view, this may not

always be practical. It may also involve dropping your nose below a minimum altitude. With the JHMCS, you can both designate a target off your nose. It also allows you to see exactly where your target is. The back-seat JHMCS has a symbol that allows the WSO to see where the pilot is looking, which eliminates a lot of the "it's over there" communications.'

ABOVE: 'Aerial gas station' for the fleet: this F/A-18F 'buddy tanker' wears the markings of VFA-2 'Bounty Hunters'. The 'Bounty Hunters', in common with many Super Hornet operators, was formerly equipped with the F-14 Tomcat for fleet defence.

LEFT: A mechanic adjusts the instruments in the cockpit of a VFA-137 F/A-18E embarked on USS *Abraham Lincoln*. The Super Hornet's cockpit takes advantage of advances in technology that have been made since the appearance of the 'legacy' Hornet, and is therefore fully compatible with night vision goggles and the Joint Helmet-Mounted Cueing System (JHMCS). The latter can be used for cueing the highly agile AIM-9X Sidewinder heat-seeking air-to-air missile.

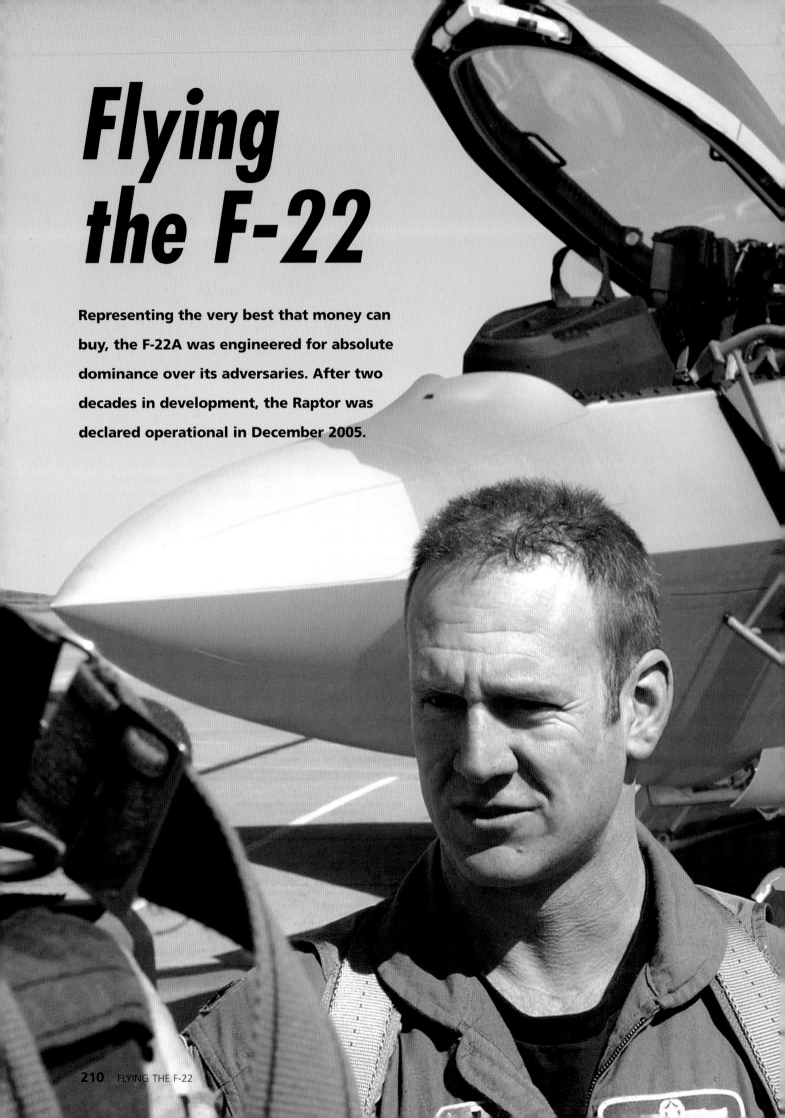

Flying the F-22

Representing the very best that money can buy, the F-22A was engineered for absolute dominance over its adversaries. After two decades in development, the Raptor was declared operational in December 2005.

From the outset, the Raptor was built to harness as many low-observable technologies as possible without compromising on its ability to find, identify and kill the best enemy fighters for decades to come.

STEALTH, SPEED AND ALTITUDE

Lt Col Mike 'Dozer' Shower, a Raptor squadron commander at Elmendorf AFB, Alaska, cites the F-22's stealth as being, *'by far the aircraft's greatest strength and most revolutionary characteristic'*. This, he says, is because, *'If I can see my adversary, track and shoot him well before he can see or shoot me, then I have an incredible advantage in combat. It would be the same as stepping into the ring to fight the world boxing champion…but with a twist: he's invisible. You're on the floor before you even know what hit you.'*

So effective are the Raptor's stealthy characteristics, Shower

MAIN PHOTOGRAPH: A Raptor pilot talks to members of the media about the jet. Media interest in the F-22A has always been high, but most of its capabilities and tactics will remain classified for decades.

PILOT'S VERDICT

"It's the fighter aircraft fighter pilots have been dreaming about. There were so few compromises made for the aircraft's performance that it excels in virtually every arena. It's an absolute thoroughbred for raw power and speed."

Lt Col Mike 'Dozer' Shower
F-22 Squadron Commander

RIGHT: An F-22A over the extensive test ranges in the Nevada desert. The Raptor has been painted in at least three different experimental camouflage patterns, including the one seen here.

confides, that *'one of our challenges is convincing other units to come fly with us for training. It's hard to train and fight against something you don't see.'*

Like the ability to remain undetected, the Raptor was also designed to operate at very high altitudes and at supersonic speeds for the majority of the time that it is airborne. Shower, who shot down a Yugoslavian Air Force MiG-29 Fulcrum during Operation Allied Force in March of 1999, explains why speed and height are key:

'Speed is probably not far behind stealth in terms of its importance. You can imagine that the faster we are, the more complicated the problem for our adversary becomes. Imagine that same boxing match, already an

[MISSION REPORT]
+++++++++++++++++++++++++++++++
ADVANCED COCKPIT

The F-22's cockpit is obviously a key factor in allowing the pilot to get the most from the Raptor's sensors, and in doing so maximizes the potential that the jet has to offer. Lt Col Shower, who has flown F-15s, and flown in F-16s and F-18s, had this to say: 'The cockpit is fairly roomy for a fighter and overall it's well designed with a lot of human factors engineering inputs, and very importantly, pilot inputs during the design and development phases. It's night compatible and is essentially an all-glass cockpit. So, there is very little for the pilot to do after starting up the jet and loading all the critical mission data. Overall, I find it a little more comfortable than the Eagle cockpit and seat because it has a slightly better seat designed to alleviate stress on the body.

'The Raptor start-up sequence is very easy. It has a battery. You turn it on, start the APU [auxiliary power unit – a small turbine engine], and then push the throttles over the cut off. The start sequence is automatic after that, to include loading of the mission data required to make the Raptor come alive. After you close the [weapons bay] doors and do a flight-control system check, you're pretty much ready to go. There's normally some manual data you might program for your mission, but that takes a minute or two and then you're ready to taxi,' he adds.

ELECTRONIC CHECKLIST
The Raptor also boasts a unique pilot aid: a series of electronic checklists displayed to the pilot on one of his screens at various times. 'The electronic checklist is a great addition that helps the pilots out a great deal, and not just during emergencies. It also has most of the normal checklist

ABOVE: The Raptor's advanced cockpit, which features four liquid crystal displays of various dimensions, gives the pilot both comfort and simplicity beyond that offered by any other operational jet fighter.

the jet has a problem, 'it's announced via an electronic message to the pilot and he can select the checklist that tells him what is wrong with the airplane and what actions need to be taken to fix the problem or get the jet safely on the ground. The Raptor has multiple back-up systems for virtually everything, so it's very robust in that sense. And the aircraft constantly monitors thousands of system inputs so it's very aware of what is going on inside itself. Incidentally, this is a great help to maintenance who can quickly narrow down the problem to fix any issues with the jet.'

'The displays have a ton of information but it's filtered and presented well, so after just a few flights its easy to interpret everything the jet is telling you – and that's a lot incredibly tough problem, but now the invisible guy can move nearly twice as fast as you in his "combat" configuration – it makes a significant difference. Altitude is important, too. The higher we are and the faster we are, the more we are able to neutralize most threats by simply avoiding the areas where they can shoot us. This is especially true of anti-aircraft artillery and most surface-to-air missile systems.'

'Another advantage is range. The higher you are, the less fuel you burn for a given speed (generally), so in super cruise we do very well at high altitude. And, quite honestly, the jet was built for, and loves to be, high and fast.'

SENSOR FUSION

'Sensor fusion allows the pilot to stop being a sensor operator, so he can stop spending precious brain time working the system. In an F-15 for example, the pilot has to operate the radar, look at the data-link display, the radar-warning receiver, listen to the

RIGHT: The different colour flush-mounted panels on the Raptor's upper surface denote the presence of air conditioning, exhaust, refuelling and avionics equipment installed beneath them.

radio, watch his wingman, etc. and build a three-dimensional picture in his head all while still having to fly the jet and shoot at targets while also defending himself when being shot at', states Shower.

Shower, now with almost 500 hours' flying time and 4 years' experience in the Raptor, explains that fusing data from all of the jet's onboard systems, as well as those from other aircraft, allows 'the pilot to spend almost all of his time looking at the big picture and figuring out what targets need to

MAIN PHOTOGRAPH: Two F-22As of Langley AFB's 1st Fighter Wing take the scenic route home. Although its composition is classified, the paint scheme applied to operational Raptors has a metallic finish which, when viewed from certain angles, suggests the presence of an additive to help absorb radar waves from hostile radars.

RIGHT: The Raptor was for a short time redesignated the F/A-22 to denote its dual capability as both air-to-air fighter and precision striker. The F/A designation was later replaced by simply F-22A.

be engaged, where to go with his airplane, etc. It's also a lot easier when you are not being shot at because they don't see you. Sensor fusion has greatly simplified the problem for a fighter pilot and made us much more lethal and efficient in combat.'

This new level of capability has meant that the Raptor community has had to rethink traditional fighter tactics. As a result, they *'employ different tactics than previous aircraft, which take advantage of our information sharing and other unique characteristics the jet brings to the fight – it's an amazing thing to watch a group of F-22s work, it really is,'* Shower concludes.

Unclassified statistics and recent air-show performances in the US have left few observers with any doubt that the Raptor has the ability to out-fly any other jet fighter in the world.

Naturally, Shower concurs. *'It's the fighter aircraft fighter pilots have been dreaming about. There were so few compromises*

[MISSION REPORT]
+++++++++++++++++++++++++++++

ATAGS

In addition to the Combat Edge anti-G vest and Combat Edge helmet and oxygen mask worn by fast jet aircrew in the US Air Force, the F-22A pilot also wears a CSU-23/P Advanced Technology Anti-G Suit (ATAGS). This garment, which completely wraps around the pilot's legs and buttocks, sits lower on the torso than previous G-suits, preventing it from pushing against the chest when it inflates. Because of these two design features, it provides increased protection from the effects of prolonged high-G environments. On its own, ATAGS provides a 60 per cent increase in aircrew endurance; combined with Combat Edge, it increases aircrew endurance by 350 per cent over the level currently achieved by F-15 and F-16 pilots.

Shower says that, 'the new G-suit, combined with a better seat design, seems to allow us to pull Gs better than previous jets. 9+ Gs still hurts, but not as bad as it did in an Eagle and I do not feel as fatigued as I used to.' He adds, 'We are

ABOVE: an F-22 Raptor pilot with the 27th Fighter Squadron at Langley AFB, Virginia. As one F-22 pilot put it, ATAGS allows 'More G, less pain.'

allowed to operate above 50,000 feet [15,000m] without having to wear a partial pressure suit so we're not artificially restricted from operating where we need to', alluding to previous Air Force rules that required pilots to wear pressure suits when operating in the rarefied atmosphere at very high altitude.

made for the aircraft's performance that it excels in virtually every arena. We lose virtually none of that performance when loaded for combat like you do in every other aircraft because all our weapons are carried internally. It's an absolute thoroughbred for raw power and speed, it turns as tight as anything out there (or better), and has all of the super manoeuvrability you see other thrust-vectored aircraft performing.'

PHENOMENAL ACCELERATION

Of the Raptor's ability to fly at very low speeds, which is sometimes necessary when a dogfight has gone on for a while and each aircraft has used up all of its airspeed and altitude trying to outmanoeuvre the other, Shower grades the Raptor as 'phenomenal', adding, 'as is its acceleration from post-stall to its maximum speed.' He's quick to qualify these remarks, though: 'But that's all just window dressing. We hope to never need the manoeuvring

capability – the goal is to destroy our adversaries long before we ever hit a visual merge [see each other] by taking advantage of its stealth and speed. And, so far, we're doing really well in our training and test [programmes].'

The F-22A will replace the stalwart F-15 as America's premier air-superiority fighter and interceptor, so how does it compare to the Eagle? Shower answers, but not before prefacing his comments first: 'I love the Eagle, so I will never say a bad word about it. In my opinion it might very well be written in history as the best overall fighter ever produced. It certainly has the combat record to prove it as the only aircraft never to be shot down in aerial combat. But, it can't hold a candle to the F-22, nor was it meant to. The whole point of designing a super fighter is to make it absolutely dominant over everything else out there – and I believe that the F-22 has achieved that goal. The F-22 is a revolutionary, not evolutionary, leap very, very far forward.'

ABOVE: The F-22A features an air refueling receptacle towards the rear of the fuselage to permit in-flight refueling from USAF KC-10 and KC-135 tankers. Doors cover the receptacle when not in use to keep the jet stealthy.

BELOW: The Raptor's clean lines serve not only to keep it as stealthy as possible, but also confirm the age-old fighter pilot saying, 'If an airplane looks great, it'll fly great!'

Flying the F-35 Lightning II

The Joint Strike Fighter (JSF), or F-35 Lightning II as it is now known, is the result of more than a decade of collaboration between the governments and defence contractors of Britain and America. The F-35 combines exceptional stealth qualities with the latest suite of sensors to provide a strike capability that will remain unmatched for many years.

While America's primary contractor, Lockheed Martin, has provided the bulk of the technical know-how required to build this stealthy multi-role fighter, Britain's BAe Systems and America's Northrop Grumman have also been major partners. In fact, the F-35 is the result of a multinational collaboration that also includes the financial contributions of Australia, Canada, Denmark, Italy, the Netherlands, Norway and Turkey.

DESIGN SPECIFICATIONS

The American-led JSF project was conceived in the mid-1990s with a view to replacing a number of ageing aircraft in the Air Forces of the US and UK. From the outset, three different variants of the F-35 were planned, each offering unique capabilities tailored to specific customer requirements, while retaining at least 80 percent parts commonality. The F-35A offers conventional takeoff and landing (CTOL) capabilities, and is intended to equip land-based customers like the US Air Force, and the air forces of Italy, the Netherlands, Turkey, and others. By contrast, the F-35B is heavily modified to allow short-takeoff and vertical landing (STOVL), making it ideally suited to the likes of the US Marine Corps and Britain's Royal Navy. Finally, the F-35C is a carrier-based variant that will equip the US Navy.

The basic design specifications behind the JSF were that it had to be four times as effective in air-to-air combat as 'legacy' fighters like the F-15 and F-16; that it had to be eight times more effective in the air-to-ground role; that it had to be three times more effective in the reconnaissance role, and in suppressing enemy air defence systems; and that it had to do all of this while being able to fly further than any legacy fighter, while all the time remaining less maintenance-intensive.

COCKPIT COMPATIBILITY

Lockheed Martin's X-35 demonstrator aircraft first flew in 2000, after which it competed against Boeing's X-32 for the JSF contract. Lockheed Martin won the competition in October 2001, and the first F-35A flew on 19 February 2006. Unsurprisingly, the more complex F-35B STOVL variant took much longer to make its maiden flight, but on 11 June 2008 it finally did so. At the controls was the lead STOVL test pilot, Graham Tomlinson, of BAe Systems.

Tomlinson, a veteran pilot of the vertical takeoff and landing Harrier, has more than 5,000 hours of flying experience, much of it on the Harrier with the Royal Air Force. Explaining the philosophy behind the three different F-35 variants, he said:

'They are designed to be easy for a pilot to be able to flit between. It is a bit like the Airbus family of airliners – where it is simple to convert a pilot of an A320 to an A330 – in that the cockpits of the three types are almost identical. A pilot can go from one version to the another and accordingly require very little retraining.

'I have to say that retaining this familiarity for the F-35B STOVL variant is something of a miracle. If you look at the cockpit of a Harrier, it is like no other cockpit

ABOVE: Graham Tomlinson prepares for flight in the F-35B demonstrator, sporting the futuristic-looking helmet-mounted display that will be integral to the F-35's pilot interface. Note the forward-hinging canopy – a somewhat unusual configuration.

MAIN PHOTOGRAPH: The strong contour of the F-35's engine bay is evident in this head-on shot. The F-35's engine generates around 178kN (40,000lb thrust) in afterburner, giving the Lightning II exceptional performance.

PILOT'S VERDICT

"The beauty of the F-35's stealth is that you can see and kill the enemy before he sees you; it's very difficult to kill a JSF when you cannot see it."

Graham Tomlinson
lead STOVL test pilot
BAe Systems

aircraft. Don't crash. Here are some golden rules, make sure you remember them. And don't crash," was what they told us. "And by the way, with what little spare capacity you have left, we want you to complete a difficult and demanding mission," they would add. Well, this aircraft reverses that situation. I would actually go as far as to say that it's trivial to fly this aircraft. I tell people that it's akin to hiring and driving a rental car: you turn the key and drive away without really even thinking about it. So, the focus for a pilot flying the F-35 will be on the mission, the bad guys, where the target it, where the threats are, and so on.'

ADVANCED COCKPIT SYSTEMS
But can too much information lead to cognitive saturation – a 'helmet fire', as fighter pilots call it?

'That's always a possibility. It's not enough to just display this information,' Tomlinson concedes. 'We have to ensure that the information is presented sensibly. Getting the balance right is not always easy: test pilots will often instruct the software engineers to take some information away from the displays, arguing that it will confuse the operational pilots who fly it. When we do this, the operational pilots invariably turn around and ask that we give them more information – in fact, the guys just seem to want more and more data. Another advancement that we have made with the F-35 is the quality of our simulations and training tools. We also now have excellent desktop simulations that an F-35 pilot can "fly" in order to improve the quality of his training, and his understanding of the aircraft.'

Unique to the F-35 is a fully integrated helmet-mounted sight (HMS) that replaces the ubiquitous heads up display (HUD), says Tomlinson.

'We don't have HUD, and this is the first aircraft not to have one for a long time. The first generation of our HMS has been flying for a year, and our second generation is coming later in 2008. One of the symbols on the display is a symbol called "flight path", and it is used all the time.'

ABOVE: Angular lift surfaces – the wings and horizontal tails – do little to endear the Joint Strike Fighter to the eye, but confer a significant advantage to the stealthy radar cross-section of the aircraft.

RIGHT: Like its stablemate the F-22A Raptor, the F-35's nose and forward fuselage are intersected by a highly defined mould line that runs from the tip of the nose to the air intakes. This chine-like line is another design feature incorporated with stealth in mind.

you will see – there are three main controls in the form of the stick, throttle and nozzle lever. Well, the Harrier was great for the 1960s, when we all had black-and-white TV and there were no computers!'

The F-35 cockpit is very different. 'We have a very large 20 inch by 8 inch [50 by 20cm] display that is touch-sensitive and can be divided up into a number of "pages" according to what the pilot wants. The rest of the cockpit looks remarkably blank, and we don't have rows of switches – we just have a battery, engine start, IPP [integrated power package] start switch and a few others. We call the display a "chin up" display, and it combines with our HOTAS [hands on throttle and stick controllers] and our Direct Voice Input system. The left and

right half of the display have independent computers controlling them, so there is redundancy built in, and if one computer fails we can still control the other half of the screen. To be even safer, there is also what you might call a "get you home" flight display that is activated following serious failures, and this gives basic information on attitude, airspeed and altitude so that the pilot can make a safe landing.'

These highly configurable displays, and the overall intuitiveness of programming them, amounts to much more than just 'eye candy'. 'In the Harrier,' Tomlinson revealed, 'you had 10 percent spare capacity to do a mission, with 90 percent spent on not crashing. "Fly the aircraft. Don't crash. Fly the

[MISSION REPORT]

++++++++++++++++++++++++++++++

F-35 DETAILED VARIANT BRIEFING

The F-35A is the conventional takeoff and landing (CTOL) F-35A and uses standard runways for takeoffs and landings. Internal fuel capacity is 8,382kg (18,480lb), providing an unrefueled range of more than 2,200km (1,200 nautical miles) without external tanks. The F-35A carries a 25mm GAU-22/A cannon internally, and has a standard internal weapons load of two AIM-120C air-to-air missiles and two 907kg (2,000lb) GBU-31 JDAM guided bombs. When stealth is no longer required, the F-35A external pylons are loaded with ordnance, giving the aircraft a weapons payload of more than 8,000kg (18,000lb).

The F-35B is *'the first aircraft in history to combine stealth with short takeoff/vertical landing capability and supersonic speed,'* Lockheed Martin states. The F-35B deploys near combat zones, dramatically shrinking the distance from base to target, increasing sortie rates and decreasing the need for logistics support. Internal fuel capacity is 6,352kg (14,003lb), providing an unrefueled range of more than 1,600km (900 nautical miles) without external tanks. The F-35B standard weapons load is two AIM-120C air-to-air missiles and two

453kg (1,000lb) GBU-32 JDAM guided bombs. The F-35B's external pylons are can carry more than 6,800kg (15,000lb) of stores.

The F-35C boasts larger wings and control surfaces and the addition of wingtip ailerons to allow improved control and precision during carrier approaches. The aircraft incorporates larger landing gear and a stronger internal structure to withstand the forces of carrier launches and recoveries. *'Ruggedized exterior materials mean low maintenance requirements for preserving the aircraft's Very Low Observable radar signature, even in harsh shipboard conditions,'* according to Lockheed Martin. The F-35C internal fuel capacity is 9,110kg (20,085lb), providing an unrefueled range of well over 2,500km (1,400 nautical miles) without external tanks. Like the F-35A, the C-model Lightning II has external pylons rated to carry more than 8,000kg (18,000lb) of weapons.

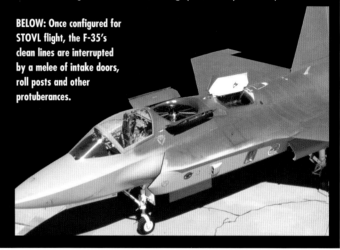

BELOW: Once configured for STOVL flight, the F-35's clean lines are interrupted by a melee of intake doors, roll posts and other protuberances.

While not an innovation new to the F-35, its integration with the HMS does make life simpler for the pilot. *'You put it where you want it to go, and it always displays where the aircraft is going. It's very useful on recovery to the ship, for example. All the clever sensors around the aeroplane will be displayed on this visor, allowing the pilot to look "through" the aircraft,'* adds Tomlinson. *'It's a bit like a video game or like flying with night vision goggles. It's a green world, and one that uses electro-optical, infrared and RF [radar sniffing] sensors that have very high resolutions and can be used for targeting.'*

The technology for the HMS is continually being refined, and Tomlinson reveals that one key area of continued development is the system's 'latency', or its ability to update the display several times per second: *'The important thing is to get the update rate on the display good enough to sense where your head is*

and do the calculations, even when the aircraft and the pilot are vibrating. The challenge is to be able to do this without any latency. We have also changed the visor for the next display; our existing display has a crease down the middle of it, but the new one will be totally smooth.'

Completing the F-35's cockpit interface will be the direct voice input

(DVI) system. *'We will use the DVI to do altimeter changes, radio changes, input waypoint information, etc. It's a tool that we will tend to use for what I call "domestic issues". We have a five-way switch on the throttle, one position of which allows you to talk to the aeroplane. You*

BELOW: The process of converting to vertical flight is initiated with a single button push by the pilot, and is seamless as far as the pilot is concerned.

[MISSION REPORT]
++++++++++++++++++++++++++++++

F-35 WEAPONS AND AVIONICS

At the heart of the F-35's offensive capability is the APG-81 AESA radar. It will work in tandem with the planned Electro-Optical Targeting System (EOTS), and a multitude of electro-optical sensors belonging to the AAS-37 missile warning system, to find, identify and target the enemy.

Once found, the enemy can be engaged by a wide range of weapons, including a GAU-22/A four-barrel 25mm cannon equipped with 180 rounds. The F-35A is the only variant to carry this weapon internally, and the B- and C-model will feature an external pod with 220 rounds, as required.

Two weapons bays, one either side of the jet, can carry up to two air-to-air missiles and two air-to-ground weapons: two 907kg (2,000lb) bombs in A- and C-models; two 453kg (1,000lb) bombs in the B-model. These weapons include: AIM-120 AMRAAM, AIM-132 ASRAAM, Joint Direct Attack Munition (JDAM) Joint Standoff Weapon (JSOW), Small Diameter Bomb (SDB), Brimstone anti-tank missile, Wind Corrected Cluster Munitions Dispenser (WCMD) and High Speed Anti-Radiation Missile (HARM). The European MBDA Meteor air-to-air missile is currently under evaluation for carriage.

Four wing pylons and two wingtip pylons increase payload for sorties when stealth is not the priority. The two wingtip pylons carry only AIM-9X Sidewinder, while the AIM-120 AMRAAM, Storm Shadow cruise missile, Joint Air to Surface Stand-off Missile (JASSM) cruise missiles, and 1,800l (480 gallon) fuel tanks to extend range, can be carried in addition to the those stores in the internal bays.

MAIN PHOTOGRAPH: F-35 AA-1 was the first Lightning II to be rolled out by Lockheed Martin, the JSF's prime contractor. The A-model F-35 has none of the complex systems associated with STOVL, and is therefore somewhat lighter than the F-35B.

could say "Comm A. one-two-three-decimal-five. Go!" and the Comm A radios will change to a new frequency of 123.5. DVI is not in the jet at the moment, but it is planned for operational service.'

STOVL FLIGHT

As the lead STOVL pilot for the F-35B, Tomlinson was the first person to fly this variant. He also worked extensively on the pilot interface and control laws that govern the jet's STOVL

capability. 'The magic with the F-35 is that when you get down to the STOVL flight parameters the throttle seamlessly transitions to an "acceleration controller". Our system means that there will be initial training for those pilots who fly the STOVL variant, but nothing like that required for the Harrier, for which there was a tremendous amount of training because of the complexity. With the F-35, your left hand on the throttle controls thrust to make the jet go faster or slower, but the

acceleration controller will now hold airspeed in the neutral position, decelerate when pulled back, and accelerate when pushed forward. Sitting in the hover, you push the stick forward to descend at zero airspeed, or pull back to climb. We enter this "blending" mode at about 50 knots [93km/h] – above that the wing is still generating lift and the pilot can still control the flight path by moving the stick back and forward.'

Naturally, computers control the process from start to finish.

'There's 40,000lb of thrust [178kN] *squirting out of the bottom of the aircraft,'* says Tomlinson, *'so there's lots of induced airflow moving us around. In the hover, the aeroplane corrects its attitude to keep it at an ideal pitch. There are some very sophisticated control laws governing the process.'*

The F-35B's Pratt & Whitney F135 (or General Electric/Rolls-Royce F136) uses Lockheed Martin's LiftSystem that is comprised of a lift fan, driveshaft, clutch, two 'roll posts' and a Three-Bearing Swivel Module (3BSM) thrust vectoring nozzle.

'When we want to enter STOVL mode, the pilot hits a button that initiates conversion. It is a complex process that starts by opening up a bunch of doors for the lift fan and auxiliary intakes for the main engine. Roll post doors open under the wing to *maintain roll control, and this entire process takes about six seconds,'* Tomlinson elucidates.

He adds, *'The motor simultaneously repositions a clutch that drives a lift fan just behind the cockpit, taking about seven seconds. The next stage is for the lift fan to spool up, then the clutch is engaged by bolts to take the torque, and then the lift fan is spun up to maximum thrust – 18,000lb [80kN]. The main engine, meanwhile, is generating 17,000lbs [75.5kN], and the roll posts are generating about 4,000lb [17.7kN] from bleed air taken from the main engine. Underneath the lift fan, a variable area guide vane exchange box can change the vector angle of the thrust. In total, it takes about 15 seconds for all of these changes to complete.'*

CLOSING THOUGHTS

Tomlinson is highly impressed with the F-35 so far, and shrugs off the comparisons between it and the Lockheed Martin F-22A Raptor, the only other Fifth Generation Fighter. *'It's at least as good as the F-22 in many of the mission systems, but of course it was designed to be a jack-of-all-trades, and is not going to be better than the F-22 or the RAF's Typhoon in dogfighting. That said, the F-35 is a 9g fighter with a good post-stall manoeuvring capability, and we have a 50° angle-of-attack limit.*

'The F-35 is going to be by far the best choice of aircraft for the first few days of any future war, when we will need to stealthily destroy the enemy's air defences. From days five or six onwards, we are going to be able to add pylons to the wings and use the F-35 as a bomb truck, because by then we won't need the jet to be at its stealthiest any more. The beauty of the F-35's stealth is that you can see and kill the enemy before he sees you; it's very difficult to kill a JSF when you cannot see it.'

ABOVE: Bumps beneath the nose of AA-1 betray the eventual location of an optical and Infra Red sensor suite (Electro-Optical Targeting System) that will eventually be incorporated into the Lightning II. Additional electro-optical sensors are distributed over the aircraft as part of the missile warning system, targeting and navigation system.

LEFT: The F-35B required thinner skin, smaller weapons bays and scaled down vertical tails in order to meet the required weight limits stipulated by Lockheed Martin's customers. The wing mating joint, elements of the electrical system, and the fuselage behind the cockpit were also redesigned or modified to prevent the STOVL variant from going over weight.

Index

Entries in *italics* refer to photographs